Contents

30-31

Home Plans

Designer's Sketchbook

Make wise design decisions with these insightful excerpts from *Home Plan Buyer's Guide,* an upcoming book by Larry W. Garnett.

110

Designer's Perspective

Gain the designer's viewpoint with these helpful home plan narratives from D. Jarret Magbee, President of Architectural Design.

211

274

Photograph courtesy of the designer

The Best Baby Boomer
HOME PLANS

FOR THOSE OF US WHO COUNT OURSELVES AMONG THE EIGHTY MILLION OR SO AMERICANS WHO WERE BORN BETWEEN 1946 AND 1964, WE'VE BECOME WELL AWARE OF OUR STATUS AS "BABY BOOMERS." For years, boomer-related statistics and trivia have pointed out the ways in which the sheer number of us has affected almost every aspect of life in this country. New home design, for example, has steadily kept pace with our ever-changing stages of life and lifestyles. Today, as the leading edge of the boomer pack has begun to "mature," the most perceptive residential architects and home designers are attentively addressing the look and layout of homes with our coming years in mind.

The Best Baby Boomer Home Plans offers a selection of over 300 home designs that reflect the needs and desires of those of us over forty – specifically, those of us who appreciate thoughtful room arrangements, flexible living spaces and most importantly, the placement of master bedrooms on the main floor. This collection of home plans was gleaned from among the

Photographs courtesy of the designer

The Best Baby Boomer
HOME PLANS

the Garlinghouse company

HELPING TO BUILD DREAMS SINCE **1907**

Marie L. Galastro
CEO & Publisher

Millions of home plan buyers have been introduced to world-class home designs through Marie's publishing and marketing expertise. Marie's commitment to producing high-quality home plan books and magazines has been the hallmark of her extensive publishing career. Her experience in the home plan publishing and design industries includes her participation in nationally publicized home shows, speaking engagements and industry events.

Bruce Arant
Editorial Director

With years of experience editing publications in the stock home plan industry, Bruce has gained a thorough understanding of the unique needs of homebuilders and buyers alike. His extensive work with residential architects and home designers has provided him valuable insights regarding trends in single-family housing, as well as regional preferences of those who seek the "perfect" home design.

D. Jarret Magbee
President of Architectural Design

In 1997 Jarret conceived a "COOL" idea and co-founded the Internet's first home plans web site, COOLhouseplans.com. Today, he is responsible for revolutionizing the home-plan industry by delivering a wide array of home-plan designs to a boundless online community. In doing so, Jarret has utilized the power of the Internet to help millions of people realize the American Dream of home ownership.

The Best Baby Boomer HOME PLANS

Published by
The Garlinghouse Company
A COOL House Plans Company

CEO & Publisher
Marie L. Galastro

President of Architectural Design
D. Jarret Magbee

Editorial/Sales Director
Bruce Arant

Accounting Manager
Monika Jackson

Customer Service Manager
Jeremy Priest

Telesales Team
Jessica Salazar
Rick Miller
Richard Kay
Rodney Roussy

Fulfillment Operations
Daniel Fuentes

Graphics Design Consultant
Pamela Stant

Technology Consultant
Philip Kearney

Financial Consultant
Karen A. Bavis

For Home Plan Orders in United States
4125 Lafayette Center Drive, Suite 100
Chantilly, Va 20151
800-235-5700

For Home Plan Orders in Canada
The Garlinghouse Company
102 Ellis Street,
Penticton, BC V2A 4L5
800-361-7526

On the Cover : Plan #63181, page 253
Photograph courtesy of the designer

Photographs courtesy of the designers

best home design professionals throughout North America and spans a wide range of styles and square footage. The designs are presented within square footage categories to help simplify your discovery of a plan that captures your heart and satisfies the needs of your day-to-day life within the home.

The better you understand and recognize good home design, the more successful you'll be in selecting a plan that's right for you. With that in mind, we've included special sections throughout this book titled *Designer's Sketchbook* and *Designer's Perspective*. These beautifully illustrated presentations highlight both the fundamentals and finer points of home design to aid you in "thinking through" each plan as it relates to you own unique requirements.

If you find yourself returning to a plan that's "almost perfect," but not quite, remember that any plan can be changed, and almost any change can be made through our convenient, affordable modifications service. See details on page 282, or visit us online at www.familyhomeplans.com. In one way or another, we trust that with this book we'll help you discover *The Best Baby Boomer Home Plans.*

"How do we build this house with the features we really want – and stay within our budget?"

"All the bells and whistles." Know what they're going to cost before you build, with BuildQuote™. Unlike any other construction cost estimating system, BuildQuote™ allows you to compare the costs of various building material choices on the same house plan. BuildQuote™ is easy to use and puts you in control of construction costs by calculating how your choices in flooring, siding, roofing and more, will affect the final cost to build.

At $29.99, BuildQuote™ is one of the wisest investments you can make before you build. Learn more at www.familyhomeplans.com

With BuildQuote™, your cost is your choice.

BuildQuote™ is a licensed trademark of RSMeans.

Quick and Easy Customizing
Make changes to your home plans in 4 easy steps

1 Here's an affordable and efficient way to make custom changes to your home plan.

Select the house plan that most closely meets your needs. Purchase of reproducible master (vellum) is necessary to make changes to a plan.

2 Order customized changes online at www.familyhomeplans.com, or call 800-235-5700 to place your order and tell the sales representative you're interested in customizing a plan. A $50 refundable consultation fee will be charged. Then you'll need to complete a customization checklist indicating all the changes you wish to make to your plan, attaching sketches if necessary. If you proceed with the custom changes, the $50 will be credited to the total amount charged.

3 Fax the completed customization checklist to us at 703-222-9705 or e-mail us at info@garlinghouse.com. Within 24 to 48* business hours you will be provided with a written cost estimate to modify your plan. Our design consultant will contact you by phone if you wish to discuss any of your changes in greater detail.

4 Once you approve the estimate, a 75% retainer fee is collected and customization work gets underway. Preliminary drawings can usually be completed within 10 to 15 business days. Following approval of these preliminary drawings, your design changes are completed within 10 to 15 business days. Your remaining 25% balance due is collected prior to shipment of your completed drawings. You will be shipped five sets of revised blueprints, or a reproducible master.

BEFORE

This original stock plan was customized by the owners to fit on a narrow waterfront lot.
Changes made include:

Garage was reversed to the street side

Interior layout was reorganized to provide waterfront views from the kitchen and family room on the first floor, and from the master suite on the second floor.

Entry hall, laundry facilities and half-bath were moved to the street side

Original covered porch was relocated to the side of the home facing the water and redesigned to become a three-side covered porch

*Terms and conditions are subject to change without notice

AFTER

original first floor

original second floor

customized first floor

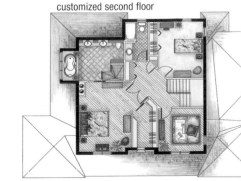
customized second floor

What comes first
HOUSE PLANS or THE SITE ?

Perhaps you already own your property as you begin selecting a plan. If so, you have the advantage of knowing the characteristics of the land and can select a design that takes advantage of the overall site. On the other hand, if you have a plan that has been your "dream home" for years and years, you will be faced with the challenge of finding an appropriate building site.

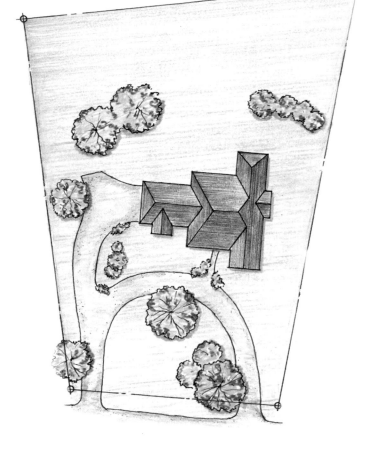

Be aware that each of these situations will probably require some compromises. For example, say your "dream home" plan has expansive windows that your building site dictates must face west towards the harsh afternoon sunlight. You might consider revising the plan or at least attempt to adjust the placement on the lot.

FIRST, SUPPOSE YOU HAVE THE PROPERTY. If a survey was not provided at the time of purchase, make arrangements to have one completed. The typical survey will include property boundaries and dimensions, along with such information as utility easements. If the property is located in any type of planned development or subdivision, you will also need to verify any setback requirements. These are the minimum (and sometimes maximum) distances that your home can be located in relation to the street, along with your side and rear property boundaries.

Next, you should review any deed restrictions that affect your property. This is a legal document that outlines an assortment of requirements and restrictions regarding the construction of your home and perhaps the landscaping and future maintenance. Spend some time visiting the site. The more time you're able to spend at the site, the better prepared you'll be to make the final decision regarding house placement.

Excerpted from *Home Plan Buyer's Guide,* an upcoming book by **Larry W. Garnett**

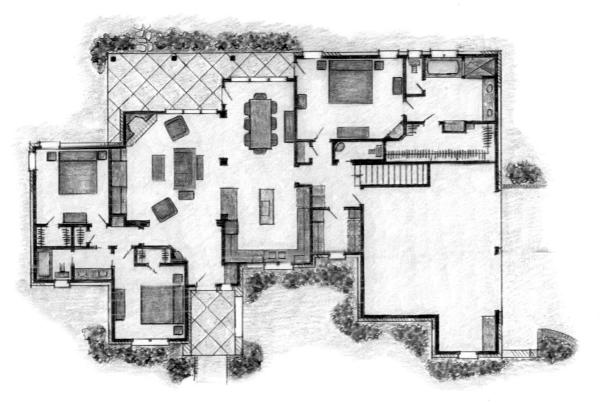

If the "home of your dreams" is too wide for your property, you may be able to make some simple revisions instead of finding a completely new plan. Opening the garage doors to the front can save at least 25 feet. ▲

This home, as shown on the photographs, is a modified version of the original plan #65001 and may differ from the actual blueprints.

Great Views - Inside and Out

Contemporary lifestyles love this open-minded design. The steep-pitched roof with the aura of an A-frame triggers vacation mode. Double porches with slender pillars interact beautifully with the great outdoors. Inside, a bounty of significantly sized windows and sleek doors with bright sidelights draw the natural light and magnify the view. The interior layout – 1480 sq. ft. – opens to a spatially rich arrangement where each of two levels is endowed with its own large bedroom, and private full bath. A cathedral ceiling hovers over the family room with fireplace and open dining area. The country-style kitchen features a crowd-pleasing lunch counter. A nearby smaller bedroom can become a study. The master bedroom owns an enormous walk-in closet and full bath. Upstairs, the secondary bedroom slips easily into its own snug family room and convenient full bath. For an inspired overview, peer from the airy mezzanine into the family room.

Outdoor living space is enjoyed on the covered rear porch and patio. ▲

Light, bright, airy spaces provide the perfect setting for casual dining at the kitchen's comfortable breakfast / lunch counter. ▶

A second-level mezzanine offers towering views of the family room below. ▶

The private master bedroom is a calm, quiet hideaway. ▼

Plan ID	65001	Price Code: A
Total Living Area	1,480 sq.ft.	
Main Living	1,024 sq.ft.	
2nd Level	456 sq.ft.	
Bedrooms	2	
Bathrooms	2	
Dimensions	32'-0" x 40'-0"	
Foundation	Full basement with walkout	

Main Living

14-8 x 12-0

40-0

14-0 x 22-8

14-8 x 12-0

© Copyright by designer

◀ 32-0 ▶

2nd Level

9-4 x 12-0

10-0 x 13-0

OPEN TO BELOW

© Copyright by designer

Main Living

12-0 X 11-4

14-8 13-4

10-0 X 16-8

10-0 X 26-8

30-0

◄ 26-0 ►

2nd Level

15-0 X 11-4

12-2 X 13-4

© Copyright by designer

Plan ID **65003** Price Code: A

Total Living Area	1,295 sq.ft.
Main Living	772 sq.ft.
2nd Level	523 sq.ft.
Bedrooms	2
Bathrooms	2
Dimensions	26'-0" x 30'-0"
Foundation	Basement

Main Living

12-8 X 11-0

12-0 X 14-0

12-4 X 14-0

30-0

© Copyright by designer

◄ 25-8 ►

2nd Level

14-4 X 11-0

10-6 X 11-0

© Copyright by designer

Plan ID **64983** Price Code: A

Total Living Area	1,168 sq.ft.
Main Living	730 sq.ft.
2nd Level	438 sq.ft.
Bedrooms	3
Bathrooms	2
Dimensions	25'-8" x 30'-0"
Foundation	Basement

Plan ID **64985**   Price Code: A

Total Living Area	1,484 sq.ft.
Main Living	908 sq.ft.
2nd Level	576 sq.ft.
Bedrooms	3
Bathrooms	2
Dimensions	26'-0" x 48'-0"
Foundation	Full basement with walkout

Main Living

10-0 X 11-0

14-4 X 10-0

12-0 X 12-8

12-8 X 11-6

48-0

14-0 X 11-6

© Copyright by designer

26-0

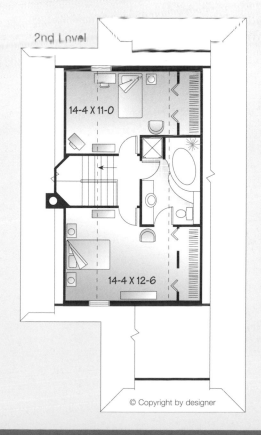

2nd Level

14-4 X 11-0

14-4 X 12-6

© Copyright by designer

Plan ID 24402 Price Code: A

Total Living Area	1,346 sq.ft.
Main Living	1,346 sq.ft.
Bedrooms	3
Bathrooms	2
Dimensions	46'-1" x 53'-1"
Garage Type	Two-car garage
Foundation	Crawlspace, Slab

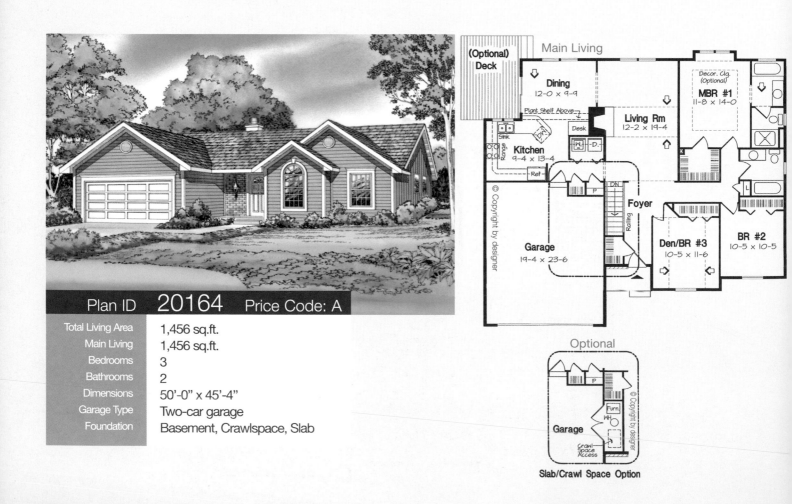

Plan ID 20164 Price Code: A

Total Living Area	1,456 sq.ft.
Main Living	1,456 sq.ft.
Bedrooms	3
Bathrooms	2
Dimensions	50'-0" x 45'-4"
Garage Type	Two-car garage
Foundation	Basement, Crawlspace, Slab

Plan ID 97137   Price Code: A

Total Living Area	1,461 sq.ft.
Main Living	1,461 sq.ft.
Bedrooms	3
Bathrooms	2
Dimensions	56'-0" x 42'-0"
Garage Type	Two-car garage
Foundation	Basement, Crawlspace*, Slab*

Main Living

WOOD DECK
20'0" x 10'0"

MBR.
12'10" x 15'0"

GRT. RM.
CATHEDRAL CEILING
14'6" x 19'0"

DIN.
CATH. CLG.
10'6" x 11'4"

KIT.
CATH. CLG.
11'0" x 11'4"

OPTIONAL DOOR

BR. #2/
DEN
11'0" x 11'0"

BR. #3
10'0" x 10'6"

2 CAR GARAGE
19'8" x 23'4"

© Copyright by designer

Main Living

MBR.
11'4"x13'4"

LIV.
15'6"x13'4"

DIN.
11'4"x9'8"

EATING BAR

KIT.
11'6"x11'0"

LIN.

DN.

PAN.

BR. #3
9'10"x10'0"

BR. #2
9'10"x11'4"

E.

2 CAR GAR.
19'4"x20'0"

47'-4"

46'-0"

© Copyright by designer

Plan ID	**97334**	Price Code: A

Total Living Area	1,295 sq.ft.
Main Living	1,295 sq.ft.
Bedrooms	3
Bathrooms	2
Dimensions	46'-0" x 47'-4"
Garage Type	Two-car garage
Foundation	Basement

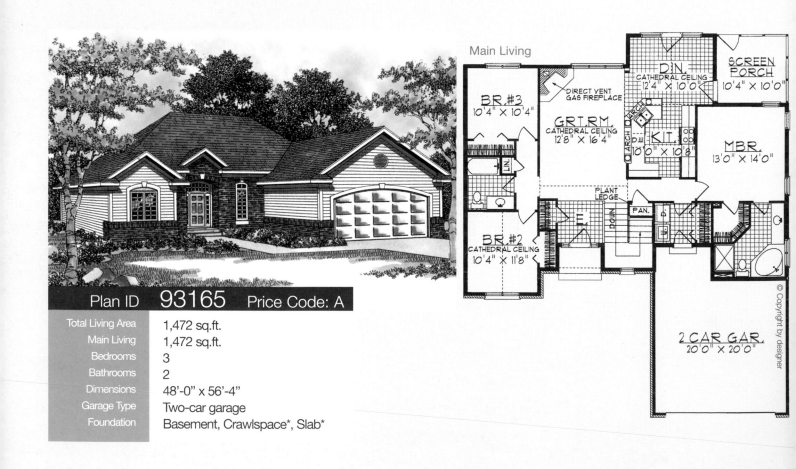

Main Living

BR. #3
10'4" X 10'4"

DIRECT VENT GAS FIREPLACE

DIN.
CATHEDRAL CEILING
12'4" X 10'0"

SCREEN PORCH
10'4" X 10'0"

GR. RM.
CATHEDRAL CEILING
12'8" X 16'4"

KIT.
10'0" X 10'8"

MBR.
13'0" X 14'0"

LIN.

PLANT LEDGE

ARCH

PAN.

E.

DOWN

BR. #2
CATHEDRAL CEILING
10'4" X 11'8"

2 CAR GAR.
20'0" X 20'0"

© Copyright by designer

Plan ID	**93165**	Price Code: A

Total Living Area	1,472 sq.ft.
Main Living	1,472 sq.ft.
Bedrooms	3
Bathrooms	2
Dimensions	48'-0" x 56'-4"
Garage Type	Two-car garage
Foundation	Basement, Crawlspace*, Slab*

Plan ID 97332 Price Code: A

Total Living Area	1,340 sq.ft.
Main Living	1,340 sq.ft.
Bedrooms	3
Bathrooms	2
Dimensions	51' 0" x 40'-0"
Garage Type	Two-car garage
Foundation	Basement

Main Living

MBR. 13'0"X13'4"

LIN.

LIV. RM. 16'8"X13'4"

DIN. 13'0"X8'0"

KIT. 13'4"X11'4"

DN.

BR. #3 11'0"X10'2"

BR. #2 11'0"X11'2"

E.

2 CAR GAR. 21'4"X19'8"

© Copyright by designer

40'-0"

51'-0"

Plan ID 58310 Price Code: A

Total Living Area	1,312 sq.ft.
Main Living	915 sq.ft.
2nd Level	397 sq.ft.
Bedrooms	3
Bathrooms	2.5
Dimensions	44'-0" x 45'-0"
Garage Type	Two-car garage
Foundation	Basement, Slab

Plan ID 58301 Price Code: A

Total Living Area	1,495 sq.ft.
Main Living	1,495 sq.ft.
Bedrooms	3
Bathrooms	2.5
Dimensions	59'-0" x 59'-0"
Garage Type	Two-car garage
Foundation	Basement, Slab

Plan ID 58311 Price Code: A

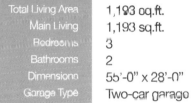

Total Living Area	1,193 sq.ft.
Main Living	1,193 sq.ft.
Bedrooms	3
Bathrooms	2
Dimensions	55'-0" x 28'-0"
Garage Type	Two-car garage
Foundation	Basement, Slab

Main Living

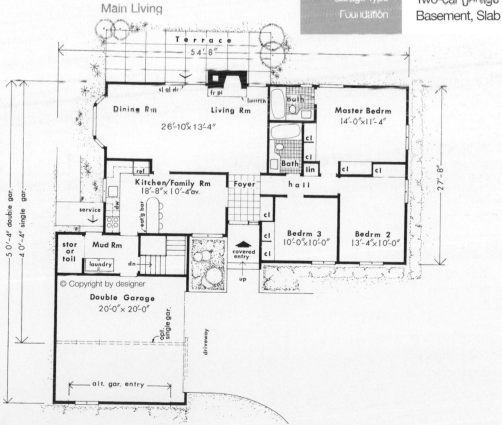

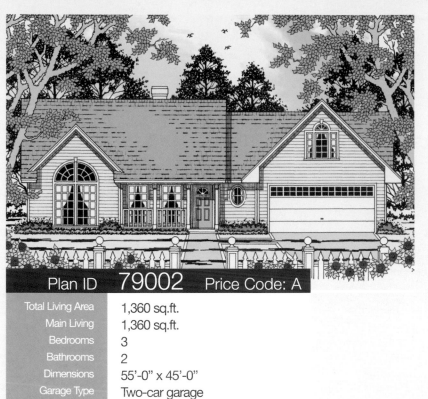

Plan ID 79002 Price Code: A

Total Living Area	1,360 sq.ft.
Main Living	1,360 sq.ft.
Bedrooms	3
Bathrooms	2
Dimensions	55'-0" x 45'-0"
Garage Type	Two-car garage
Foundation	Crawlspace, Slab

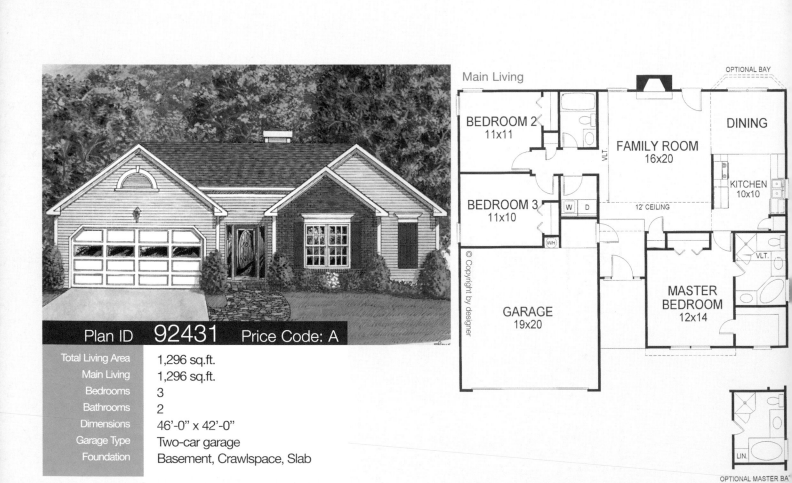

Plan ID 92431 Price Code: A

Total Living Area	1,296 sq.ft.
Main Living	1,296 sq.ft.
Bedrooms	3
Bathrooms	2
Dimensions	46'-0" x 42'-0"
Garage Type	Two-car garage
Foundation	Basement, Crawlspace, Slab

Plan ID 77015 Price Code: A

Total Living Area	1,418 sq. ft.
Main Living	1,418 sq. ft.
Bedrooms	3
Bathrooms	2
Dimensions	52'-0" x 45' 0"
Garage Type	Two car garage
Foundation	Crawlspace, Slab

Main Living

52'-0"

45'-0"

BATH 1

WALK IN CLOSET

SITTING AREA

MASTER SUITE
12'-0" X 14'-0"

PORCH

DINING RM.
11'-6" X 11'-0"

KITCH.
12'-0" X 12'-0"

10'-0" HIGH CEILING
LIVING RM.
20'-0" X 14'-0"

MEDIA CENTER

W/H

UT.

STORAGE

B.2

LINEN STOR.

BED RM.3
11'-0" X 10'-0"

ENT.

© Copyright by designer

GARAGE
20'-0" X 22'-0"

BED RM.2
11'-0" X 10'-0"

PORCH

WOOD POSTS & RAIL

Main Living

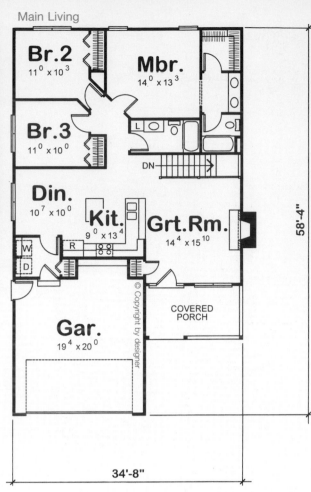

Plan ID 68096 — Price Code: A

Total Living Area	1,311 sq.ft.
Main Living	1,311 sq.ft.
Bedrooms	3
Bathrooms	2
Dimensions	34'-8" x 58'-4"
Garage Type	Two-car garage
Foundation	Basement*, Crawlspace*, Slab

Br.2 11⁰ x 10³ · Mbr. 14⁰ x 13³ · Br.3 11⁰ x 10⁰ · DN · Din. 10⁷ x 10⁰ · Kit. 9⁰ x 13⁴ · Grt.Rm. 14⁴ x 15¹⁰ · W D R · Gar. 19⁴ x 20⁰ · COVERED PORCH · 58'-4" · 34'-8"

© Copyright by designer

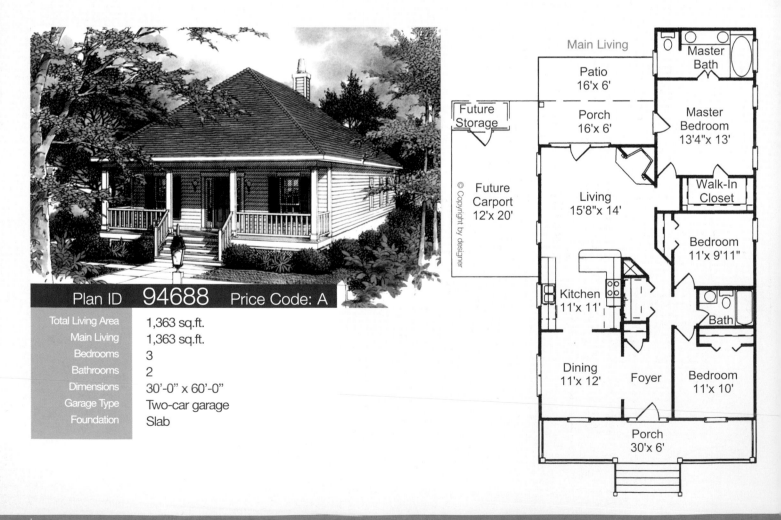

Plan ID 94688 — Price Code: A

Total Living Area	1,363 sq.ft.
Main Living	1,363 sq.ft.
Bedrooms	3
Bathrooms	2
Dimensions	30'-0" x 60'-0"
Garage Type	Two-car garage
Foundation	Slab

Main Living

Patio 16'x 6' · Porch 16'x 6' · Master Bath · Master Bedroom 13'4"x 13' · Future Storage · Walk-In Closet · Future Carport 12'x 20' · Living 15'8"x 14' · Bedroom 11'x 9'11" · Kitchen 11'x 11' · Bath · Dining 11'x 12' · Foyer · Bedroom 11'x 10' · Porch 30'x 6'

© Copyright by designer

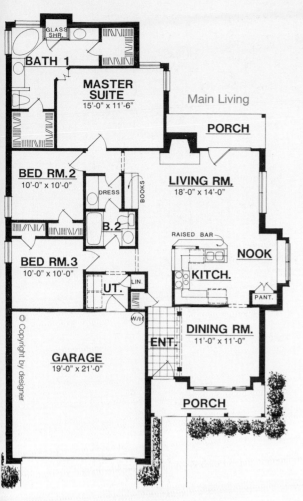

BATH 1

MASTER SUITE
15'-0" x 11'-6"

Main Living

PORCH

BED RM.2
10'-0" x 10'-0"

DRESS

BOOKS

LIVING RM.
18'-0" x 14'-0"

B.2

RAISED BAR

BED RM.3
10'-0" x 10'-0"

NOOK

UT.

LIN.

KITCH.

PANT.

© Copyright by designer

GARAGE
19'-0" x 21'-0"

ENT.

W/H

DINING RM.
11'-0" x 11'-0"

PORCH

Plan ID **77017** Price Code: A

Total Living Area	1,434 sq.ft.
Main Living	1,434 sq.ft.
Bedrooms	3
Bathrooms	2
Dimensions	39'-0" x 65'-0"
Garage Type	Two-car garage
Foundation	Crawlspace, Slab

Main Living

GREAT RM
vault cl'g
15'4 x 13'4

WI Closet

DIN
10'4 x 9'6

M BATH

SNACK BAR

MBR
11'4 x 13'8

KIT
13'8 x 9'0

Two Story FOYER

Entry

Pdr

Covered Entry

© Copyright by designer

GARAGE
19'4 x 20'4

2nd Level

Great Room Below

BR 3
11'4 x 10'

© Copyright by designer

BR 2
10' x 12'6

Balcony

Foyer Below

LINEN

BATH 2

Optional Sunken
BONUS ROOM
302 SF

SLOPED CL'G   FLAT CL'G   SLOPED CL'G

Plan ID **94154** Price Code: A

Total Living Area	1,477 sq.ft.
Main Living	976 sq.ft.
2nd Level	501 sq.ft.
Bedrooms	3
Bathrooms	2.5
Dimensions	41'-4" x 50'-8"
Garage Type	Two-car garage
Foundation	Basement

Plan ID 97731 Price Code: A

Total Living Area	1,315 sq.ft.
Main Living	1,315 sq.ft.
Bedrooms	3
Bathrooms	2
Dimensions	50'-0" x 54'-8"
Garage Type	Two-car garage
Foundation	Basement

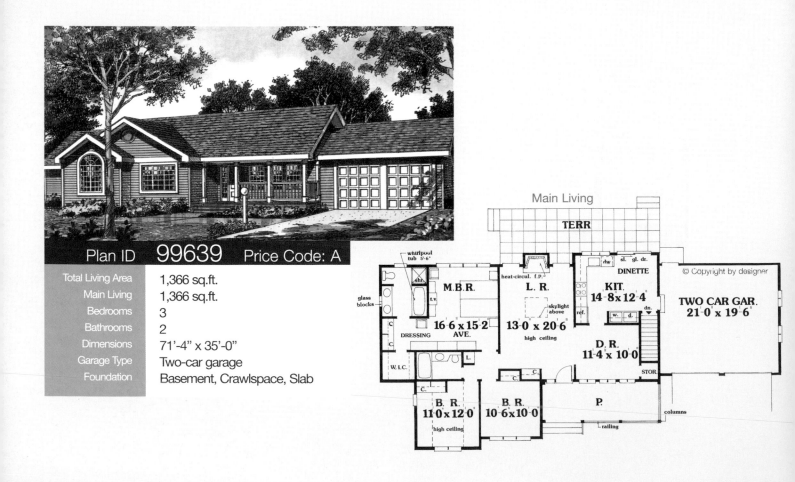

Plan ID 99639 Price Code: A

Total Living Area	1,366 sq.ft.
Main Living	1,366 sq.ft.
Bedrooms	3
Bathrooms	2
Dimensions	71'-4" x 35'-0"
Garage Type	Two-car garage
Foundation	Basement, Crawlspace, Slab

Plan ID 99673 **Price Code: A**

Total Living Area	1,380 sq.ft.
Main Living	1,380 sq.ft.
Bedrooms	3
Bathrooms	2
Dimensions	40'-0" x 43'-4"
Foundation	Basement, Crawlspace, Slab

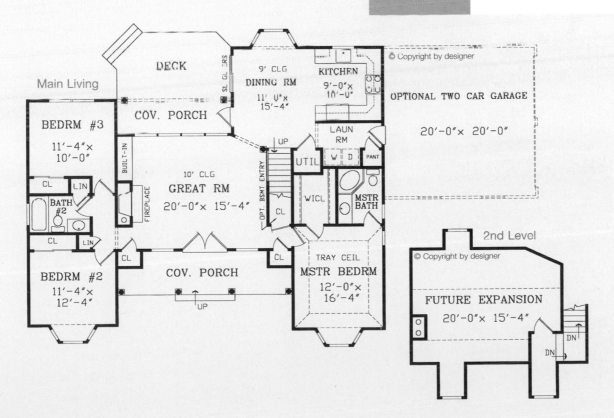

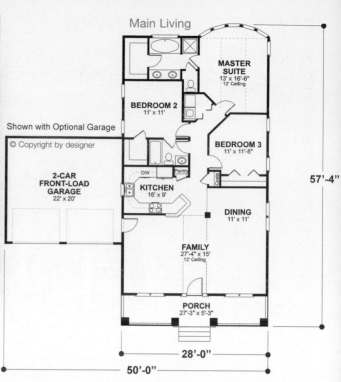

Main Living

Shown with Optional Garage

© Copyright by designer

MASTER SUITE
13' x 16'-6"
12' Ceiling

BEDROOM 2
11' x 11'

BEDROOM 3
11' x 11'-8"

2-CAR FRONT-LOAD GARAGE
22' x 20'

KITCHEN
16' x 9'

DINING
11' x 11'

FAMILY
27'-4" x 15'
12' Ceiling

PORCH
27'-3" x 5'-3"

57'-4"

28'-0"

50'-0"

Plan ID	92459	Price Code: A

Total Living Area	1,420 sq.ft.
Main Living	1,420 sq.ft.
Bedrooms	3
Bathrooms	2
Dimensions	50'-0" x 57'-4"
Garage Type	Two-car garage
Foundation	Crawlspace

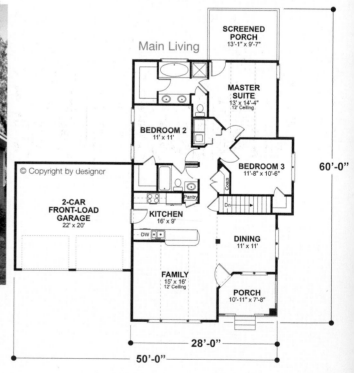

SCREENED PORCH
13'-1" x 9'-7"

Main Living

MASTER SUITE
13' x 14'-4"
12' Ceiling

BEDROOM 2
11' x 11'

BEDROOM 3
11'-8" x 10'-6"

© Copyright by designer

2-CAR FRONT-LOAD GARAGE
22' x 20'

KITCHEN
16' x 9'

DINING
11' x 11'

FAMILY
15' x 16'
12' Ceiling

PORCH
10'-11" x 7'-8"

60'-0"

28'-0"

50'-0"

Plan ID	92458	Price Code: A

Total Living Area	1,343 sq.ft.
Main Living	1,343 sq.ft.
Bedrooms	3
Bathrooms	2
Dimensions	50'-0" x 60'-0"
Garage Type	Two-car garage
Foundation	Basement

Plan ID 92372 Price Code: A

Total Living Area	1,334 sq. ft.
Main Living	953 sq.ft.
2nd Level	381 sq.ft.
Bedrooms	3
Bathrooms	2.5
Dimensions	49'-0" x 28'-0"
Foundation	Crawlspace

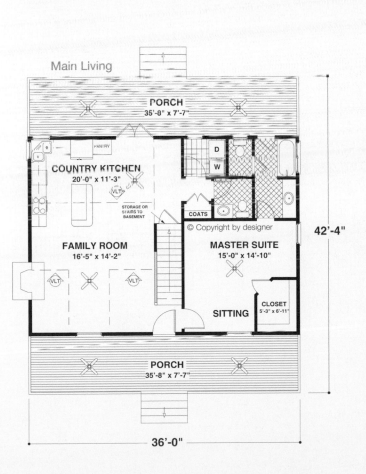

Main Living

PORCH
35'-8" x 7'-7"

PANTRY

COUNTRY KITCHEN
20'-0" x 11'-3"
VLT

STORAGE OR
STAIRS TO
BASEMENT

COATS

D
W

© Copyright by designer

42'-4"

FAMILY ROOM
16'-5" x 14'-2"
VLT

MASTER SUITE
15'-0" x 14'-10"

SITTING

CLOSET
5'-3" x 6'-11"

PORCH
35'-8" x 7'-7"

36'-0"

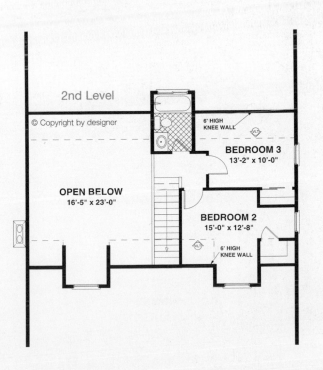

2nd Level

© Copyright by designer

6' HIGH
KNEE WALL
VLT

OPEN BELOW
16'-5" x 23'-0"

BEDROOM 3
13'-2" x 10'-0"

BEDROOM 2
15'-0" x 12'-8"
VLT

6' HIGH
KNEE WALL

Plan ID 82003 Price Code: A

Total Living Area	1,379 sq.ft.
Main Living	1,379 sq.ft.
Bedrooms	3
Bathrooms	2
Dimensions	38'-4" x 68'-6"
Garage Type	Two-car garage
Foundation	Crawlspace, Slab

Plan ID 62143 Price Code: A

Total Living Area	1,485 sq.ft.
Main Living	1,485 sq.ft.
Bedrooms	3
Bathrooms	2
Dimensions	46'-10" x 56'-10"
Garage Type	Two-car garage
Foundation	Crawlspace, Slab

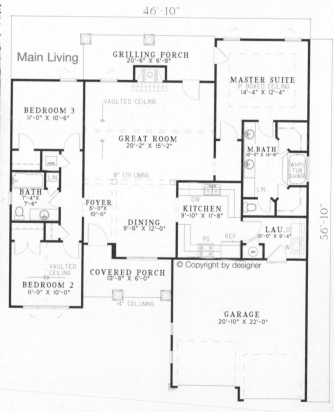

Plan ID 61033 Price Code: A

Total Living Area	1,485 sq.ft.
Main Living	1,485 sq ft
Bedrooms	3
Bathrooms	2
Dimensions	51'-6" x 49'-10"
Garage Type	Two-car garage
Foundation	Crawlspace, Slab

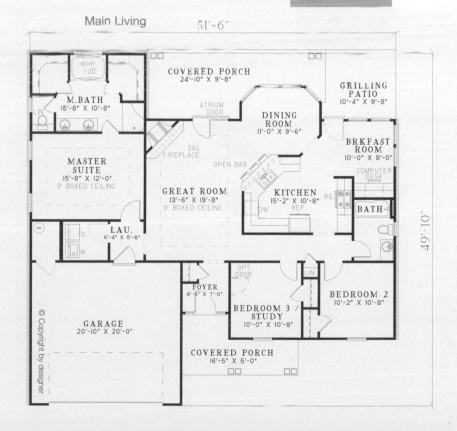

Affordably Upscale

The concept behind this house was simple; design an affordable house with as many upscale features as possible. We wanted to cater to the first time home buyer, or the growing family needing more space, without sacrificing budget. We believe we hit a home run with this design. Square footage was maximized by using an open floor plan concept. Notice the size of the dining room, a generous 11'4 x 14'3. The only elements separating the dining room from the vaulted great room and kitchen/breakfast areas are strategically placed, elegant columns (see interior illustration). Another feature that adds to the family-friendly floor plan is the back foyer/laundry room off the garage. The cabinet area can be used for storing coats, shoes, etc. We also decided to split the bedrooms to give mom and dad a little privacy. The master bedroom has its own foyer and access to the covered rear porch.

ORDER NOW 1-800-235-5700 or at www.familyhomeplans.com

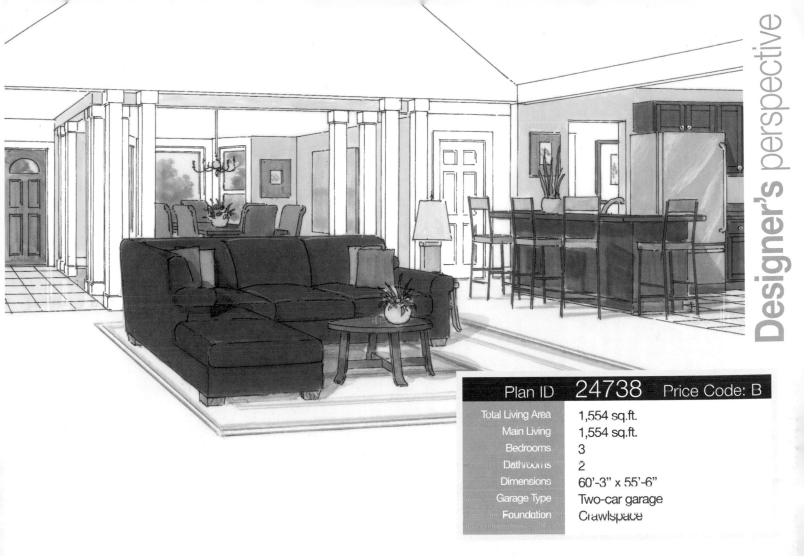

Plan ID	24738	Price Code: B
Total Living Area	1,554 sq.ft.	
Main Living	1,554 sq.ft.	
Bedrooms	3	
Bathrooms	2	
Dimensions	60'-3" x 55'-6"	
Garage Type	Two-car garage	
Foundation	Crawlspace	

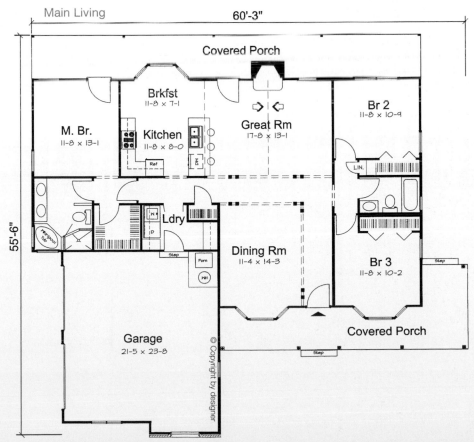

Main Living

60'-3"

55'-6"

Covered Porch

Brkfst
11-8 x 7-1

M. Br.
11-8 x 13-1

Kitchen
11-8 x 8-0

Great Rm
17-8 x 13-1

Br 2
11-8 x 10-9

LIN.

Ldry

Dining Rm
11-4 x 14-3

Br 3
11-8 x 10-2

Garage
21-5 x 23-8

Covered Porch

© Copyright by designer

Plan ID **20075** Price Code: B

Total Living Area	1,682 sq.ft.
Main Living	1,682 sq.ft.
Bedrooms	3
Bathrooms	2
Dimensions	68'-0" x 44'-0"
Garage Type	Two-car garage
Foundation	Basement

Main Living

DECK

WALK

© Copyright by designer

BRKFST
10'-0" X 7'-0"

SLOPE DOWN

KITCHEN
10'-0"
X
9'-0"

LIVING
14'-0"
X
21'-4"
(10'-0" CLG)

M. BEDROOM
14'-2"
X
13'-4"
7-1/2" VAULT

2-CAR GARAGE
21'-8"
X
21'-4"

DINING
11'-4"
X
11'-8"
5-1/2" VAULT

FOYER

PORCH

BEDROOM 2
12'-6"
X
13'-4"

BEDROOM 3
11'-6"
X
11'-8"

B

SHWR

DRIVEWAY

WALK

LEDGE

44'-0"

68'-0"

Plan ID 24250   **Price Code: B**

Total Living Area	1,700 sq.ft.
Main Living	1,700 sq.ft.
Bedrooms	3
Bathrooms	2
Dimensions	55'-4" x 53'-3,5"
Garage Type	Two-car garage
Foundation	Basement, Crawlspace

Main Living

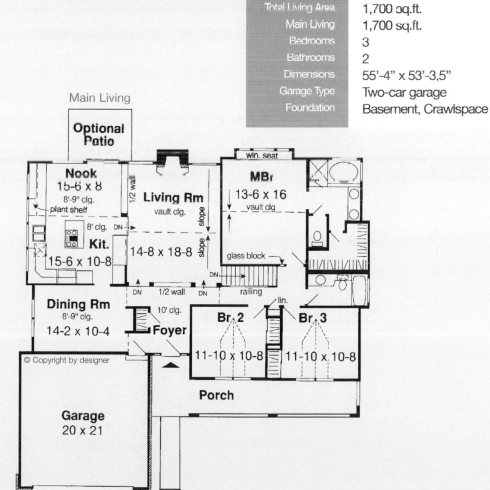

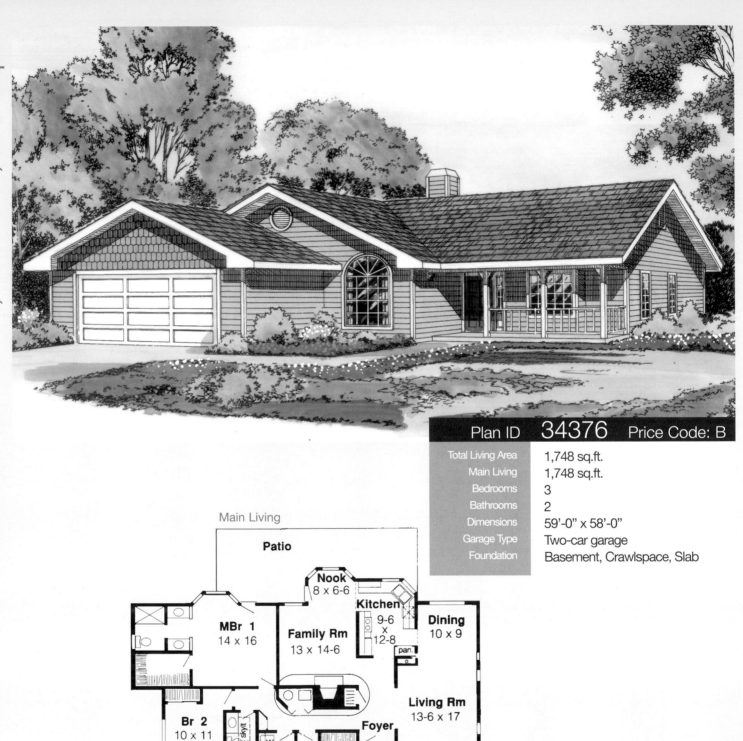

Plan ID **34376** **Price Code: B**

Total Living Area	1,748 sq.ft.
Main Living	1,748 sq.ft.
Bedrooms	3
Bathrooms	2
Dimensions	59'-0" x 58'-0"
Garage Type	Two-car garage
Foundation	Basement, Crawlspace, Slab

Main Living

Patio

Nook
8 x 6-6

Kitchen
9-6 x 12-8

MBr 1
14 x 16

Family Rm
13 x 14-6

Dining
10 x 9

pan.

Living Rm
13-6 x 17

Br 2
10 x 11

skylt

W
D

U

Foyer

Br 3
10 x 11

© Copyright by designer

Garage
22-4 x 23-2

DN

Crawlspace Option

Plan ID 24743 Price Code: C

Total Living Area	1,000 sq. ft.
Main Living	1,990 sq. ft.
Bedrooms	3
Bathrooms	2
Dimensions	62'-0" x 40'-0"
Garage Type	Two-car garage
Foundation	Basement

Main Living

© Copyright by designer

Deck

DN

Creal Rm
21'-7" X 18'-9"

M. Dr
17'-8" X 15'-2"

Br 3
13'-5" X 10'-10"

LIN.

WP TUB

Kitchen
13'-2" X 13'-6"

DW

REF.

Dining Rm
13'-10" X 14'-0"

SLOPE SLOPE

Br 2
11'-5" X 13'-9"

Brkfst
10'-10" X 9'-7"

Porch

Plan ID **20220** Price Code: B

Total Living Area	1,568 sq.ft.
Main Living	1,568 sq.ft.
Bedrooms	3
Bathrooms	2
Dimensions	54'-0" x 48'-4"
Garage Type	Two-car garage
Foundation	Basement, Crawlspace, Slab

Main Living

Master Br
15-4 x 13-4

Kitchen
10-7 x 11-1

Dining Rm
12-8 x 13-8

Br 2
11-7 x 11-2

Pantry

Corner Fireplace & Hearth

Laund.

Flat Clg. @ 10'

Living Rm
13-6 x 15-4

Books

DN

© Copyright by designer

Garage
21-5 x 21-8

Vaulted
Porch

Br 3
11-7 x 11-1

Deck

Bkfst Bar

D.W.

Ref.

Shelves

Crawl Space Access

Pantry

Furn

ORDER NOW 1-800-235-5700 or at www.familyhomeplans.com

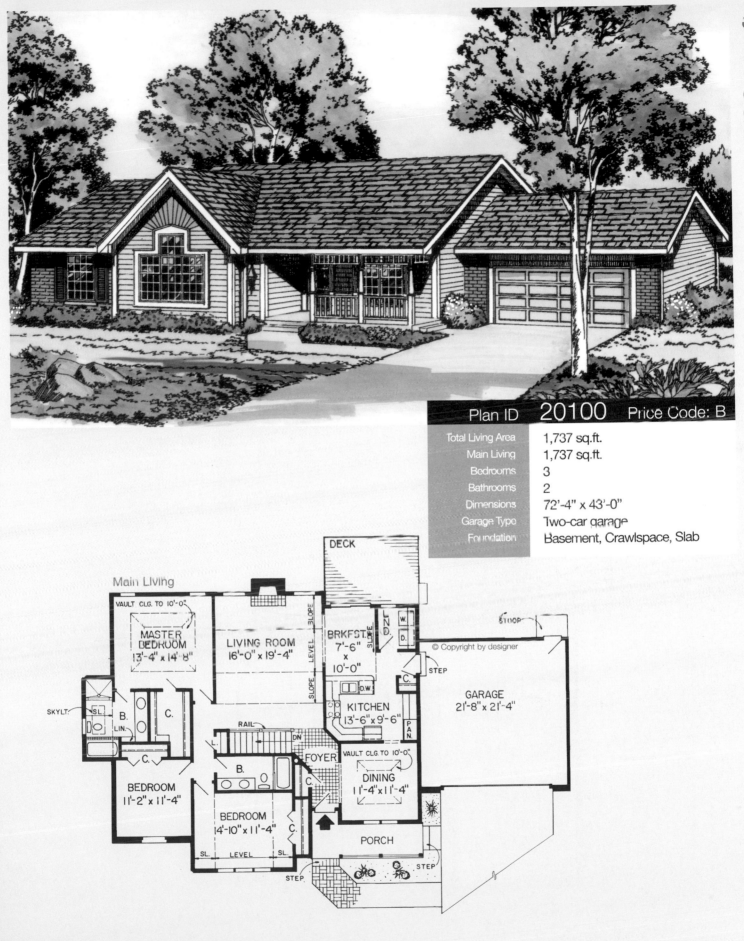

Plan ID 20100 Price Code: B

Total Living Area	1,737 sq.ft.
Main Living	1,737 sq.ft.
Bedrooms	3
Bathrooms	2
Dimensions	72'-4" x 43'-0"
Garage Type	Two-car garage
Foundation	Basement, Crawlspace, Slab

Plan ID 24651 Price Code: C

Total Living Area	1,821 sq.ft.
Main Living	1,821 sq.ft.
Bedrooms	3
Bathrooms	2
Dimensions	56'-0" x 42'-0"
Garage Type	Two-car garage
Foundation	Basement

Main Living

© Copyright by designer

Deck

Brkfst 8-10 x 10-5

pantry

Br 3 11-11 x 13-2

Kit. 11-2 x 9-8

Dining 12-6 x 14-1
flat clg. @ 12'-0"

DN

whirlpool tub

books

skylight

Mstr. Br 13-0 x 15-4

tray clg.

Br 2 11-11 x 12-0

Living 15-5 x 21-3

flat clg. @ 12'-0"

Porch

ORDER NOW 1-800-235-5700 or at www.familyhomeplans.com

Plan ID 24721   Price Code: B

Total Living Area	1,539 sq.ft.
Main Living	1,539 sq.ft.
Bedrooms	3
Bathrooms	2
Dimensions	50'-0" x 45'-4"
Garage Type	Two-car garage
Foundation	Basement, Crawlspace, Slab

Main Living

© Copyright by designer

What is "GOOD DESIGN" ?

ASK ANY GROUP OF PEOPLE WHAT THEY THINK "GOOD DESIGN" MEANS AND YOU'RE LIKELY TO RECEIVE A VARIETY OF RESPONSES. For most of us, the easier question might be, what is "bad design." We seem to immediately recognize what we consider unattractive. When the question relates to home design, the large variety of houses built all across the country would seem to prove that as a society, we have some extremely diverse opinions of what we consider to be "good" home designs.

Throughout this book, you'll find recurring references to such terms as scale, proportion, and functionality. Essentially, a "good design" will possess all three of these basic elements.

Although most people never take the time to analyze why they are attracted to certain homes, they often find themselves drawn to those that have been designed and built with particular attention to such details. One of the reasons many individuals find older homes built in the early part of the 20th century attractive is that these residences were constructed during a period when architects and builders paid strict attention to craftsmanship and details.

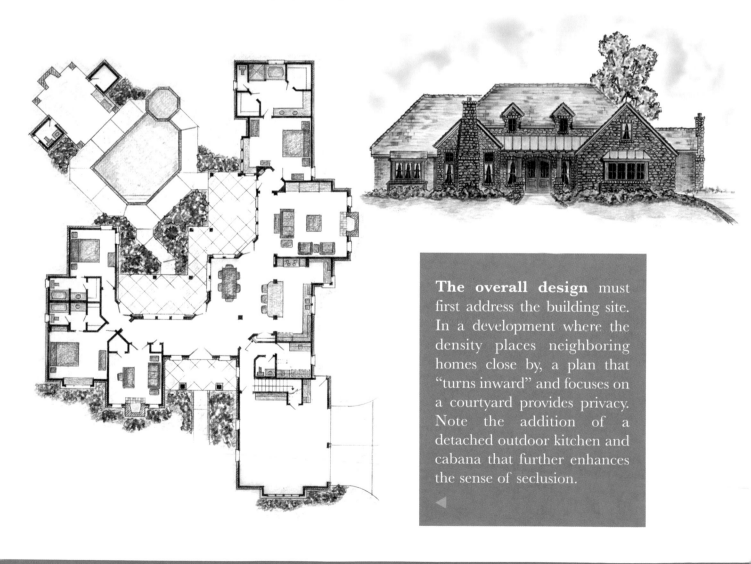

The overall design must first address the building site. In a development where the density places neighboring homes close by, a plan that "turns inward" and focuses on a courtyard provides privacy. Note the addition of a detached outdoor kitchen and cabana that further enhances the sense of seclusion.

◄

These same elements of scale and proportion relate to the interior of homes as well. Some houses seem to possess a certain feeling of permanence. A sense of warmth and sincerity exists when careful attention is paid to color, texture and scale.

Any definition of "good design" must take into consideration Individual requirements. The old saying that "you can't judge a book by its cover" readily applies to home design. Even though we typically pay a great deal of attention to the "surface" appeal of our homes, the true measure of enduring design also relates to function. Homes that offer practical solutions to the challenges of our daily routines often become more valuable in the long term than those with elaborate ornamental elements.

Unfortunately, "good design" is not the result of a special formula or distinct set of rules. However, the more you understand about the various elements of design, the better prepared you'll be to recognize both "good" and "bad" design when you see it.

Excerpted from *Home Plan Buyer's Guide,* an upcoming book by **Larry W. Garnett**

Proper Proportions become essential when designing exterior details such as porch columns.

Plan ID 24242 Price Code: B

Total Living Area	1,595 sq.ft.
Main Living	931 sq.ft.
2nd Level	664 sq.ft.
Bedrooms	4
Bathrooms	2.5
Dimensions	32'-4" x 40'-0"
Foundation	Basement, Crawlspace, Slab

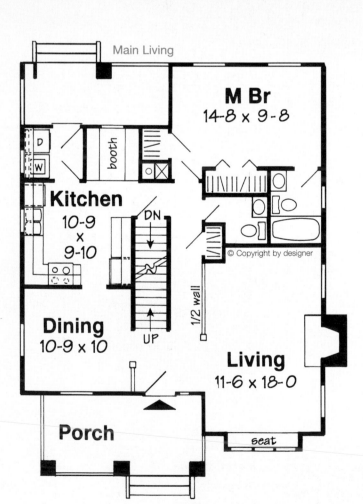

Main Living

M Br
14-8 x 9-8

Kitchen
10-9
x
9-10

DN

Dining
10-9 x 10

UP

1/2 wall

Living
11-6 x 18-0

Porch

seat

© Copyright by designer

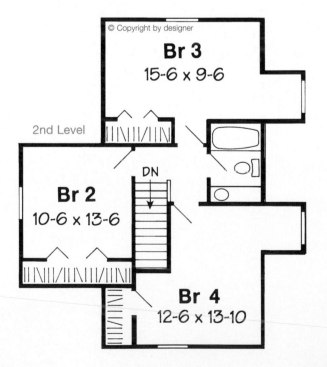

© Copyright by designer

2nd Level

Br 3
15-6 x 9-6

Br 2
10-6 x 13-6

DN

Br 4
12-6 x 13-10

Plan ID 24717 Price Code: B

Total Living Area	1,842 sq. ft.
Main Living	1,642 sq. ft.
Bedrooms	3
Bathrooms	2
Dimensions	59'-0" x 44' 0"
Garage Type	Two-car garage
Foundation	Basement, Crawlspace, Slab

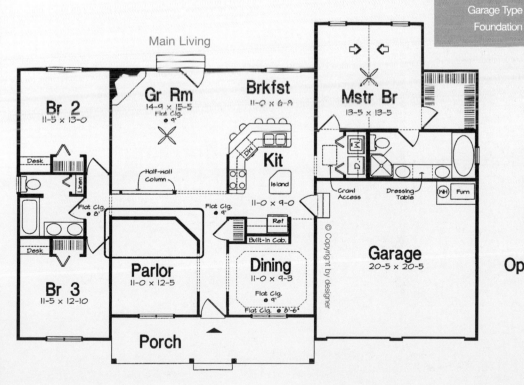

Main Living

Br 2 11-5 x 13-0

Desk

Linen

Gr Rm 14-9 x 15-5 Flat Clg. 9'

Brkfst 11-0 x 8-9

Mstr Br 13-5 x 13-5

Half-Wall Column

Flat Clg. 8'

Kit 11-0 x 9-0 Flat Clg. 9'

Dw

Island

Crawl Access

Dressing Table

Furn

© Copyright by designer

Ref

Built-In Cab.

Parlor 11-0 x 12-5

Dining 11-0 x 9-3 Flat Clg. 9'

Garage 20-5 x 20-5

Desk

Br 3 11-5 x 12-10

Flat Clg. 8'-6"

Porch

2nd Level

DN 14R

Optional Basement Stairs

Airy, Open and *Warm*

Although this design has an open floor plan layout, it still allows one to sense the separation between the different living areas. This separation is accomplished by the placement of the fireplace. Notice how effectively it defines the dining area. We also wanted to design a house where the "shell" was economical to build, i.e. a rectangular form, yet would still boast of some upscale features. The stone faced fireplace, vaulted ceilings, and wood floors satisfy this requirement quite nicely. These features in themselves are not expensive, but together they add tremendously to the overall architectural satisfaction (see interior rendering). We have found that nothing beats a front porch for welcoming guests, relaxing, or doubling as an outside playroom, and this house boasts a generous one. The porch even wraps the corner, which gives the front of the house more depth and visual interest. The basement also doubles as a two-car garage and storage area.

Plan ID	**24249**	Price Code: B
Total Living Area	1,741 sq.ft.	
Main Living	1,741 sq.ft.	
Bedrooms	3	
Bathrooms	2	
Dimensions	61'-0" x 36'-0"	
Foundation	Basement	

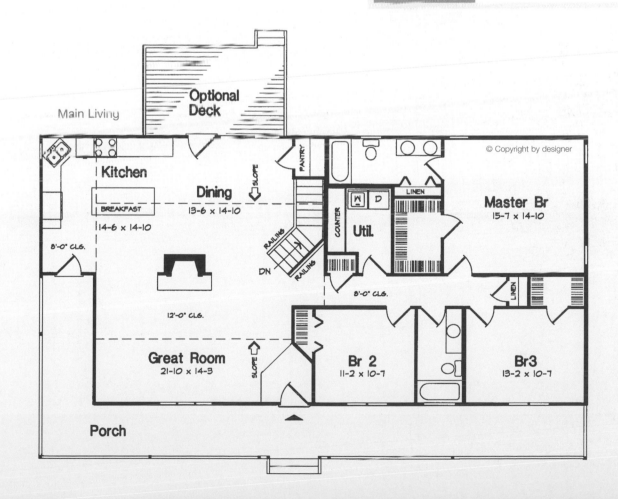

Main Living

Optional Deck

© Copyright by designer

Kitchen

Dining
13-6 x 14-10

PANTRY

SLOPE

LINEN

Master Br
15-7 x 14-10

BREAKFAST
14-6 x 14-10

W D

COUNTER

Util.

8'-0" CLG.

RAILING

DN

RAILING

8'-0" CLG.

LINEN

12'-0" CLG.

Great Room
21-10 x 14-3

SLOPE

Br 2
11-2 x 10-7

Br3
13-2 x 10-7

Porch

Main Living

Kitchen
8-1 x 12-7

Dining
9-8 x 12-7
8' clg

Optional Deck w/ Hot Tub

privacy fence

stor.

8' clg

17' flat clg

DN

Master Br
12 x 14-6
vault clg

Great Room
19-7 x 14-10
vault clg

UP

flat clg @15'-7"

© Copyright by designer

Porch

Plan ID	34603	Price Code: B

Total Living Area	1,560 sq.ft.
Main Living	1,061 sq.ft.
2nd Level	499 sq.ft.
Bedrooms	3
Bathrooms	2.5
Dimensions	40'-0" x 34'-0"
Foundation	Basement, Crawlspace, Slab

2nd Level

Br 2
10-10 x 12-6

Br 3
11-6 x 12-6

railing

DN

© Copyright by designer

open to great room below

open to master bedroom below

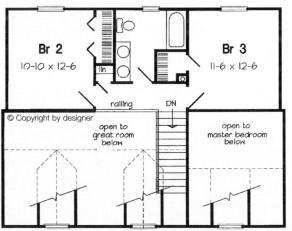

Optional Deck w/ Hot Tub

privacy fence

wh

furn

crawl space access

Master Br
12 x 14-6

Alternate Foundation Plan

Plan ID 34602 Price Code: B

Total Living Area	1,560 sq.ft.
Main Living	1,061 sq ft
2nd Level	499 sq.ft.
Bedrooms	3
Bathrooms	2.5
Dimensions	44'-0" x 34'-0"
Foundation	Basement, Crawlspace, Slab

Main Living

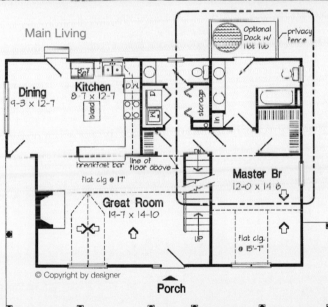

Dining
9-3 x 12-7

Kitchen
8-7 x 12-7

Island

Ref

DW

W
D

Optional Deck w/ Hot Tub

privacy fence

storage

Master Br
12-0 x 14-6

breakfast bar

line of floor above

flat clg @ 17'

Great Room
19-7 x 14-10

UP

flat clg @ 15'-7"

© Copyright by designer

Porch

2nd Level

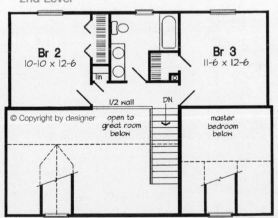

Br 2
10-10 x 12-6

Br 3
11-6 x 12-6

1/2 wall

DN

© Copyright by designer

open to great room below

master bedroom below

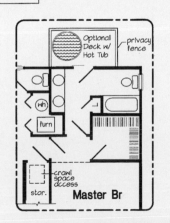

Optional Deck w/ Hot Tub

privacy fence

w/h

furn

crawl space access

stor.

Master Br

Alternate Foundation Plan

Plan ID 24725 Price Code: B

Total Living Area	1,661 sq.ft.
Main Living	1,661 sq.ft.
Bedrooms	3
Bathrooms	2
Dimensions	56'-0" x 46'-0"
Garage Type	Two-car garage
Foundation	Basement, Crawlspace, Slab

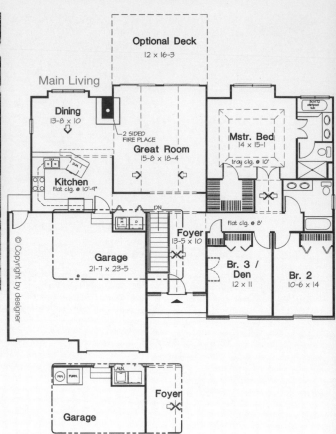

ALTERNATE SLAB /
CRAWLSPACE PLAN

Plan ID 24701 Price Code: B

Total Living Area	1,625 sq.ft.
Main Living	1,625 sq.ft.
Bedrooms	3
Bathrooms	2
Dimensions	54'-0" x 48'-4"
Garage Type	Two-car garage
Foundation	Basement, Crawlspace, Slab

Plan ID 10785   Price Code: C

Total Living Area	1,907 sq.ft.
Main Living	1,269 sq ft
2nd Level	638 sq.ft.
Bedrooms	3
Bathrooms	2.5
Dimensions	47' 0" x 30' 0"
Foundation	Basement, Crawlspace, Slab

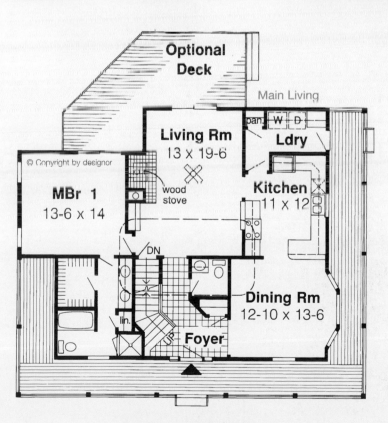

Optional Deck

Main Living

© Copyright by designor

Living Rm
13 x 19-6

pan. W D

Ldry

wood stove

MBr 1
13-6 x 14

Kitchen
11 x 12

DN

Dining Rm
12-10 x 13-6

lin.

UP

Foyer

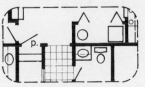

Slab/Crawl Space Option

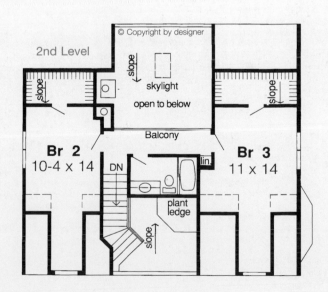

© Copyright by designer

2nd Level

slope

slope

skylight

slope

slope

open to below

Balcony

Br 2
10-4 x 14

DN

lin.

Br 3
11 x 14

plant ledge

slope

Compact *Curb Appeal*

With this design, we wanted a house that was somewhat narrow in dimension, yet was still packed with curb appeal. We feel this house definitely reached that goal. Inside the home, we also wanted to emphasize the dramatic, while maintaining a compact floor plan. When you enter the foyer, your eye is drawn to the 2-story great room which feels larger than it actually is, due to an abundance of light and a sense of airiness. Upon entering the great room, your eye is drawn to the corner fireplace and the built-in bookshelves along the wall. As you continue to the back of the room and turn around, you encounter a nice surprise; an upper bedroom foyer area at the top of the staircase (see illustration). This element enhances our dramatic theme. Back on the first floor, in the master bedroom, we've included a window seat. Since the master bedroom is the parent's refuge, a window seat provides a great place to enjoy a favorite book or just be still. The master bath offers additional comforts, with his/her walk-in-closets and vanities.

Plan ID 20230 Price Code: C

Total Living Area	1,995 sq.ft.
Main Living	1,365 sq.ft.
2nd Level	630 sq.ft.
Bedrooms	4
Bathrooms	2.5
Dimensions	44'-0" x 53'-8"
Garage Type	Two-car garage
Foundation	Basement, Crawlspace, Slab

Main Living

Nook
10-11 x 10-0

Great Room
18-6 x 15-6

(Open to Above)

Master Bedroom
13-5 x 13-0

Seat

Kitchen
10-11 x 15-11

Open Rail

Up   Dn

Lin.

M. Bath

Dining Room
10-11 x 12-0

Pass-Thru   Ref.

Step
Step

Covered Porch

Step

© Copyright by designer

SLAB/CRAWLSPACE
OPTION

Garage
19-5 x 21-11

2nd Level

© Copyright by designer

Bedroom #2
10-11 x 13-0

(Open to Below)

1/2 Wall

Dn

Lin.

1/2 Wall

Bedroom #4
10-5 x 11-4

Bedroom #3
11-0 x 10-8

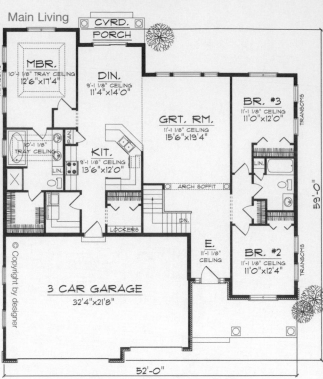

Main Living

CVRD. PORCH

MBR.
12'6"x17'4"
10'-1 1/8" TRAY CEILING

DIN.
11'4"x14'0"
9'-1 1/8" CEILING

BR. #3
11'0"x12'0"
11'-1 1/8" CEILING

GRT. RM.
15'6"x19'4"
11'-1 1/8" CEILING

KIT.
13'6"x12'0"
9'-1 1/8" CEILING

10'-1 1/8" TRAY CEILING

ARCH SOFFIT

LOCKERS

E.
11'-1 1/8" CEILING

BR. #2
11'0"x12'4"
11'-1 1/8" CEILING

3 CAR GARAGE
32'4"x21'8"

© Copyright by designer

52'-0"

59'-0"

Plan ID 73005   Price Code: C

Total Living Area	1,867 sq.ft.
Main Living	1,867 sq.ft.
Bedrooms	3
Bathrooms	2
Dimensions	52'-0" x 59'-0"
Garage Type	Three-car garage
Foundation	Basement

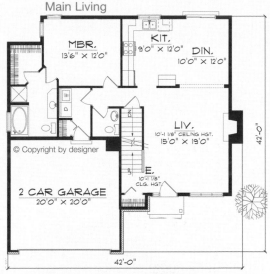

Main Living

MBR.
13'6" x 12'0"

KIT.
9'0" x 12'0"

DIN.
10'0" x 12'0"

LIV.
15'0" x 19'0"
10'-1 1/8" CEILING HGT.

© Copyright by designer

E.
10'-1 1/8" CLG. HGT.

2 CAR GARAGE
20'0" x 20'0"

42'-0"

42'-0"

2nd Level

BR. #2
11'4" x 12'0"

BR. #4
11'4" x 12'0"

BR. #3
11'4" x 10'10"

© Copyright by designer

Plan ID 99187   Price Code: B

Total Living Area	1,683 sq.ft.
Main Living	1,062 sq.ft.
2nd Level	621 sq.ft.
Bedrooms	4
Bathrooms	2.5
Dimensions	42'-0" x 42'-0"
Garage Type	Two-car garage
Foundation	Basement

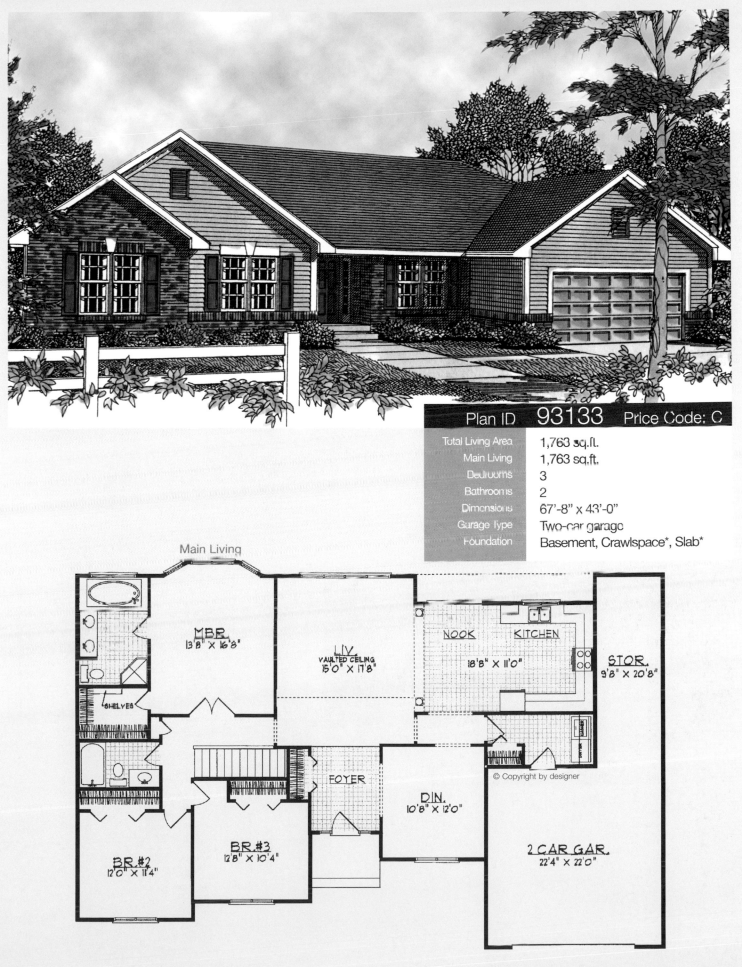

Plan ID 93133 Price Code: C

Total Living Area	1,763 sq.ft.
Main Living	1,763 sq.ft.
Bedrooms	3
Bathrooms	2
Dimensions	67'-8" x 43'-0"
Garage Type	Two-car garage
Foundation	Basement, Crawlspace*, Slab*

Main Living

MBR
13'8" X 16'8"

LIV
VAULTED CEILING
15'0" X 17'8"

NOOK

KITCHEN
18'8" X 11'0"

STOR.
9'8" X 20'8"

SHELVES

FOYER

DIN.
10'8" X 12'0"

© Copyright by designer

BR #2
12'0" X 11'4"

BR #3
12'8" X 10'4"

2 CAR GAR.
22'4" X 22'0"

Main Living

Plan ID 99175 Price Code: B

Total Living Area	1,649 sq.ft.
Main Living	1,649 sq.ft.
Bedrooms	3
Bathrooms	2
Dimensions	54'-0" x 49'-4"
Garage Type	Two-car garage
Foundation	Basement

Main Living

Plan ID 93171 Price Code: B

Total Living Area	1,642 sq.ft.
Main Living	1,642 sq.ft.
Bedrooms	3
Bathrooms	2.5
Dimensions	59'-0" x 66'-0"
Garage Type	Two-car garage
Foundation	Basement

Main Living

Plan ID 97178 Price Code: B

Total Living Area	1,591 sq.ft.
Main Living	1,591 sq.ft.
Bedrooms	3
Bathrooms	2
Dimensions	64'-8" x 57'-0"
Garage Type	Three-car garage
Foundation	Basement, Crawlspace*, Slab*

MBR.
10'-11 1/8"
TRAY CEILING
16'8" X 12'0"

DIN.
10'4 1/8"
TRAY CEILING
12'4" X 10'4"

SCREEN PORCH
11'0" X 19'0"

GRT. RM.
VAULT CEILING
14'0" X 20'4"

KIT.
12'4" X 10'0"

© Copyright by designer

BR. #2
12'0" X 11'4"

BR. #3
11'-11 1/8" CEILING HGT.
11'0" X 11'0"

E.
VAULT CEILING

DN.

3 CAR GAR.
31'8 X 29'4"

Plan ID	93161	Price Code: B
Total Living Area	1,540 sq.ft.	
Main Living	1,540 sq.ft.	
Bedrooms	3	
Bathrooms	2	
Dimensions	60'-4" x 46'-0"	
Garage Type	Two-car garage	
Foundation	Basement, Crawlspace*, Slab*	

Main Living

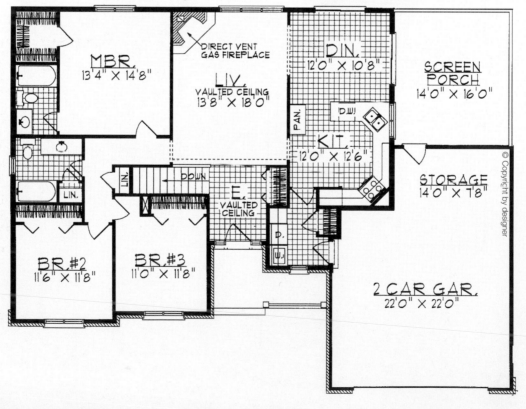

© Copyright by designer

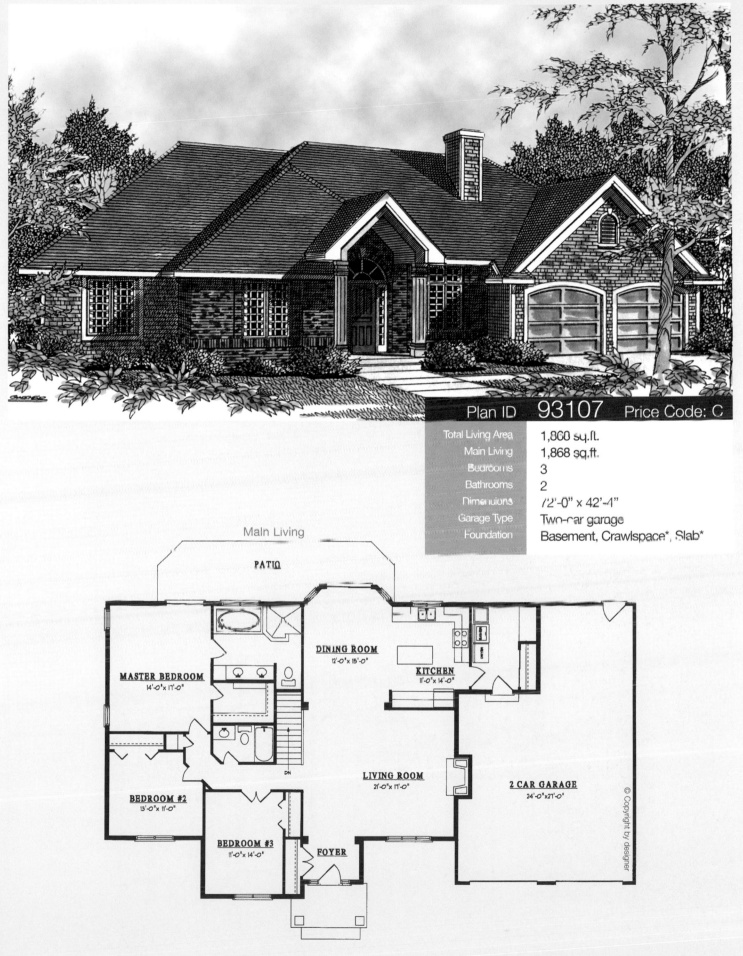

Plan ID 93107 Price Code: C

Total Living Area	1,800 sq. ft.
Main Living	1,868 sq. ft.
Bedrooms	3
Bathrooms	2
Dimensions	72'-0" x 42'-4"
Garage Type	Two-car garage
Foundation	Basement, Crawlspace*, Slab*

Main Living

PATIO

MASTER BEDROOM
14'-0" x 17'-0"

DINING ROOM
12'-0" x 15'-0"

KITCHEN
11'-0" x 14'-0"

BEDROOM #2
13'-0" x 11'-0"

LIVING ROOM
21'-0" x 17'-0"

2 CAR GARAGE
24'-0" x 21'-0"

DN

BEDROOM #3
11'-0" x 14'-0"

FOYER

© Copyright by designer

Plan ID 65635 Price Code: B

Total Living Area	1,655 sq.ft.
Main Living	1,655 sq.ft.
Bedrooms	3
Bathrooms	2
Dimensions	52'-0" x 66'-0"
Garage Type	Two-car garage
Foundation	Crawlspace, Slab

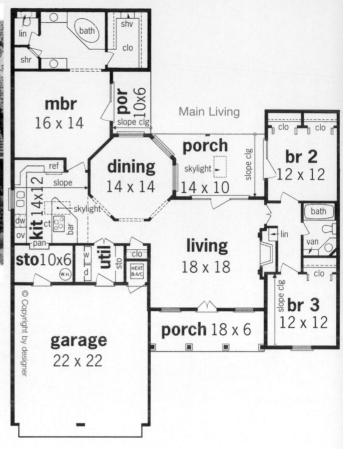

Plan ID 65624 Price Code: C

Total Living Area	1,891 sq.ft.
Main Living	1,891 sq.ft.
Bedrooms	2
Bathrooms	2
Dimensions	49'-0" x 64'-0"
Garage Type	Two-car garage
Foundation	Crawlspace, Slab

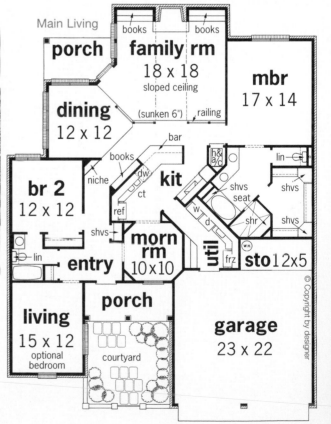

Plan ID	65677	Price Code: B
Total Living Area	1,682 sq.ft.	
Main Living	1,682 sq.ft.	
Bedrooms	4	
Bathrooms	2	
Dimensions	55'-0" x 50'-0"	
Garage Type	Two car garage	
Foundation	Basement, Slab	

Main Living

patio
16' x 12'

sitting
8' x 9'

wic
8' x 7'

br 2
16' x 10' - 6"

dining
12' x 10'

kit
12' x 13'

mbr
16' x 12'

wic

bath

living
17' x 15'

AC

util

bath
15' x 6'

fireplace

hair dryer stor.

stor.

stor.

br 3
12' x 12'

hall

stor.

stairs

foy

br 4
12' x 11'

clo

porch

clo

garage
21' x 21'

© Copyright by designer

Plan ID	**65616**	Price Code: B

Total Living Area	1,704 sq.ft.
Main Living	1,704 sq.ft.
Bedrooms	3
Bathrooms	2.5
Dimensions	71'-0" x 50'-0"
Garage Type	Two-car garage
Foundation	Crawlspace, Slab

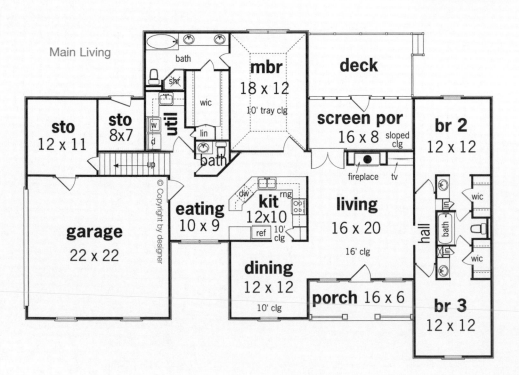

Main Living

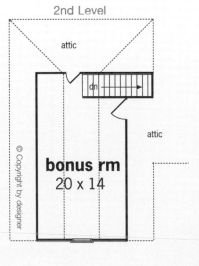

2nd Level

Plan ID **69017**   Price Code: C

Total Living Area	1,791 sq. ft.
Main Living	1,791 sq. ft.
Bedrooms	4
Bathrooms	2
Dimensions	67'-4" x 48'-0"
Garage Type	Two-car garage
Foundation	Basement

Main Living

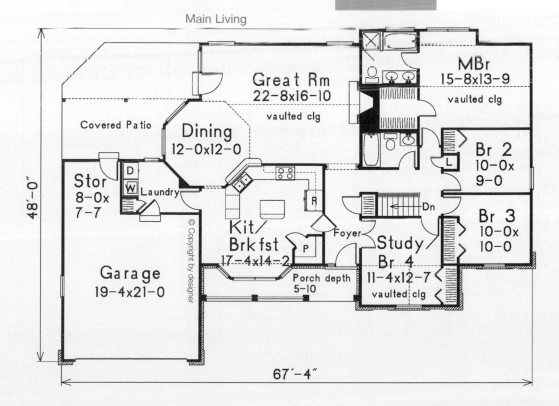

Plan ID **67046** Price Code: C

Total Living Area	1,905 sq.ft.
Main Living	1,905 sq.ft.
Bedrooms	3
Bathrooms	2
Dimensions	56'-0" x 59'-3"
Garage Type	Two-car garage
Foundation	Slab

Main Living

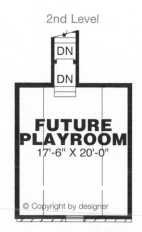

2nd Level

Plan ID 67042 Price Code: C

Total Living Area	1,795 sq.ft.
Main Living	1,795 sq.ft.
Bedrooms	3
Bathrooms	2
Dimensions	55'-0" x 57'-10"
Garage Type	Two-car garage
Foundation	Crawlspace, Slab

Main Living

MASTER SUITE
13'-0" x 16'-0"

DECORATIVE CEILING

SHOWER

LIN

MASTER BATH

CTS

PLANT LEDGE

CL.

ENTRY

PORCH

GREAT ROOM
15'-0' X 21'-3"

EATING BAR

D.W.

KIT

REF

DINING
13'-0" X 10'-0"

PANT

UTIL

D W

F/P

BRK.

CL.

STOR

BEDROOM 2
10'-0" X 11'-6"

HALL

BATH-2

LIN

CL.

BEDROOM 3
10'-0" X 11'-6"

UP

D

N

STOR

57'-10"

55'-0"

DOUBLE GARAGE
20'-0' X 22'-0"

© Copyright by designer

2nd Level

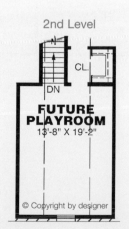

DN

FUTURE PLAYROOM
13'-8" X 19'-2"

CL.

© Copyright by designer

Plan ID 67036 Price Code: C

Total Living Area	1,974 sq.ft.
Main Living	1,480 sq.ft.
2nd Level	494 sq.ft.
Bedrooms	3
Bathrooms	2.5
Dimensions	62'-9" x 38'-6"
Garage Type	Two-car garage
Foundation	Crawlspace, Slab

Main Living

CL.

GREAT ROOM
18'-0" X 15'-6"
(VAULTED)

UTIL

D W

F

LIN

SHOWER

F/P

1/2 BATH

CL.

© Copyright by designer

MASTER BATH

CTS

REF

DOUBLE GARAGE
20'-0" X 21'-0"

38'-6"

UP

PANT

ISLAND

MASTER SUITE
13'-0" X 16'-0"
(VAULTED)

FOYER

DINING
10'-0" X 12'-4"

R

KIT

S

D.W.

PORCH

EATING BAR

BRK.
12'-0" X 11'-0"

62'-9"

2nd Level

GREAT ROOM BELOW

FLUE

BALCONY

FUTURE PLAYROOM
20'-5" X 12'-0"

© Copyright by designer

DN

BATH

W.I.C.

BEDR'M-3
10'-0" X 12'-4"

LIN

CL

BEDR'M-2
12'-0" X 12'-0"

ORDER NOW 1-800-235-5700 or at www.familyhomeplans.com

Plan ID	67044	Price Code: B

Total Living Area	1,593 sq.ft.
Main Living	1,503 sq.ft.
Bedrooms	3
Bathrooms	2
Dimensions	64'-4" x 41'-9"
Garage Type	Two-car garage
Foundation	Slab

Main Living

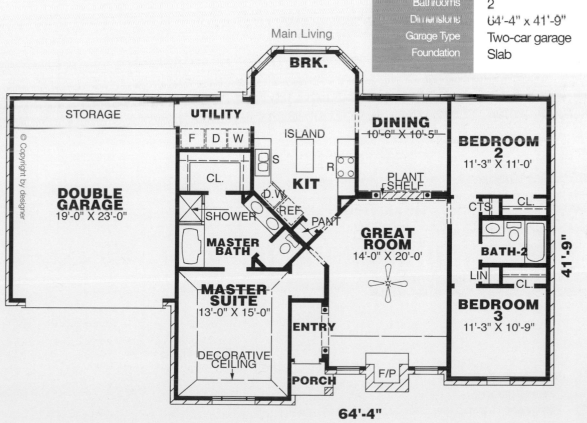

BRK.

STORAGE

UTILITY

F D W

ISLAND

DINING
10'-6" X 10'-5"

BEDROOM 2
11'-3" X 11'-0"

© Copyright by designer

CL.

S

KIT

R

PLANT SHELF

DOUBLE GARAGE
19'-0" X 23'-0"

D.W

REF

PANT

CTS

CL.

SHOWER

BATH-2

MASTER BATH

GREAT ROOM
14'-0" X 20'-0"

LIN

CL.

MASTER SUITE
13'-0" X 15'-0"

ENTRY

BEDROOM 3
11'-3" X 10'-9"

41'-9"

DECORATIVE CEILING

PORCH

F/P

64'-4"

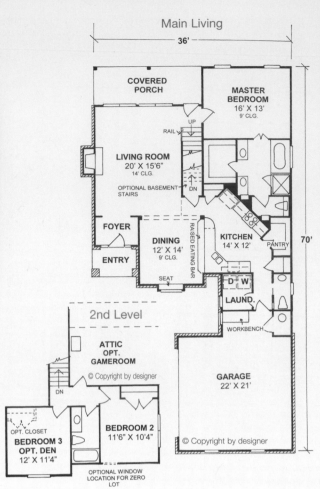

Main Living

36'

COVERED PORCH

MASTER BEDROOM
16' X 13'
9' CLG.

LIVING ROOM
20' X 15'6"
14' CLG.

OPTIONAL BASEMENT STAIRS

RAIL

UP

DN

70'

FOYER

ENTRY

DINING
12' X 14'
9' CLG.

RAISED EATING BAR

KITCHEN
14' X 12'

PANTRY

SEAT

D W

LAUND.

WORKBENCH

2nd Level

ATTIC
OPT.
GAMEROOM

© Copyright by designer

DN

GARAGE
22' X 21'

OPT. CLOSET

BEDROOM 3
OPT. DEN
12' X 11'4"

BEDROOM 2
11'6" X 10'4"

© Copyright by designer

OPTIONAL WINDOW LOCATION FOR ZERO LOT

Plan ID 68525 Price Code: B

Total Living Area	1,688 sq.ft.
Main Living	1,297 sq.ft.
2nd Level	391 sq.ft.
Bedrooms	3
Bathrooms	2.5
Dimensions	36'-0" x 70'-0"
Garage Type	Two-car garage
Foundation	Basement, Crawlspace, Slab

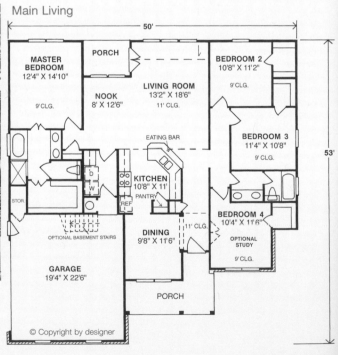

Main Living

50'

MASTER BEDROOM
12'4" X 14'10"
9' CLG.

PORCH

BEDROOM 2
10'8" X 11'2"
9' CLG.

NOOK
8' X 12'6"

LIVING ROOM
13'2" X 18'6"
11' CLG.

53'

EATING BAR

BEDROOM 3
11'4" X 10'8"
9' CLG.

STOR.

W

KITCHEN
10'8" X 11"
PANTRY

REF

BEDROOM 4
10'4" X 11'6"

OPTIONAL BASEMENT STAIRS

DINING
9'8" X 11'6"
11' CLG.

OPTIONAL STUDY
9' CLG.

GARAGE
19'4" X 22'6"

PORCH

© Copyright by designer

Plan ID 68432 Price Code: B

Total Living Area	1,694 sq.ft.
Main Living	1,694 sq.ft.
Bedrooms	4
Bathrooms	2
Dimensions	50'-0" x 53'-0"
Garage Type	Two-car garage
Foundation	Basement, Crawlspace, Slab

ORDER NOW 1-800-235-5700 or at **www.familyhomeplans.com**

Plan ID 97405 Price Code: C

Total Living Area	1,984 sq. ft.
Main Living	1,487 sq. ft.
2nd Level	497 sq. ft.
Bedrooms	3
Bathrooms	2.5
Dimensions	62' 0" x 42'-0"
Garage Type	Two-car garage
Foundation	Basement, Crawlspace*, Slab*

Main Living

STORAGE 7'-4" X 6'-10"

UTILITY 8' CH

PDWR 9' CH

2 CAR GARAGE 21'-4" X 22'6" + STORAGE AREA 9' CH

© Copyright by designer

BREAKFAST ROOM 12'-0" X 9'-0"

KITCHEN 11'-8" X 13'-0" 9' CH

LIVING ROOM 14'-0" X 19'-4" 18' CH

MASTER BED ROOM 12' 0" X 16' 0" 9'-11" CH

PANT

DINING ROOM 11'-8" X 12'-0" 9' CH

ENTRY 18' CH

PORCH 9' CLG.

UP TO 2ND FL

CLO.

MASTER BATH 9' CH

MASTER CLOSET 9' CH

LINEN   SEAT

42'-6"

62'-0"

2nd Level

© Copyright by designer

BEDROOM 3 11'-8"X10'-0" 8'-10" CH

CLOSET

248 SQ.FT. OPTIONAL ATTIC 15'-0" X 15'-0" 8' CH

BATHROOM 8' CH

CLOSET

BEDROOM 2 11'-8" X 11'-0" 8'-10" CH

LIVING ROOM 14'-0"X19'-4" 18' CH

OPTIONAL ATTIC 8'- X 8' + DORMER 8' CH

HALL-WAY 8' CH

DOWN

OPEN BELOW 18' CH

What's the right STYLE for you ?

Certain styles seem to be more appealing to many of us than others. Actually, the term "style" becomes increasingly difficult to define or describe. All of the labels such as *Tudor, Victorian, French, European, etc.* seem more and more vague. Many homes borrow elements from various styles to create a blend of details and features.

MUCH MORE IMPORTANT THAN ADHERING TO A CERTAIN STYLE IS TO FIND A HOME PLAN THAT SEEMS APPROPRIATE TO YOUR BUILDING SITE. The most appealing homes typically are those that appear appropriate in their surroundings. Not only does this refer to the natural conditions such as topography, but also to existing structures close by. Consider selecting an exterior design that looks as

though it belongs on the land. If the surrounding area has cedar trees and stone outcroppings, relate the home to the land by using some of these same materials. On the other hand, if you have a lot in a subdivision with homes nearby, respect the existing architecture.

Avoid trying to import that Southern California plan with low pitched tile roofing that you fell in love with on your vacation. While it's lovely in California, it will look totally out of place in an existing neighborhood in New England.

As you browse through the plans in this book or any collection of house plans, resist the urge to pass over plans with an exterior you don't like. If you

Details become critical
when creating homes with
a sense of character

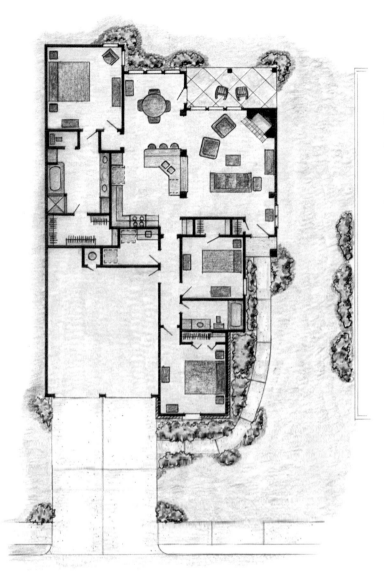

These two front elevations show how dramatically different exterior designs can be created with the same floor plan.

quickly pass by that Mediterranean design because you have your heart set on a Country French style, you just may overlook a floor plan that addresses many of your requirements. Remember, exterior design can easily be changed. In fact, exteriors can often be revised with much less effort that it takes to dramatically alter a floor plan.

Excerpted from *Home Plan Buyer's Guide,* an upcoming book by **Larry W. Garnett**

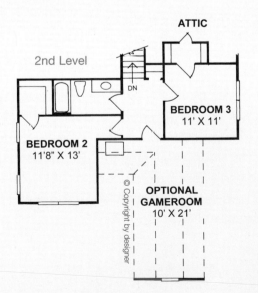

Plan ID	68170	Price Code: C

Total Living Area	1,867 sq.ft.
Main Living	1,375 sq.ft.
2nd Level	492 sq.ft.
Bedrooms	3
Bathrooms	2.5
Dimensions	49'-0" x 60'-0"
Garage Type	Two-car garage
Foundation	Basement*, Crawlspace*, Slab

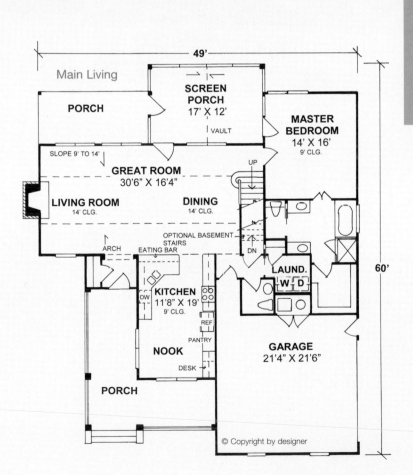

Main Living

49'

PORCH

SCREEN PORCH
17' X 12'
VAULT

MASTER BEDROOM
14' X 16'
9' CLG.

SLOPE 9' TO 14'

GREAT ROOM
30'6" X 16'4"

UP

LIVING ROOM
14' CLG.

DINING
14' CLG.

OPTIONAL BASEMENT STAIRS

ARCH

EATING BAR

DN

60'

LAUND.
W D

KITCHEN
11'8" X 19'
9' CLG.

DW

REF

PANTRY

NOOK

DESK

GARAGE
21'4" X 21'6"

PORCH

© Copyright by designer

ATTIC

2nd Level

DN

BEDROOM 3
11' X 11'

BEDROOM 2
11'8" X 13'

OPTIONAL GAMEROOM
10' X 21'

© Copyright by designer

ORDER NOW 1-800-235-5700 or at www.familyhomeplans.com

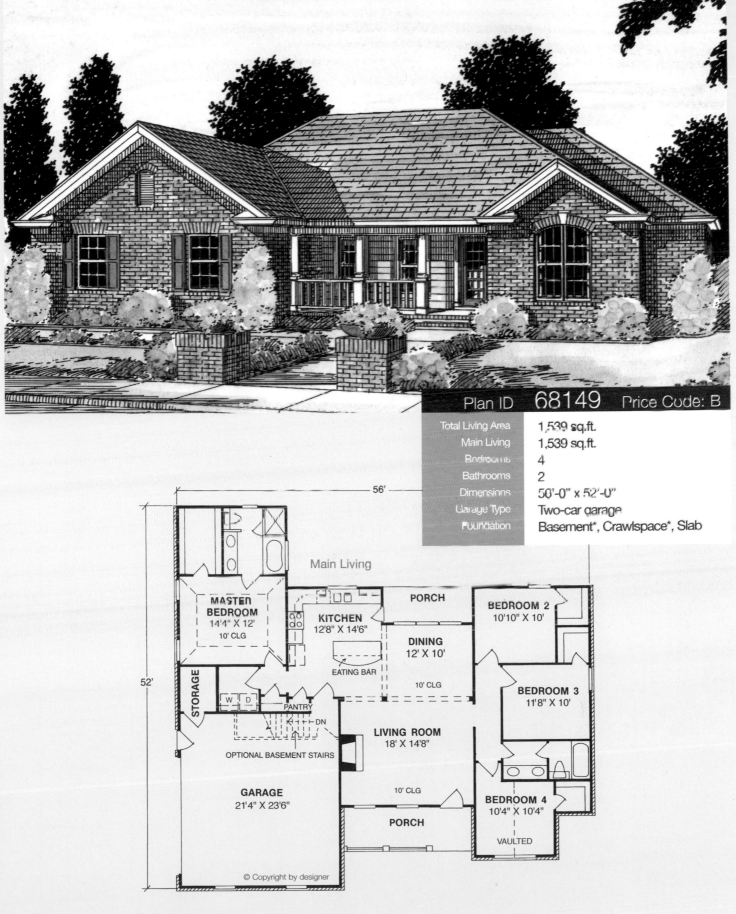

Plan ID **68149** Price Code: **B**

Total Living Area	1,539 sq.ft.
Main Living	1,539 sq.ft.
Bedrooms	4
Bathrooms	2
Dimensions	50'-0" x 52'-0"
Garage Type	Two-car garage
Foundation	Basement*, Crawlspace*, Slab

Main Living

MASTER BEDROOM
14'4" X 12'
10' CLG

KITCHEN
12'8" X 14'6"

PORCH

BEDROOM 2
10'10" X 10'

DINING
12' X 10'
10' CLG

EATING BAR

STORAGE

W D

PANTRY

DN

OPTIONAL BASEMENT STAIRS

LIVING ROOM
18' X 14'8"

BEDROOM 3
11'8" X 10'

GARAGE
21'4" X 23'6"

10' CLG

BEDROOM 4
10'4" X 10'4"

PORCH

VAULTED

56'

52'

© Copyright by designer

Main Living

Master Bedroom
14'6"x 13'

Porch

Breakfast
8'10"x 9'8"

Living
15'x 18'

Bedroom
9'6"x 11'

Bedroom
9'6"x 11'

Dining
10'x 11'

Two Car Garage
18'x 20'

© Copyright by designer

Porch

Porch

Plan ID **94517** Price Code: A

Total Living Area	1,500 sq.ft.
Main Living	1,500 sq.ft.
Bedrooms	3
Bathrooms	2
Dimensions	64'-0" x 45'-0"
Garage Type	Two-car garage
Foundation	Basement, Crawlspace, Slab

Main Living

Porch

Stor.

Master Bedroom
13'x 15'2"

Breakfast

Bedroom
12'x 10'4"

Living
13'8"x 17'

Bedroom
12'x 11'6"

© Copyright by designer

Porch

Plan ID **94522** Price Code: B

Total Living Area	1,606 sq.ft.
Main Living	1,606 sq.ft.
Bedrooms	3
Bathrooms	2
Dimensions	33'-0" x 64'-0"
Foundation	Slab

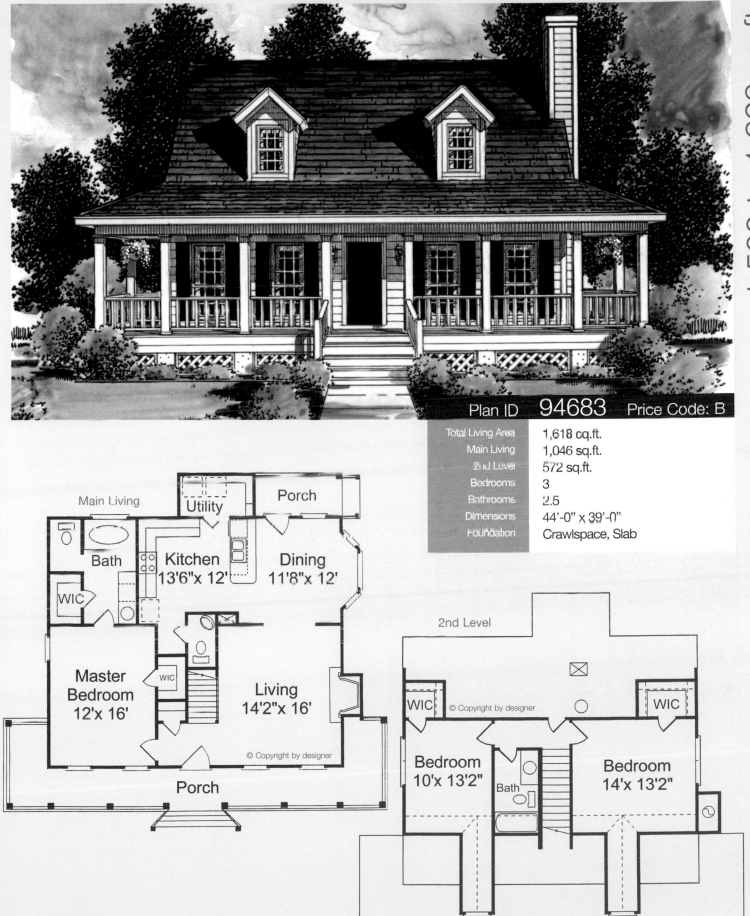

Plan ID 94683 Price Code: B

Total Living Area	1,618 sq.ft.
Main Living	1,046 sq.ft.
2nd Level	572 sq.ft.
Bedrooms	3
Bathrooms	2.5
Dimensions	44'-0" x 39'-0"
Foundation	Crawlspace, Slab

Main Living

Porch

Utility

Bath

Kitchen
13'6"x 12'

Dining
11'8"x 12'

WIC

WIC

Master
Bedroom
12'x 16'

Living
14'2"x 16'

© Copyright by designer

Porch

2nd Level

WIC

WIC

© Copyright by designer

Bedroom
10'x 13'2"

Bath

Bedroom
14'x 13'2"

Plan ID	94682	Price Code: B

Total Living Area	1,609 sq.ft.
Main Living	1,072 sq.ft.
2nd Level	537 sq.ft.
Bedrooms	3
Bathrooms	2.5
Dimensions	62'-0" x 46'-0"
Garage Type	Two-car garage
Foundation	Crawlspace, Slab

Main Living

© Copyright by designer

Patio

Utility

1/2 Ba.

Kitchen
12' x 12'

Dining
11' x 12'

Two Car
Garage

Bath

WIC

Master
Bedroom
12' x 16'

Family
13'7" x 19'

Porch

2nd Level

© Copyright by designer

Attic Storage

Hall

Bath

Bedroom
12'1" x 12'

Bedroom
13'6" x 12'

Plan ID 69515 Price Code: B

Total Living Area	1,670 sq.ft.
Main Living	1,134 sq.ft.
2nd Level	545 sq.ft.
Bedrooms	3
Bathrooms	2.5
Dimensions	42'-0" x 45'-0"
Foundation	Basement, Crawlspace, Slab

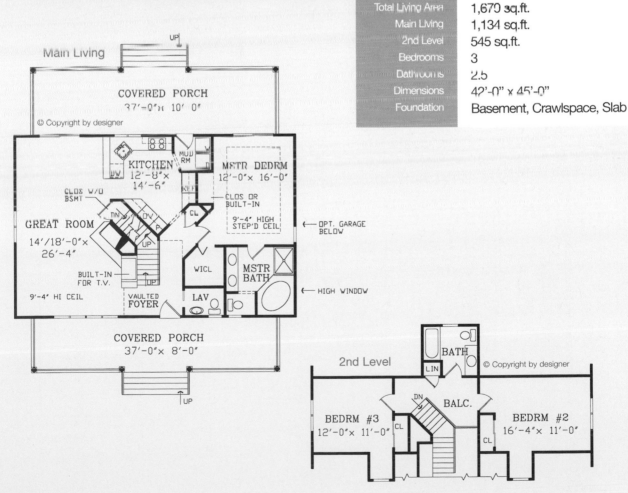

Plan ID 69503 Price Code: C

Total Living Area	1,892 sq.ft.
Main Living	1,892 sq.ft.
Bedrooms	3
Bathrooms	2.5
Dimensions	65'-0" x 44'-0"
Garage Type	Two-car garage
Foundation	Basement, Crawlspace, Slab

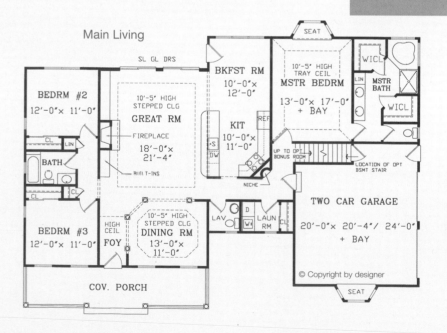

Main Living

SL GL DRS

BEDRM #2
12'-0"x 11'-0"

10'-5" HIGH
STEPPED CLG
GREAT RM
FIREPLACE
18'-0"x
21'-4"
BUILT-INS

BKFST RM
10'-0"x
12'-0"

10'-5" HIGH
TRAY CEIL
MSTR BEDRM
13'-0"x 17'-0"
+ BAY

WICL
LIN
MSTR
BATH
WICL

SEAT

KIT
10'-0"x
11'-0"
REF
S
DW

CL LIN
BATH
CL CL

NICHE

UP TO OPT
BONUS ROOM
LOCATION OF OPT
BSMT STAIR

BEDRM #3
12'-0"x 11'-0"
HIGH
CEIL
FOY

10'-5" HIGH
STEPPED CLG
DINING RM
13'-0"x
11'-0"

LAV
D
W
LAUN
RM
CL

TWO CAR GARAGE
20'-0"x 20'-4"/ 24'-0"
+ BAY

© Copyright by designer

COV. PORCH

SEAT

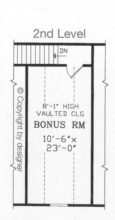

2nd Level

DN

8'-1" HIGH
VAULTED CLG
BONUS RM
10'-6"x
23'-0"

© Copyright by designer

Plan ID	99641	Price Code: B
Total Living Area	1,579 sq.ft.	
Main Living	1,579 sq.ft.	
Bedrooms	3	
Bathrooms	2	
Dimensions	67'-6" x 53'-0"	
Garage Type	Two-car garage	
Foundation	Basement, Crawlspace, Slab	

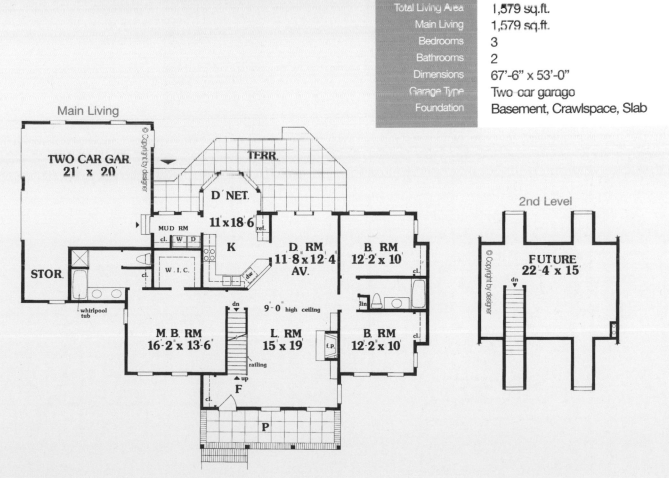

Main Living

2nd Level

Plan ID **99683**   Price Code: C

Total Living Area	1,945 sq.ft.
Main Living	1,375 sq.ft.
2nd Level	570 sq.ft.
Bedrooms	3
Bathrooms	2.5
Dimensions	65'-8" x 43'-10"
Garage Type	Two-car garage
Foundation	Basement, Crawlspace, Slab

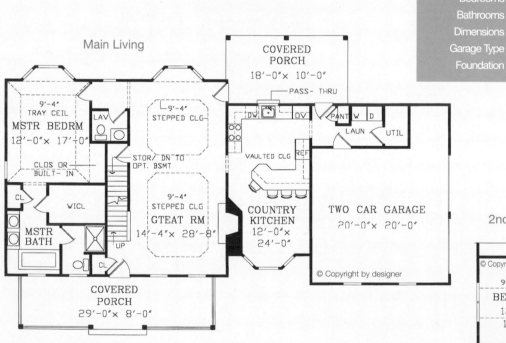

Main Living

COVERED PORCH
18'-0" x 10'-0"

PASS-THRU

9'-4" TRAY CEIL
MSTR BEDRM
12'-0" x 17'-0"

LAV

9'-4" STEPPED CLG

STOR/ DN TO OPT. BSMT

CLOS OR BUILT-IN

CL

WICL

UP

MSTR BATH

9'-4" STEPPED CLG
GTEAT RM
14'-4" x 28'-8"

DW

REF

VAULTED CLG

COUNTRY KITCHEN
12'-0" x 24'-0"

PANT

W D

LAUN   UTIL

TWO CAR GARAGE
20'-0" x 20'-0"

CL

© Copyright by designer

COVERED PORCH
29'-0" x 8'-0"

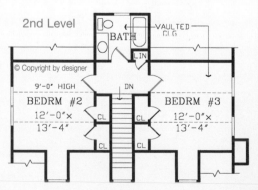

2nd Level

BATH

VAULTED CLG

LIN

© Copyright by designer

DN

9'-0" HIGH
BEDRM #2
12'-0" x 13'-4"

CL   CL

9'-0" HIGH
BEDRM #3
12'-0" x 13'-4"

CL   CL

ORDER NOW 1-800-235-5700 or at www.familyhomeplans.com

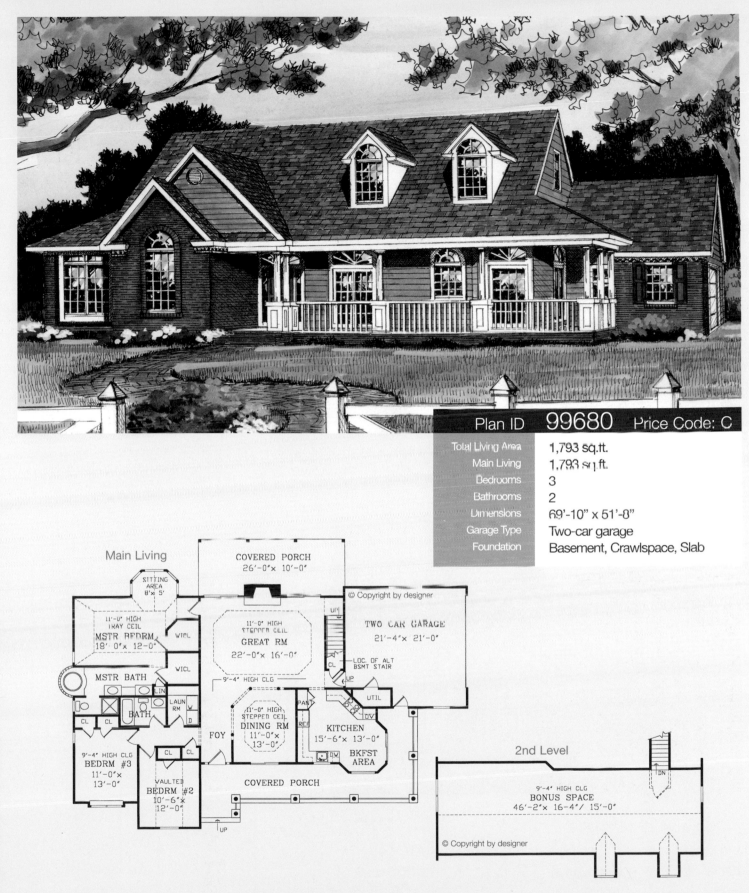

Plan ID **99680** Price Code: C

Total Living Area	1,793 sq. ft.
Main Living	1,793 sq. ft.
Bedrooms	3
Bathrooms	2
Dimensions	69'-10" x 51'-8"
Garage Type	Two-car garage
Foundation	Basement, Crawlspace, Slab

Main Living

COVERED PORCH
26'-0" x 10'-0"

SITTING AREA
8' x 5'

11'-0" HIGH TRAY CEIL
MSTR BEDRM
18'-0" x 12'-0"

WICL

11'-0" HIGH STEPPED CEIL
GREAT RM
22'-0" x 16'-0"

© Copyright by designer

UP

TWO CAR GARAGE
21'-4" x 21'-0"

WICL

MSTR BATH

9'-4" HIGH CLG

CL

LOC. OF ALT BSMT STAIR

LIN

BATH

LAUN RM

UP

UTIL

CL CL

PANT

D

DV

9'-4" HIGH CLG
BEDRM #3
11'-0" x 13'-0"

CL CL

FOY

11'-0" HIGH STEPPED CEIL
DINING RM
11'-0" x 13'-0"

REF

KITCHEN
15'-6" x 13'-0"

VAULTED
BEDRM #2
10'-6" x 12'-0"

COVERED PORCH

DW

BKFST AREA

UP

2nd Level

9'-4" HIGH CLG
BONUS SPACE
46'-2" x 16'-4" / 15'-0"

DN

© Copyright by designer

Main Living

Plan ID 62177   Price Code: C

Total Living Area	1,760 sq.ft.
Main Living	1,760 sq.ft.
Bedrooms	4
Bathrooms	2
Dimensions	53'-2" x 64'-4"
Garage Type	Two-car garage
Foundation	Basement*, Crawlspace, Slab, Walkout basement*

Main Living

Plan ID 82011   Price Code: B

Total Living Area	1,654 sq.ft.
Main Living	1,654 sq.ft.
Bedrooms	3
Bathrooms	2
Dimensions	49'-0" x 58'-6"
Garage Type	Two-car garage
Foundation	Basement, Crawlspace, Slab, Walkout basement

Plan ID 82050 Price Code: B

Total Living Area	1,746 sq.ft.
Main Living	1,746 sq.ft
Bedrooms	3
Bathrooms	2
Dimensions	67'-0" x 51'-10"
Garage Type	Two-car garage
Foundation	Basement, Crawlspace, Slab

Main Living

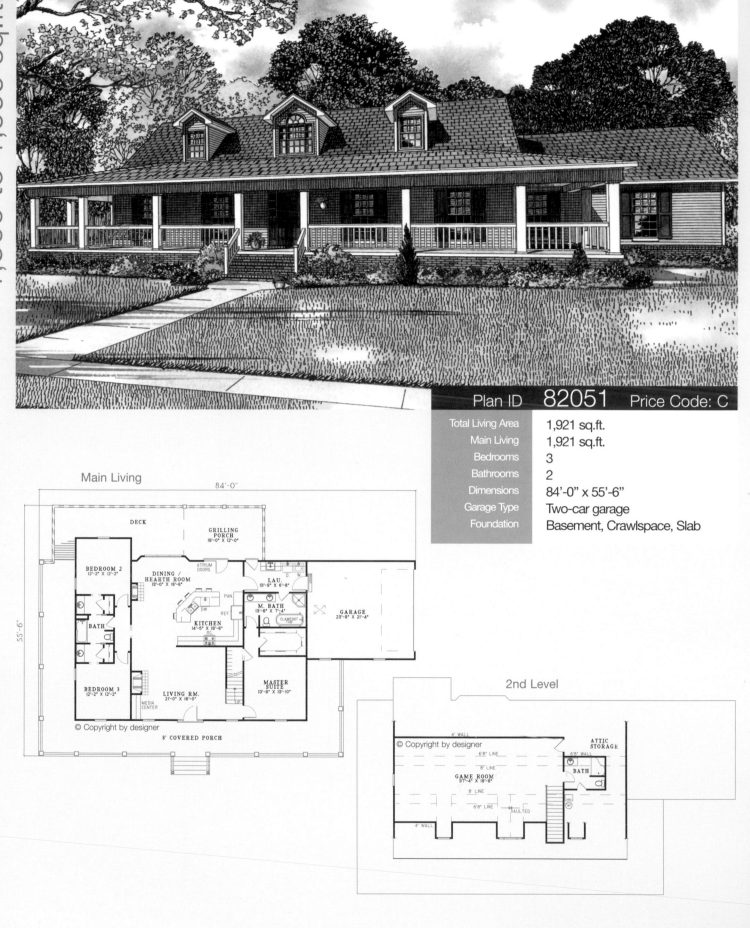

Plan ID 82051 Price Code: C

Total Living Area	1,921 sq.ft.
Main Living	1,921 sq.ft.
Bedrooms	3
Bathrooms	2
Dimensions	84'-0" x 55'-6"
Garage Type	Two-car garage
Foundation	Basement, Crawlspace, Slab

Main Living

84'-0"

DECK

GRILLING PORCH
18'-0" X 12'-0"

ATRIUM DOORS

LAU.
13'-8" X 6'-8"

BEDROOM 2
12'-2" X 12'-2"

DINING / HEARTH ROOM
13'-0" X 19'-6"

PAN

M. BATH
13'-8" X 7'-4"

GARAGE
29'-8" X 21'-4"

BATH

KITCHEN
14'-5" X 18'-8"

DW

REF

CLAW&POT

55'-6"

BEDROOM 3
12'-2" X 12'-2"

MEDIA CENTER

LIVING RM.
21'-0" X 16'-0"

UP

MASTER SUITE
13'-8" X 13'-10"

© Copyright by designer

8' COVERED PORCH

2nd Level

© Copyright by designer

4' WALL

6'-8" LINE

8' LINE

GAME ROOM
37'-4" X 18'-8"

8' LINE

6'-8" LINE

VAULTED

4' WALL

ATTIC STORAGE

6'-8" WALL

BATH

Plan ID 62086 Price Code: B

Total Living Area	1,597 sq.ft.
Main Living	1,597 sq.ft.
Bedrooms	3
Bathrooms	2
Dimensions	59'-0" x 67'-0"
Garage Type	Two-car garage
Foundation	Basement*, Crawlspace, Slab, Walkout basement*

Main Living

Plan ID **97757** **Price Code: C**

Total Living Area	1,755 sq.ft.
Main Living	1,755 sq.ft.
Bedrooms	3
Bathrooms	2
Dimensions	78'-6" x 47'-7"
Garage Type	Three-car garage
Foundation	Basement

Main Living

Master Bedroom
17'2" x 12'

Dining
11'5" x 11'4"

Porch

Great Room
20'9" x 17'

Sloped Ceiling

Stairs down

Kitchen
18' x 11'

Sloped Ceiling

Bath

Foyer

Bedroom
11'2" x 10'4"

Laun.

Three Car Garage
31'8" x 33'2"

Bedroom
12' x 10'4"

Porch

Porch

© Copyright by designer

47'-7"

78'-6"

ORDER NOW 1-800-235-5700 or at www.familyhomeplans.com

Plan ID	92461	Price Code: C

Total Living Area	1,963 sq.ft.
Main Living	1,963 sq.ft.
Bedrooms	3
Bathrooms	2
Dimensions	57'-8" x 57'-6"
Garage Type	Two-car garage
Foundation	Basement

Main Living

2nd Level

Main Living

Porch

Dining Area
11'6" x 14'2"

Master Bedroom
14' x 11'9"

Great Room
16'6" x 17'

Kitchen
18' x 10'10"

Bath

slope ceiling

slope ceiling

Foyer

Bath

Hall

Two-car Garage
20' x 22'

Laun.

Porch

Bedroom
10'6" x 10'6"

© Copyright by designer

Bedroom
11' x 10'6"

47'

60'

Plan ID 92649   Price Code: B

Total Living Area	1,508 sq.ft.
Main Living	1,508 sq.ft.
Bedrooms	3
Bathrooms	2
Dimensions	60'-0" x 47'-0"
Garage Type	Two-car garage
Foundation	Basement

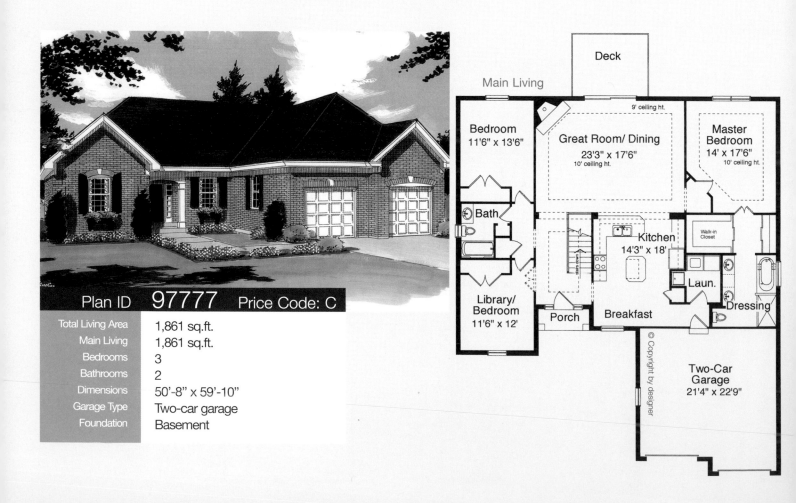

Deck

Main Living

Bedroom
11'6" x 13'6"

Great Room/ Dining
23'3" x 17'6"
10' ceiling ht.

9' ceiling ht.

Master Bedroom
14' x 17'6"
10' ceiling ht.

Bath

Kitchen
14'3" x 18'

Walk-in Closet

Library/ Bedroom
11'6" x 12'

Porch

Breakfast

Laun.

Dressing

© Copyright by designer

Two-Car Garage
21'4" x 22'9"

Plan ID 97777   Price Code: C

Total Living Area	1,861 sq.ft.
Main Living	1,861 sq.ft.
Bedrooms	3
Bathrooms	2
Dimensions	50'-8" x 59'-10"
Garage Type	Two-car garage
Foundation	Basement

Plan ID	**97760**	Price Code: B

Total Living Area	1,611 sq.ft.
Main Living	1,611 sq.ft.
Bedrooms	3
Bathrooms	2
Dimensions	66' 4" x 43'-10"
Garage Type	Two-car garage
Foundation	Basement, Crawlspace*

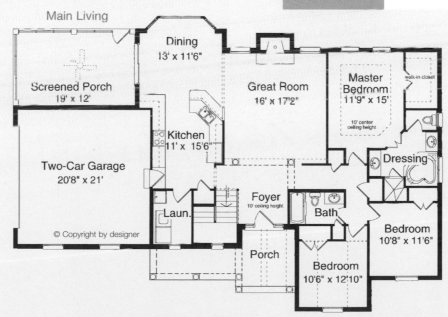

Main Living

Dining
13' x 11'6"

Screened Porch
19' x 12'

Great Room
16' x 17'2"

Master Bedroom
11'9" x 15'
10' center ceiling height

walk-in closet

Kitchen
11' x 15'6"

Two-Car Garage
20'8" x 21'

Dressing

Foyer
10' ceiling height

Laun.

Bath

© Copyright by designer

Bedroom
10'8" x 11'6"

Porch

Bedroom
10'6" x 12'10"

Plan ID 92446 Price Code: C

Total Living Area	1,992 sq.ft.
Main Living	1,992 sq.ft.
Bedrooms	3
Bathrooms	3
Dimensions	66'-2" x 62'-0"
Garage Type	Two-car garage
Foundation	Basement, Slab

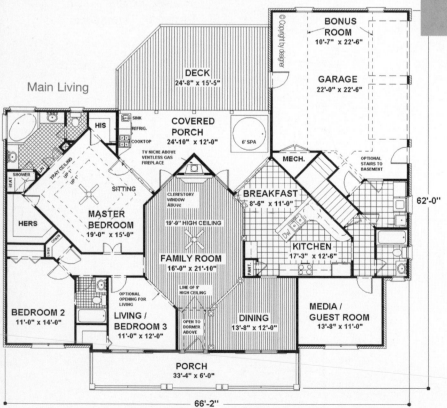

Main Living

Plan ID	92421	Price Code: C

Total Living Area	1,992 sq.ft.
Main Living	1,992 sq.ft.
Bedrooms	3
Bathrooms	2.5
Dimensions	63'-0" x 57'-2"
Garage Type	Three-car garage
Foundation	Basement, Crawlspace, Slab

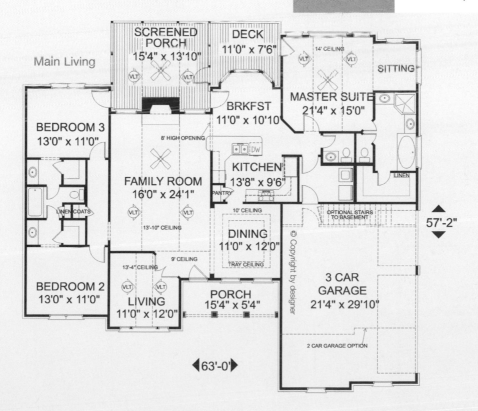

Main Living

SCREENED PORCH 15'4" x 13'10"

DECK 11'0" x 7'6"

14' CEILING

SITTING

MASTER SUITE 21'4" x 15'0"

BEDROOM 3 13'0" x 11'0"

BRKFST 11'0" x 10'10"

8' HIGH OPENING

DW

FAMILY ROOM 16'0" x 24'1"

KITCHEN 13'8" x 9'6"

PANTRY

LINEN

13'-10" CEILING

LINEN COATS

10' CEILING

OPTIONAL STAIRS TO BASEMENT

57'-2"

DINING 11'0" x 12'0"

13'-4" CEILING

9' CEILING

TRAY CEILING

BEDROOM 2 13'0" x 11'0"

LIVING 11'0" x 12'0"

PORCH 15'4" x 5'4"

© Copyright by designer

3 CAR GARAGE 21'4" x 29'10"

2 CAR GARAGE OPTION

◄ 63'-0" ►

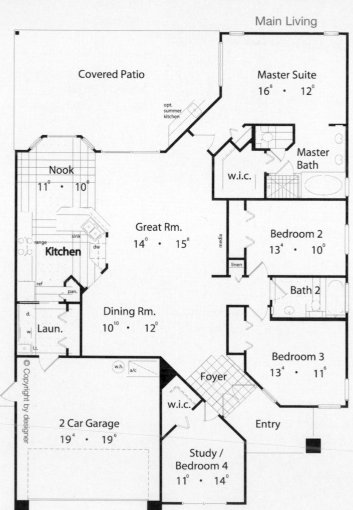

Main Living

Plan ID	63114	Price Code: C
Total Living Area		1,868 sq.ft.
Main Living		1,868 sq.ft.
Bedrooms		3
Bathrooms		2
Dimensions		45'-0" x 66'-0"
Garage Type		Two-car garage
Foundation		Slab

Covered Patio

opt. summer kitchen

Master Suite
16⁸ · 12⁰

Master Bath

w.i.c.

Nook
11⁰ · 10⁰

Kitchen

Great Rm.
14⁰ · 15⁸

media

linen

Bedroom 2
13⁴ · 10⁰

Bath 2

Dining Rm.
10¹⁰ · 12⁰

Laun.

© Copyright by designer

w.h. a/c

2 Car Garage
19⁴ · 19⁶

w.i.c.

Foyer

Bedroom 3
13⁴ · 11⁶

Entry

Study /
Bedroom 4
11⁰ · 14⁰

Plan ID	**63095**	Price Code: C

Total Living Area	1,758 sq. ft.
Main Living	1,758 sq ft
Bedrooms	3
Bathrooms	2
Dimensions	60'-0" x 45'-0"
Garage Type	Two-car garage
Foundation	Slab

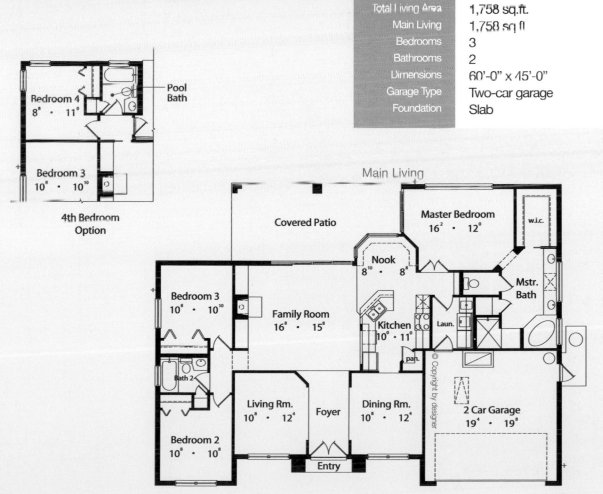

Bedroom 4
8⁸ · 11⁰

Pool Bath

Bedroom 3
10⁸ · 10¹⁰

4th Bedroom Option

Main Living

Covered Patio

Master Bedroom
16² · 12⁰

w.i.c.

Nook
8¹⁰ · 8⁸

Mstr. Bath

Bedroom 3
10⁸ · 10¹⁰

Family Room
16⁸ · 15⁸

Kitchen
10⁰ · 11⁰

Laun.

Bath 2

pan.

© Copyright by designer

Living Rm.
10⁸ · 12⁴

Foyer

Dining Rm.
10⁸ · 12⁴

2 Car Garage
19⁴ · 19⁸

Bedroom 2
10⁸ · 10⁰

Entry

Main Living

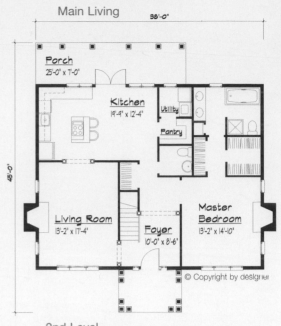

Plan ID 41008 Price Code: B

Total Living Area	1,749 sq.ft.
Main Living	1,178 sq.ft.
2nd Level	571 sq.ft.
Bedrooms	3
Bathrooms	2.5
Dimensions	38'-0" x 45'-0"
Foundation	Basement, Crawlspace

2nd Level

Main Living

Plan ID 41022 Price Code: B

Total Living Area	1,604 sq.ft.
Main Living	1,152 sq.ft.
2nd Level	452 sq.ft.
Bedrooms	3
Bathrooms	2.5
Dimensions	36'-0" x 64'-0"
Garage Type	Two-car garage
Foundation	Basement, Crawlspace

2nd Level

Plan ID 41003 Price Code: B

Total Living Area	1,094 sq. ft.
Main Living	1,216 sq. ft.
2nd Level	478 sq. ft.
Bedrooms	3
Bathrooms	3
Dimensions	37'-0" x 62'-0"
Garage Type	Two-car garage
Foundation	Basement, Crawlspace

Main Living

© Copyright by designer

Deck
14'-9" x 22'-4"

Garage
20'-0" x 20'-0"

Storage
14'-0" x 4'-0"

Kitchen
10'-0" x 14'-5"

Utility

Dining Rm.
10'-0" x 14'-5"

Pantry

Great Room
20'-0" x 16'-3"
(cathedral clg.)

Master Bedroom
13'-5" x 16'-3"

Porch
22'-8" x 6'-8"

2nd Level

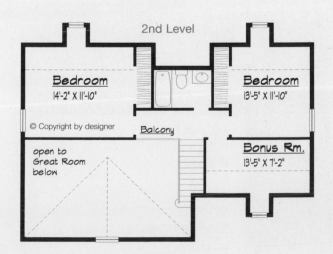

Bedroom
14'-2" x 11'-10"

Bedroom
13'-5" x 11'-10"

© Copyright by designer

Balcony

open to Great Room below

Bonus Rm.
13'-5" x 7'-2"

Plan ID 41000 Price Code: B

Total Living Area	1,694 sq.ft.
Main Living	1,216 sq.ft.
2nd Level	478 sq.ft.
Bedrooms	3
Bathrooms	2.5
Dimensions	37'-0" x 31'-0"
Foundation	Basement, Crawlspace

Plan ID 41013 Price Code: C

Total Living Area	1,974 sq.ft.
Main Living	1,152 sq.ft.
2nd Level	822 sq.ft.
Bedrooms	4
Bathrooms	2
Dimensions	56'-0" x 32'-0"
Foundation	Basement, Crawlspace, Slab

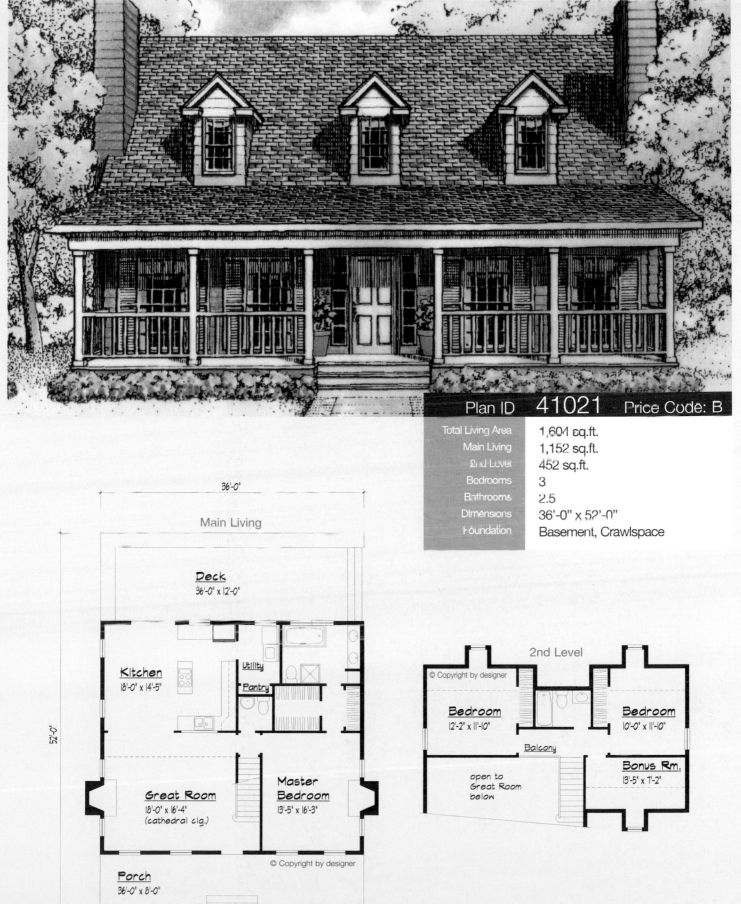

Plan ID 41021   Price Code: B

Total Living Area	1,604 sq.ft.
Main Living	1,152 sq.ft.
2nd Level	452 sq.ft.
Bedrooms	3
Bathrooms	2.5
Dimensions	36'-0" x 52'-0"
Foundation	Basement, Crawlspace

36'-0"

Main Living

Deck
36'-0" x 12'-0"

Kitchen
18'-0" x 14'-5"

Utility

Pantry

52'-0"

Great Room
18'-0" x 16'-4"
(cathedral clg.)

Master Bedroom
13'-5" x 16'-3"

© Copyright by designer

Porch
36'-0" x 8'-0"

2nd Level

© Copyright by designer

Bedroom
12'-2" x 11'-10"

Bedroom
10'-0" x 11'-10"

Balcony

open to
Great Room
below

Bonus Rm.
13'-5" x 7'-2"

Plan ID 96811 Price Code: C

Total Living Area	1,954 sq.ft.
Main Living	1,954 sq.ft.
Bedrooms	3
Bathrooms	2.5
Dimensions	74'-6" x 43'-0"
Garage Type	Two-car garage
Foundation	Crawlspace, Slab

Main Living

PATIO
42'-6"x12'-0"

STORAGE
HW
LNDRY/MUD ROOM
16'-11"x8'-5"
MECH
F

BREAKFAST
11'-7"x11'-2"

F.P.

MASTER BATH
PLANTS
JACC.

GREAT ROOM
13'-0"x29'-5"
(VAULTED)

MASTER BEDROOM
15'-0"x13'-1"
(VAULTED)

W.I.C.
SHWR.

KITCHEN
11'-7"x11'-0"

PNTRY
FRIG

GARAGE
20'-8"x20'-8"

BATH

LINEN

BEDROOM #2
11'-0"x12'-0"

W.I.C.

BEDROOM #3
11'-7"x10'-6"

W.I.C.

FORMAL DINING
11'-7"x12'-1"

OPTIONAL HALF-WALL

© Copyright by designer

COVERED PORCH
32'-6"x10'-0"

Optional

STORAGE
LNDRY
1/2 BATH
D W

MUDROOM
14'-4"x8'-11"
DN

© Copyright by designer

Plan ID 96808   PrIce Code: C

Total Living Area	1,784 sq.ft.
Main Living	1,112 sq.ft.
2nd Level	672 sq.ft.
Bedrooms	3
Bathrooms	2.5
Dimensions	51'-0" x 50'-9"
Garage Type	Two-car garage
Foundation	Basement, Crawlspace, Slab

Main Living

9' WIDE COVERED PORCH

CANTILEVERED 2nd FLOOR

MASTER BATH

SHWR · JACC · W.I.C.

SHOP/ STORAGE 7'-7"x11'-9"

OPTIONAL TWO CAR GARAGE

LNDRY 1/2 BATH · D W

COATS PNTRY

UP

DN

GARAGE 14'-0"x22'-2"

COATS

10' OVERHEAD DOOR

DINING 10'-3"x10'-5" (9' CLG)

KITCHEN 10'-6"x10'-5" (9' CLG) BAR DW LS FRIG LS

MASTER BEDROOM 12'-0"x17'-6" (9' CLG)

LIVING ROOM 20'-9"x15'-6" (9' CLG)

VENTLESS GAS FIREPLACE

OPTIONAL DOOR

8' WIDE COVERED PORCH

© Copyright by designer

2nd Level

BEDROOM #2 10'-0"x11'-1" (VAULT CLG) W.I.C.

BEDROOM #3 10'-0"x11'-1" (VAULT CLG) W.I.C.

LINEN

RIDGE OF VAULT

BATH

DN

GATHERING ROOM 18'-11"x15'-6" (VAULT CLG)

TUB/SHWR

MEDIA CENTER

8' CLG

© Copyright by designer

What makes a ROOM INVITING ?

AS WITH ANY DISCUSSION RELATING TO DESIGN ELEMENTS, AN ANALYSIS OF JUST WHAT MAKES A ROOM SEEM INVITING OR APPEALING IS OFTEN QUITE SUBJECTIVE. Diverse personal preferences make it difficult to outline specific "do's - and - don'ts'," but a few general guidelines can help increase the attraction of several areas in a home.

The front door and entry require special attention since this area normally provides the first and last impression of any home. While grand entries with elaborate staircases and 20' ceilings continue to be built, some designers and architects consider a more subdued space with lower ceilings and functional stair design to be what the market desires. Entering a home with an enormous expanse of white walls and no separation from the family room can be an overwhelming and often unwelcoming experience.

Windows certainly play a large role in the creation of comfortable and inviting spaces. Careful placement within a room actually makes the area seem much larger. Locating two windows at the corner of a bedroom extends the view diagonally across the room. Taller ceilings allow an opportunity to use

clerestory windows. These small windows offer additional natural light and become a major design element in the room. Window seats can also become focal points as they supply plenty of natural light and also create cozy alcoves for sitting. Transoms above windows not only illuminate the room with additional light, but often add to the exterior appeal of the design as well.

When quizzed about the details they find appealing in older homes, many people invariably mention the "nooks and crannies" that were abundant in homes built in the late 19th and early 20th centuries. Window seats and small alcoves with built-in bookcases seem to add a great deal of charm to any room. These areas provide private spaces to read, study, or just "get away."

In recent years, our attempts to create extremely "open" plans have often eliminated such delightful areas. However, most designs can easily be reworked to include such spaces.

Excerpted from *Home Plan Buyer's Guide,* an upcoming book by **Larry W. Garnett**

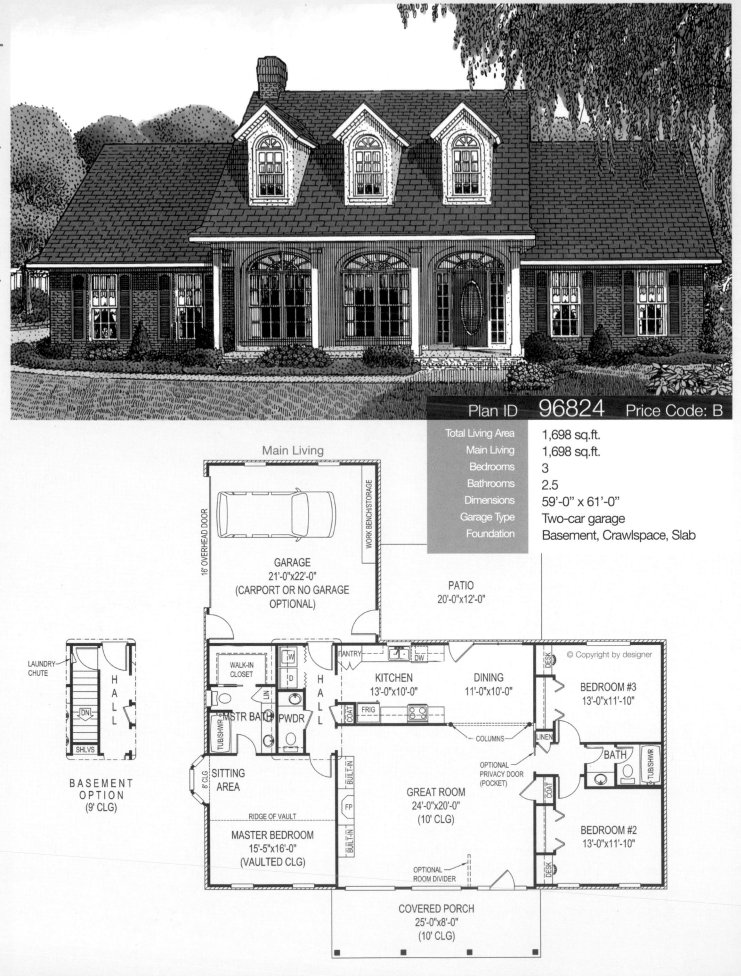

Plan ID **96824** Price Code: **B**

Total Living Area	1,698 sq.ft.
Main Living	1,698 sq.ft.
Bedrooms	3
Bathrooms	2.5
Dimensions	59'-0" x 61'-0"
Garage Type	Two-car garage
Foundation	Basement, Crawlspace, Slab

Main Living

GARAGE
21'-0"x22'-0"
(CARPORT OR NO GARAGE
OPTIONAL)

16' OVERHEAD DOOR

WORK BENCH/STORAGE

PATIO
20'-0"x12'-0"

LAUNDRY
CHUTE

H
A
L
L

DN

SHLVS

BASEMENT
OPTION
(9' CLG)

WALK-IN
CLOSET

W
D

LIN

MSTR BATH

PWDR

TUB/SHWR

PANTRY

H
A
L
L

KITCHEN
13'-0"x10'-0"

COAT

FRIG

DW

DINING
11'-0"x10'-0"

COLUMNS

DESK

© Copyright by designer

BEDROOM #3
13'-0"x11'-10"

LINEN

OPTIONAL
PRIVACY DOOR
(POCKET)

BATH

TUB/SHWR

SITTING
AREA

8' CLG

RIDGE OF VAULT

FP

BUILT-IN

BUILT-IN

GREAT ROOM
24'-0"x20'-0"
(10' CLG)

COAT

DESK

MASTER BEDROOM
15'-5"x16'-0"
(VAULTED CLG)

OPTIONAL
ROOM DIVIDER

BEDROOM #2
13'-0"x11'-10"

COVERED PORCH
25'-0"x8'-0"
(10' CLG)

ORDER NOW 1-800-235-5700 or at www.familyhomeplans.com

Plan ID 96525 Price Code: C

Total Living Area	1,771 sq.ft.
Main Living	1,771 sq.ft.
Bedrooms	3
Bathrooms	2
Dimensions	68'-0" x 50'-0"
Garage Type	Two-car garage
Foundation	Crawlspace, Slab

Main Living

9' CEILINGS TYPICAL

Main Living

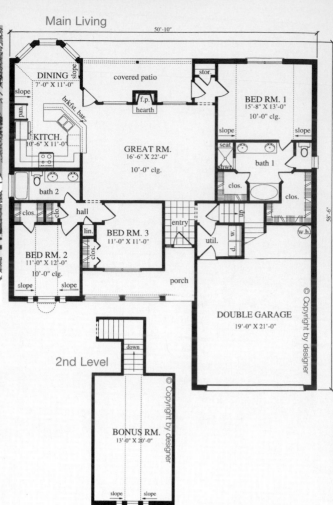

Plan ID 79005   Price Code: B

Total Living Area	1,643 sq.ft.
Main Living	1,643 sq.ft.
Bedrooms	3
Bathrooms	2
Dimensions	50'-10" x 58'-6"
Garage Type	Two-car garage
Foundation	Crawlspace, Slab

Main Living

Plan ID 79235   Price Code: B

Total Living Area	1,747 sq.ft.
Main Living	1,747 sq.ft.
Bedrooms	3
Bathrooms	2
Dimensions	52'-8" x 62'-10"
Garage Type	Two-car garage
Foundation	Crawlspace, Slab

Plan ID **79007** Price Code: B

Total Living Area	1,688 sq.ft.
Main Living	1,688 sq.ft.
Bedrooms	3
Bathrooms	2
Dimensions	59'-4" x 49'-8"
Garage Type	Two-car garage
Foundation	Crawlspace, Slab

Main Living

59'-4"

covered patio

BRK'FST.
11'-0" X 11'-0"
10'-0" clg.

brkfst. bar

GREAT RM.
17'-8" X 20'-0"
10'-0" clg.

BED RM. 1
14'-0" X 16'-0"
10'-0" clg.

bath 1
10'-0" clg.

clos.

clos.

KITCH.
11'-0" X 12'-0"
10'-0" clg.

pant.

hvac

clos.

hall

up

stor.

w.h.

seat

shwr

49'-8"

bath 2

hall

entry

util.

w.
d.

© Copyright by designer

BED RM. 3
11'-0" X 11'-0"
10'-0" clg.

DOUBLE GARAGE
20'-0" X 21'-0"

BED RM. 2
11'-0" X 11'-0"
10'-0" clg.

linen

clos.

porch

slope

2nd Level

down

stor.

slope

slope

© Copyright by designer

BONUS RM.
13'-0" X 21'-0"

Main Living

- clos.
- bath 1
- BED RM. 1
  12'-0" X 15'-0"
  10'-0" clg.
- covered patio
- slope
- f.p. hearth
- GREAT RM.
  15'-0" X 16'-8"
  10'-0" clg.
- BRK'FST.
  10'-0" X 11'-0"
  10'-0" clg.
- slope
- brkfst. bar
- KIT.
  10'-0" X 12'-8"
- clos.
- slope
- BED RM. 2
  11'-0" X 11'-8"
  10'-0" clg.
- clos.
- util.
- hall
- lin.
- clos.
- w. d.
- bath 2
- BED RM. 3
  10'-0" X 10'-0"
  10'-0" clg.
- entry
- DINING RM.
  10'-0" X 11'-0"
  10'-0" clg.
- clo.
- pan.
- w.h.
- stor.
- porch
- © Copyright by designer

DOUBLE GARAGE
20'-0" X 20'-0"

50'-0"

57'-8"

2nd Level

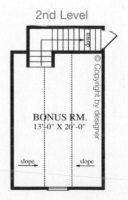

BONUS RM.
13'-0" X 20'-0"

slope   slope

© Copyright by designer

Plan ID	**79233**	Price Code: B
Total Living Area	1,573 sq.ft.	
Main Living	1,573 sq.ft.	
Bedrooms	3	
Bathrooms	2	
Dimensions	50'-0" x 57'-8"	
Garage Type	Two-car garage	
Foundation	Crawlspace, Slab	

Plan ID 79012 **Price Code: C**

Total Living Area	1,821 sq.ft.
Main Living	1,821 sq.ft.
Bedrooms	3
Bathrooms	2
Dimensions	65'-4" x 49'-10"
Garage Type	Two-car garage
Foundation	Crawlspace, Slab

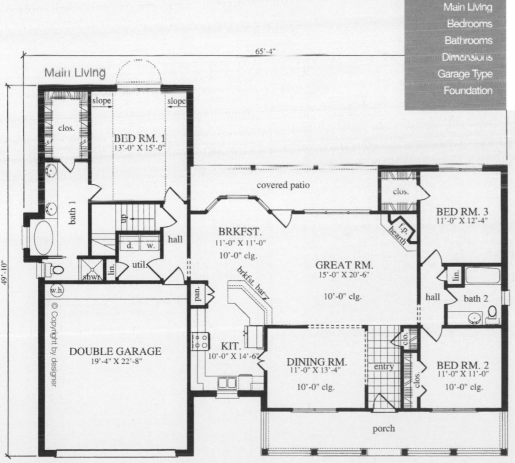

Main Living

65'-4"

49'-10"

BED RM. 1
13'-0" X 15'-0"

clos.

bath 1

slope   slope

up

hall

d.   w.

lin.

util.

shwr.

w.h.

DOUBLE GARAGE
19'-4" X 22'-8"

pan.

KIT.
10'-0" X 14'-6"

brkfst. bar

BRKFST.
11'-0" X 11'-0"
10'-0" clg.

covered patio

GREAT RM.
15'-0" X 20'-6"
10'-0" clg.

f.p.
hearth

clos.

BED RM. 3
11'-0" X 12'-4"

lin.

hall   bath 2

DINING RM.
11'-0" X 13'-4"
10'-0" clg.

entry

clos.

clos.

BED RM. 2
11'-0" X 11'-0"
10'-0" clg.

porch

© Copyright by designer

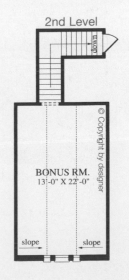

2nd Level

down

BONUS RM.
13'-0" X 22'-0"

slope   slope

© Copyright by designer

Main Living

56'-4"

MASTER SUITE 15'-0" X 12'-0"

SLOPE CLG. TO 10'-0"

NOOK 11'-0" X 10'-0"

PORCH

BED RM.3 11'-8" X 11'-6"

WALK IN CLOSET

FIRE PLACE HEARTH

8' 10'

RAISED BAR 1/2 WALL

LIVING RM. 15'-10" X 14'-10"

10'-0" HIGH CLG.

LIN.

BATH 1

KITCH. 11'-0" X 11'-0"

B.2

MARBLE TUB

GLASS SHR.

UTIL.

DRY WASH

PANT

OVEN

POWDER ROOM

WALK IN CLOSET

W/H

A/C

DINING RM. 13'-1" X 11'-0"

10'-0" HIGH CLG.

ENT.

10'-0" CLG.

STORAGE

BED RM.2 12'-3" X 11'-0"

SLOPE CLG. TO 10'-0"

GARAGE 20'-6" X 22'-0"

PORCH

52'-10"

© Copyright by designer

Plan ID 77031   Price Code: B

Total Living Area	1,720 sq.ft.
Main Living	1,720 sq.ft.
Bedrooms	3
Bathrooms	2
Dimensions	56'-4" x 52'-10"
Garage Type	Two-car garage
Foundation	Crawlspace, Slab

Main Living

58'-4"

STEP UP CEILING

MASTER SUITE 16'-0" X 12'-0"

NOOK 9'-10" X 11'-0"

PORCH

BED RM.2 11'-0" X 12'-0"

BATH 1

SHR.

RAISED BAR

D.W.

LIVING RM. 17'-10" X 16'-3"

10'-0" HIGH CEILING

WALK IN CLOSET

MARBLE TUB

WALK IN CLOSET

REF.

KITCH. 10'-0" X 11'-0"

RANGE

STOR.

LIN.

B.2

STORAGE

W/H

PANT

BED RM.3 11'-6" X 11'-0"

GARAGE 18'-9" X 20'-0"

UTIL.

DINING RM. 11'-0" X 13'-0"

SLOPE CLG. UP TO 10'-0"

ENT.

SLOPE CLG. UP

SLOPE CLG. UP

P.

49'-6"

© Copyright by designer

Plan ID 77045   Price Code: C

Total Living Area	1,791 sq.ft.
Main Living	1,791 sq.ft.
Bedrooms	3
Bathrooms	2
Dimensions	58'-4" x 49'-6"
Garage Type	Two-car garage
Foundation	Crawlspace, Slab

Plan ID 77058   Price Code: C

Total Living Area	1,896 sq.ft.
Main Living	1,235 sq.ft.
2nd Level	661 sq.ft.
Bedrooms	4
Bathrooms	2.5
Dimensions	52'-8" x 44'-0"
Garage Type	Two-car garage
Foundation	Crawlspace, Slab

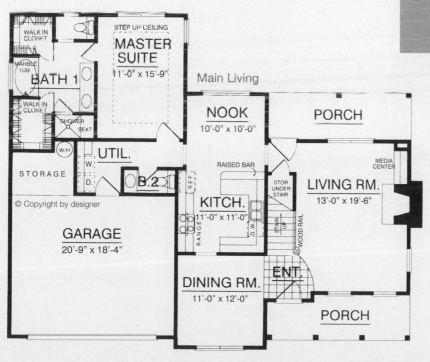

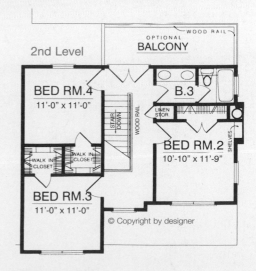

Plan ID	77063	Price Code: C

Total Living Area	1,919 sq.ft.
Main Living	1,326 sq.ft.
2nd Level	593 sq.ft.
Bedrooms	3
Bathrooms	2.5
Dimensions	75'-0" x 37'-6"
Garage Type	Two-car garage
Foundation	Basement, Crawlspace, Slab

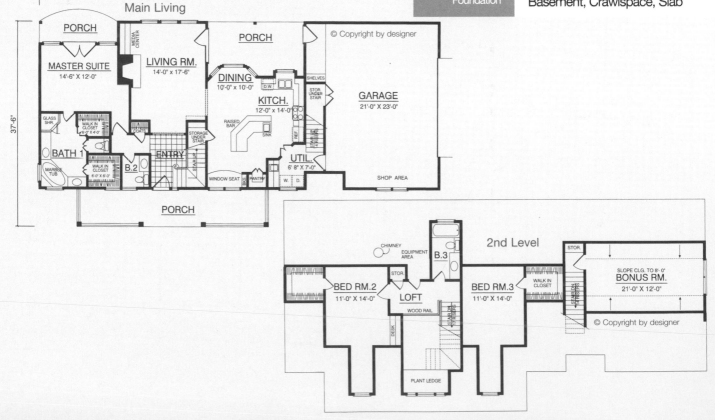

Plan ID 77049   Price Code: C

Total Living Area	1,815 sq.ft.
Main Living	1,245 sq.ft.
2nd Level	570 sq.ft.
Bedrooms	3
Bathrooms	2
Dimensions	48'-0" x 57'-0"
Garage Type	Two-car garage
Foundation	Basement, Crawlspace, Slab

GARAGE
23'-0" x 23'-0"

Main Living

P O R C H

REF.

KITCH.
9'-6" x 12'-0"

DINING RM.
11'-0" x 14'-0"

STOR. W/H

UTIL.

RAISED BAR

D.W.

BATH 1

WALK IN CLOSET

POWDER ROOM

LIN.

STOR.

LIVING RM.
20'-6" x 16'-0"

STOR. UNDER STAIR

STAIR UP

MASTER SUITE
17'-0" x 12'-6"

WD. RAIL

ENT.

© Copyright by designer

P O R C H

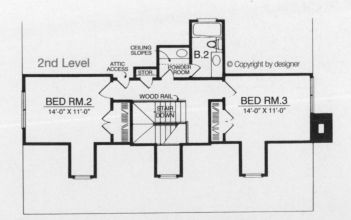

2nd Level

CEILING SLOPES

ATTIC ACCESS

STOR.

B.2

POWDER ROOM

© Copyright by designer

BED RM.2
14'-0" X 11'-0"

WOOD RAIL

STAIR DOWN

BED RM.3
14'-0" X 11'-0"

Plan ID	92442	Price Code: B

Total Living Area	1,507 sq.ft.
Main Living	1,507 sq.ft.
Bedrooms	3
Bathrooms	2
Dimensions	50'-0" x 30'-0"
Garage Type	Two-car garage
Foundation	Basement

Plan ID 58903 Price Code: C

Total Living Area	1,780 sq.ft.
Main Living	1,789 sq.ft.
Bedrooms	3
Bathrooms	?
Dimensions	55'-0" x 60'-0"
Foundation	Slab

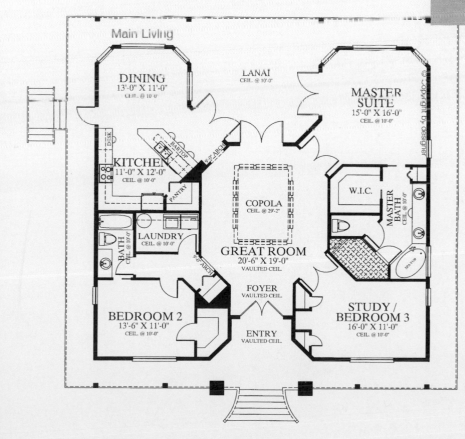

Main Living

DINING
13'-0" X 11'-0"
CEIL. @ 10'-0"

LANAI
CEIL. @ 10'-0"

MASTER SUITE
15'-0" X 16'-0"
CEIL. @ 10'-0"

KITCHEN
11'-0" X 12'-0"
CEIL. @ 10'-0"

PANTRY

W.I.C.

MASTER BATH
CEIL. @ 10'-0"

COPOLA
CEIL. @ 29'-2"

BATH
CEIL. @ 10'-0"

LAUNDRY
CEIL. @ 10'-0"

GREAT ROOM
20'-6" X 19'-0"
VAULTED CEIL.

BEDROOM 2
13'-6" X 11'-0"
CEIL. @ 10'-0"

FOYER
VAULTED CEIL.

STUDY / BEDROOM 3
16'-0" X 11'-0"
CEIL. @ 10'-0"

ENTRY
VAULTED CEIL.

Plan ID	58306	Price Code: B
Total Living Area	1,560 sq.ft.	
Main Living	1,560 sq.ft.	
Bedrooms	3	
Bathrooms	2	
Dimensions	59'-0" x 55'-0"	
Garage Type	Two-car garage	
Foundation	Basement, Slab	

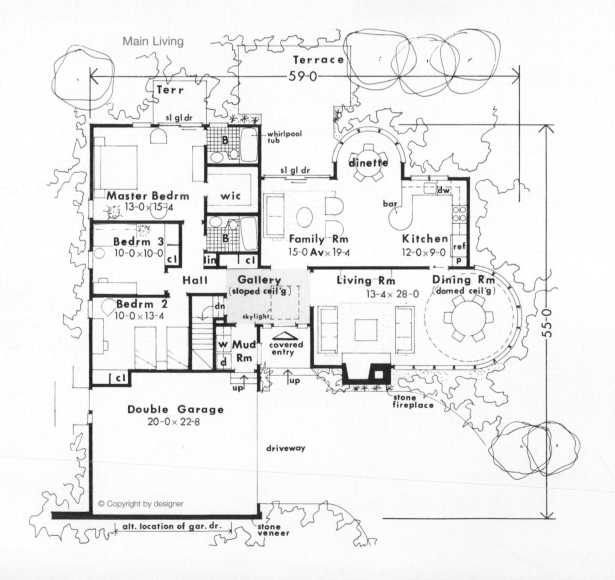

Main Living

Terrace
59-0

Terr

sl gl dr

whirlpool tub

B

dinette

sl gl dr

dw

Master Bedrm
13-0 x 15-4

wic

bar

Family Rm
15-0 Av x 19-4

Kitchen
12-0 x 9-0

ref

Bedrm 3
10-0 x 10-0

cl

B

cl

Hall

Gallery
(sloped ceil'g)

Living Rm
13-4 x 28-0

Dining Rm
(domed ceil'g)

Bedrm 2
10-0 x 13-4

dn

skylight

w Mud
Rm
d

covered entry

up

up

stone fireplace

cl

Double Garage
20-0 x 22-8

driveway

© Copyright by designer

alt. location of gar. dr.

stone veneer

55-0

Plan ID 58309 Price Code: C

Total Living Area	1,948 sq.ft.
Main Living	1,948 sq.ft
Bedrooms	4
Bathrooms	2.5
Dimensions	60' 0" x 62'-0"
Garage Type	Two-car garage
Foundation	Basement, Slab

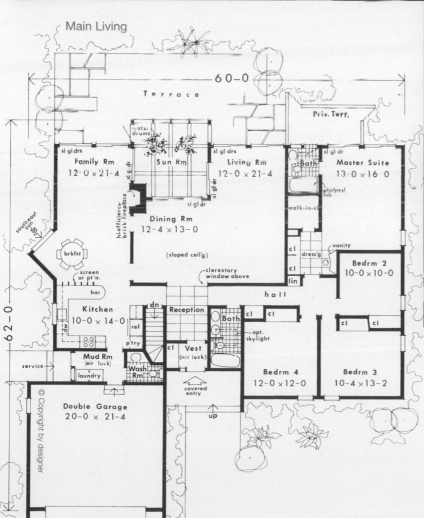

Main Living

Terrace

60-0

Priv. Terr.

sl gl drs — Family Rm 12-0 x 21-4

Sun Rm

sl gl drs — Living Rm 12-0 x 21-4

sl gl dr — Master Suite 13-0 x 16 0

Bath

whirlpool tub

walk-in cl

metal drums

hi-efficiency brick fireplace

Dining Rm 12-4 x 13-0

(sloped ceil'g)

vanity

cl dress'g

southeast sun

brkfst

screen or pt'n.

bar

clerestory window above

cl lin

Bedrm 2 10-0 x 10-0

hall

Kitchen 10-0 x 14-0

dn

Reception

ref

p'try

Bath

cl cl

opt. skylight

cl cl

62-0

wd

Mud Rm (air lock)

cl Vest (air lock)

Wash Rm

laundry

service

covered entry

up

Bedrm 4 12-0 x 12-0

Bedrm 3 10-4 x 13-2

© Copyright by designer

Double Garage 20-0 x 21-4

driveway

REAR ELEVATION

Plan ID 59052 Price Code: B

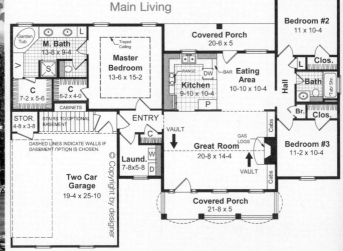

Main Living

Total Living Area	1,502 sq.ft.
Main Living	1,502 sq.ft.
Bedrooms	3
Bathrooms	2
Dimensions	61'-8" x 45'-8"
Garage Type	Two-car garage
Foundation	Basement, Crawlspace, Slab

Plan ID 59050 Price Code: A

Total Living Area	1,500 sq.ft.
Main Living	1,500 sq.ft.
Bedrooms	3
Bathrooms	2
Dimensions	61'-0" x 47'-4"
Garage Type	Two-car garage
Foundation	Basement, Crawlspace, Slab

REAR ELEVATION

Plan ID	59012	Price Code: C
Total Living Area		1,799 sq.ft.
Main Living		1,799 sq.ft.
Bedrooms		3
Bathrooms		2.5
Dimensions		78'-0" x 46'-0"
Garage Type		Two-car garage
Foundation		Basement, Crawlspace, Slab

Main Living

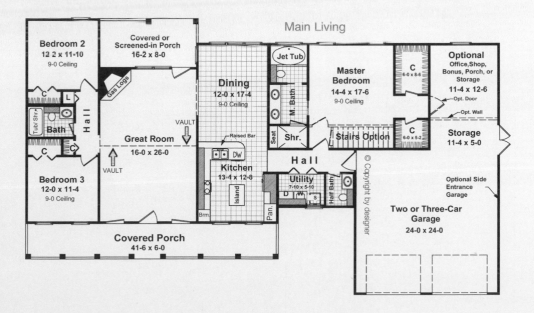

2nd Level

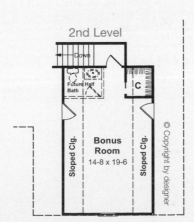

Main Living

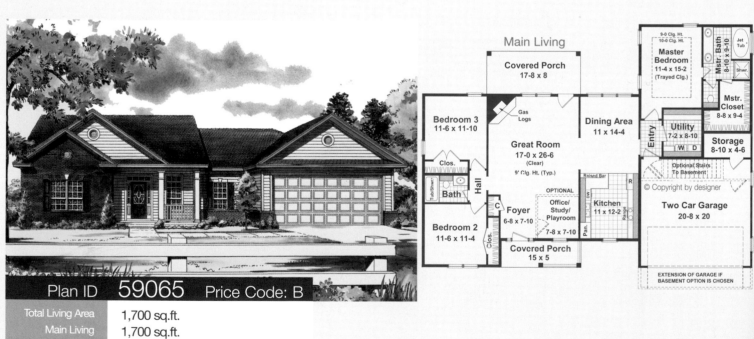

Plan ID	59009	Price Code: B

Total Living Area	1,654 sq.ft.
Main Living	1,654 sq.ft.
Bedrooms	3
Bathrooms	2
Dimensions	64'-0" x 39'-0"
Garage Type	Two-car garage
Foundation	Crawlspace, Slab

Main Living

Plan ID	59065	Price Code: B

Total Living Area	1,700 sq.ft.
Main Living	1,700 sq.ft.
Bedrooms	3
Bathrooms	2
Dimensions	62'-2" x 45'-8"
Garage Type	Two-car garage
Foundation	Basement, Crawlspace, Slab

Plan ID **59017** Price Code: C

Total Living Area	1,802 sq.ft.
Main Living	1,802 sq.ft.
Bedrooms	3
Bathrooms	2
Dimensions	65'-0" x 50'-10"
Garage Type	Two-car garage
Foundation	Basement, Crawlspace, Slab

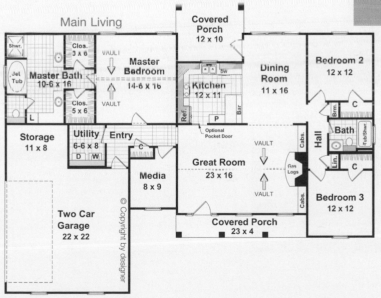

Main Living

Basement option

Plan ID 40005 Price Code: B

Total Living Area	1,680 sq.ft.
Main Living	1,680 sq.ft.
Bedrooms	3
Bathrooms	2
Dimensions	56'-6" x 68'-6"
Garage Type	Two-car garage
Foundation	Basement, Crawlspace, Slab

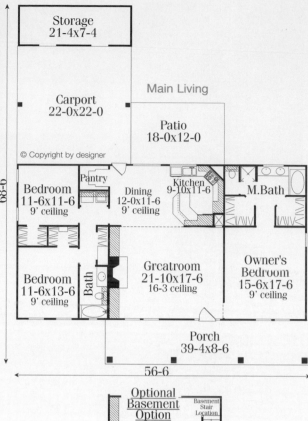

Storage
21-4x7-4

Carport
22-0x22-0

Main Living

Patio
18-0x12-0

© Copyright by designer

Bedroom
11-6x11-6
9' ceiling

Pantry

Dining
12-0x11-6
9' ceiling

Kitchen
9-10x11-6

M.Bath

Bedroom
11-6x13-6
9' ceiling

Bath

Greatroom
21-10x17-6
16-3 ceiling

Owner's
Bedroom
15-6x17-6
9' ceiling

Porch
39-4x8-6

68-6

56-6

Optional Basement Option

Basement Stair Location

Greatroom
16-8x17-6
16-3 ceiling

© Copyright by designer

Plan ID 40027 Price Code: B

Total Living Area	1,501 sq.ft.
Main Living	1,501 sq.ft.
Bedrooms	3
Bathrooms	2
Dimensions	52'-8" x 59'-10"
Garage Type	Two-car garage
Foundation	Basement, Crawlspace, Slab

52-8

Main Living

M.Bath

Master
Bedroom
14-1x15-9

Courtyard

Garage
21-5x21-5

© Copyright by designer

Bedroom/
Office
10-2x11-0

Porch
16-0x6-10

Laun.

Kitchen
13-8x10-9

59-10

Bath

Greatroom
15-9x15-5

Dining
11-9x8-9

Bedroom
11-8x10-0

Foyer

Porch
21-4x5-6

Basement option

© Copyright by designer

Garage

Storage
9-0x6-10

Laun.

Plan ID 40004 Price Code: C

Total Living Area	1,927 sq.ft.
Main Living	1,927 sq.ft
Bedrooms	3
Bathrooms	2.5
Dimensions	64' 0" x 56'-0"
Garage Type	Two-car garage
Foundation	Basement, Crawlspace, Slab

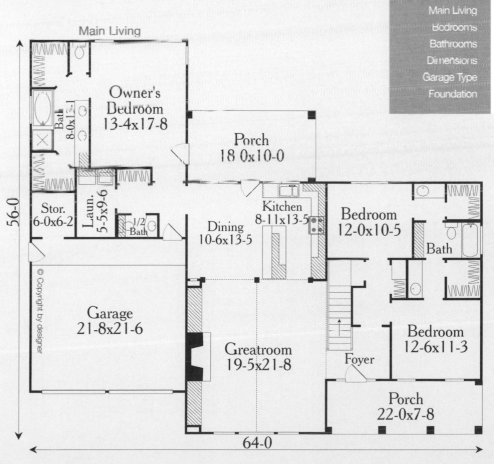

Main Living

Owner's Bedroom
13-4x17-8

Bath
8-0x13-5

Porch
18 0x10-0

Stor.
6-0x6-2

Laun.
5-5x9-6

1/2 Bath

Kitchen
8-11x13-5

Dining
10-6x13-5

Bedroom
12-0x10-5

Bath

Garage
21-8x21-6

© Copyright by designer

Greatroom
19-5x21-8

Foyer

Bedroom
12-6x11-3

Porch
22-0x7-8

56-0

64-0

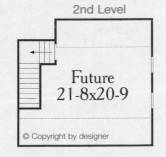

2nd Level

Future
21-8x20-9

© Copyright by designer

Plan ID 40030   Price Code: B

Total Living Area	1,730 sq.ft.
Main Living	1,730 sq.ft.
Bedrooms	3
Bathrooms	2
Dimensions	61'-0" x 62'-0"
Garage Type	Two-car garage
Foundation	Basement, Crawlspace, Slab

Plan ID 40014   Price Code: C

Total Living Area	1,997 sq.ft.
Main Living	1,997 sq.ft.
Bedrooms	4
Bathrooms	2.5
Dimensions	56'-4" x 67'-4"
Garage Type	Two-car garage
Foundation	Basement, Crawlspace, Slab

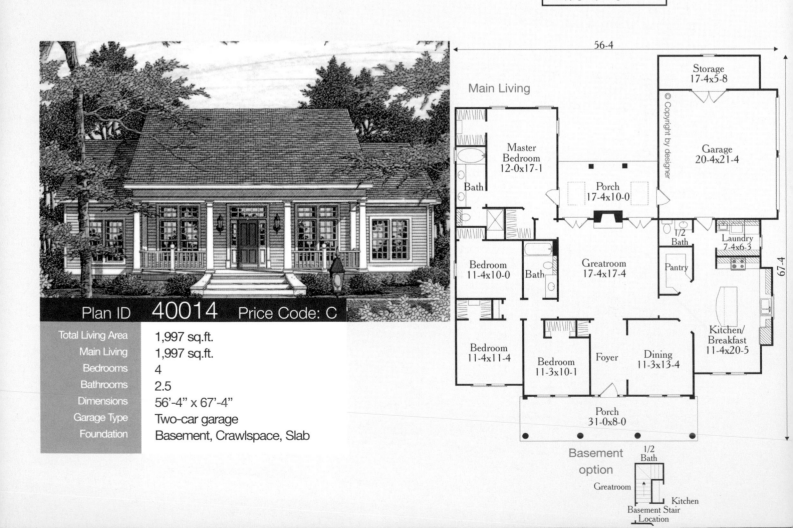

REAR ELEVATION

Plan ID	40010	Price Code: B
Total Living Area		1,688 sq. ft.
Main Living		1,688 sq. ft.
Bedrooms		3
Bathrooms		2
Dimensions		70'-1" x 48' 0"
Garage Type		Two-car garage
Foundation		Basement, Crawlspace, Slab

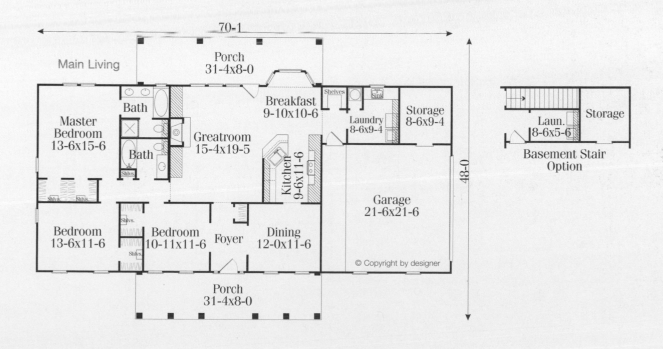

Plan ID **40021** Price Code: C

Total Living Area	1,833 sq.ft.
Main Living	1,833 sq.ft.
Bedrooms	3
Bathrooms	2
Dimensions	68'-0" x 49'-5"
Garage Type	Two-car garage
Foundation	Basement, Crawlspace, Slab

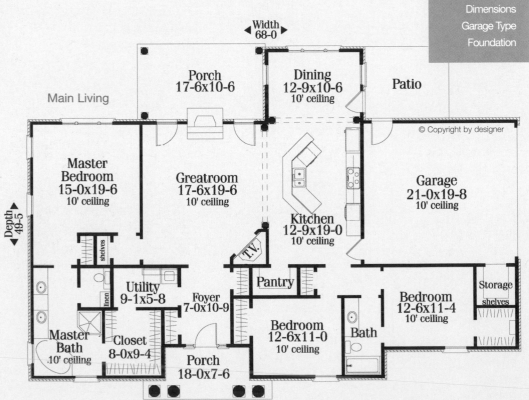

Width 68-0

Depth 49-5

Main Living

Porch 17-6x10-6

Dining 12-9x10-6 10' ceiling

Patio

© Copyright by designer

Master Bedroom 15-0x19-6 10' ceiling

Greatroom 17-6x19-6 10' ceiling

Garage 21-0x19-8 10' ceiling

Kitchen 12-9x19-0 10' ceiling

shelves

Utility 9-1x5-8

Pantry

Storage shelves

Bedroom 12-6x11-4 10' ceiling

linen

Master Bath 10' ceiling

Closet 8-0x9-4

Foyer 7-0x10-9

T.V.

Bedroom 12-6x11-0 10' ceiling

Bath

Porch 18-0x7-6

Basement Option

Kitchen

Foyer

Down to Basement

Bedroom

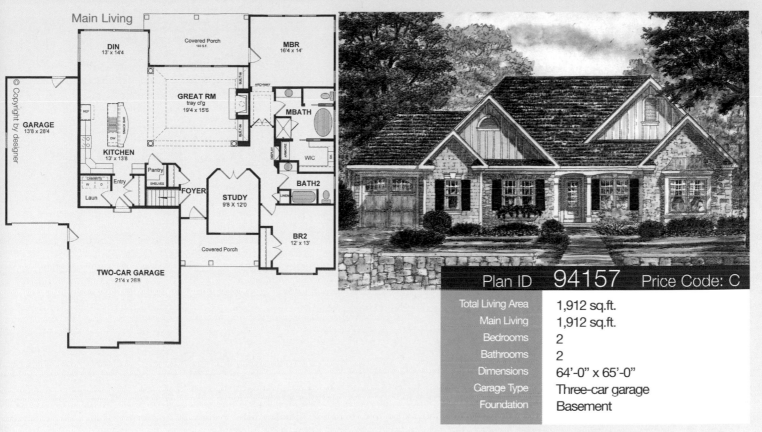

Main Living

GARAGE
13'8 x 28'4

DIN
13' x 14'4

Covered Porch
193 S.F.

MBR
16'4 x 14'

GREAT RM
tray cl'g
19'4 x 15'6

MBATH

KITCHEN
13' x 13'8

WIC

Pantry
SHELVES

BATH2

FOYER

STUDY
9'8 X 12'0

Entry

Laun

BR2
12' x 13'

Covered Porch

TWO-CAR GARAGE
21'4 x 26'8

© Copyright by designer

Plan ID 94157   Price Code: C

Total Living Area	1,912 sq.ft.
Main Living	1,912 sq.ft.
Bedrooms	2
Bathrooms	2
Dimensions	64'-0" x 65'-0"
Garage Type	Three-car garage
Foundation	Basement

54-0

Patio / Deck

Main Living

Bdrm.3
10⁸ x 11⁶

Living
15⁶ x 22⁶
12' High Ceil.

Brkfst.
11⁰ x 9⁰

Master Bdrm.
13⁶ x 17⁴

Kit.
11⁸ x 12⁰

Bth.2

Bdrm.2
10⁸ x 11⁶

Foyer
6⁰ x 10⁶
12' Ceil.

Dining
11⁰ x 12⁰
12' High Ceil.

Laund.

M.Bath
Vaulted

Plant Shelf Above

Opt. Location
For Bsmt.Stairs

60-6

2nd Level

Double Garage
21⁸ x 21⁸

© Copyright by designer

Bonus
13⁴ x 23⁸

© Copyright by designer

Plan ID 71032   Price Code: C

Total Living Area	1,869 sq.ft.
Main Living	1,869 sq.ft.
Bedrooms	3
Bathrooms	2
Dimensions	54'-0" x 60'-6"
Garage Type	Two-car garage
Foundation	Basement, Crawlspace, Slab

Tudor Cottage Charm

Designed for a narrow lot, this Tudor style cottage provides charming curb appeal with the combined use of board and batton, and shake shingle siding. The modest front entry is highlighted by a dormer that opens to the cathedral ceiling of the spacious, open great room. The living/dining rooms and kitchen all flow together to provide the impression of a much larger home. The curved bar separating the kitchen can house a bench seat to service a small café style table while defining the kitchen space from the rest of the living area. The split bedroom design allows for maximum privacy. The volume master suite offers a separate sunlit sitting area. Although, originally designed for a slab, a basement option is also available.

The homeowners modified this design with a comfortable front porch, bordered by tapered columns. ▲

Secondary bedrooms are well separated from the master bedroom and are brightened by plenty of natural sunlight. ▶

The free-flowing living and dining areas are graced by the gently curved kitchen ▲

Plan ID	71022	Price Code: B
Total Living Area	1,532 sq.ft.	
Main Living	1,532 sq.ft.	
Bedrooms	3	
Bathrooms	2	
Dimensions	38'-0" x 66'-0"	
Garage Type	Two-car garage	
Foundation	Basement, Crawlspace*, Slab*	

Main Living

Master Bdrm. 130 x 146 Vaults to 9'-5" High

Sitting 8⁴ x 7⁸

Patio

M.Bath

Kit. 11⁸ x 10⁸

Dining 10⁰ x 11⁸

Opt. Bench

Pant.

Dw.

Ref.

Bth.2

Lin.

Cts.

Living Area 19⁰ x 15⁴ Vaults to 10'-8" High

Bdrm.2 10⁰ x 10⁸

W. D.

Whl. Furn.

Foyer

Bdrm.3 10⁸ x 10⁴

Opt. Study 10⁸ x 12⁸

Disp. Stairs

Double Garage 19⁸ x 19⁸

© Copyright by designer

Basement Option

Bdrm.2

Cts.

W. D.

Dn

© Copyright by designer

Plan ID 71067 Price Code: B

Total Living Area	1,715 sq.ft.
Main Living	1,046 sq.ft.
2nd Level	669 sq.ft.
Bedrooms	3
Bathrooms	2.5
Dimensions	38'-0" x 40'-0"
Garage Type	Two-car garage
Foundation	Basement, Crawlspace*, Slab*

Main Living

38-0

32-0

8-0

Deck
16-0 x 12-0

Skylights

Breakfast

Kitchen
9-0 x 9-6

Dining Area
9-10 x 11-4

Bath

M. Bath

Living Area
18-0 x 13-6

Up

Master Bedroom
15-6 x 13-6

W D

© Copyright by designer

Porch

2nd Level

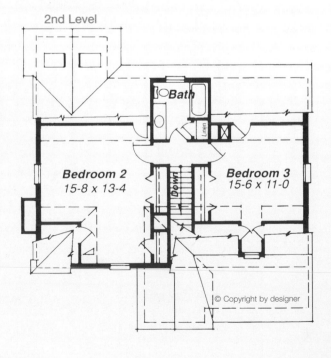

Bath

Linen

Bedroom 2
15-8 x 13-4

Down

Bedroom 3
15-6 x 11-0

© Copyright by designer

Plan ID **93293** Price Code: C

Total Living Area	1,803 sq.ft.
Basement	85 sq.ft.
Main Living	1,718 sq.ft.
Bedrooms	3
Bathrooms	2
Dimensions	54'-0" x 34'-0"
Garage Type	Three-car garage
Foundation	Basement

Basement

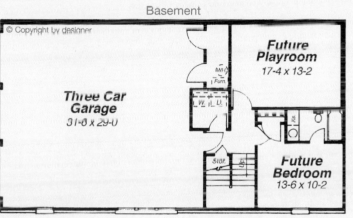

© Copyright by designer

Three Car Garage
31-8 x 29-0

Future Playroom
17-4 x 13-2

Future Bedroom
13-6 x 10-2

Main Living

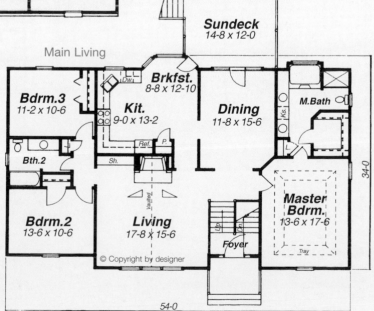

Sundeck
14-8 x 12-0

Bdrm.3
11-2 x 10-6

Brkfst.
8-8 x 12-10

Kit.
9-0 x 13-2

Dining
11-8 x 15-6

M.Bath

Bth.2

Bdrm.2
13-6 x 10-6

Living
17-8 x 15-6

Foyer

Master Bdrm.
13-6 x 17-6

© Copyright by designer

54-0

34-0

Plan ID 98956 — Price Code: C

Total Living Area	1,869 sq.ft.
Main Living	1,869 sq.ft.
Bedrooms	3
Bathrooms	2
Dimensions	54'-0" x 60'-0"
Garage Type	Two-car garage
Foundation	Basement, Crawlspace, Slab

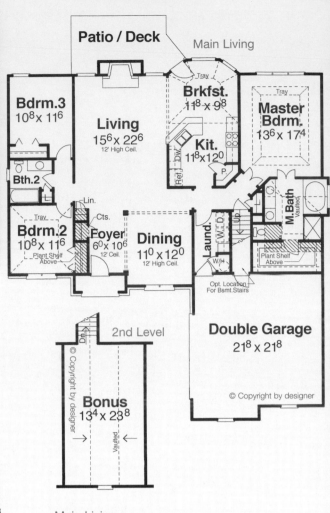

Plan ID 94153 — Price Code: C

Total Living Area	1,916 sq.ft.
Main Living	1,916 sq.ft.
Bedrooms	2
Bathrooms	2
Dimensions	58'-0" x 63'-6"
Garage Type	Two-car garage
Foundation	Basement, Walkout basement

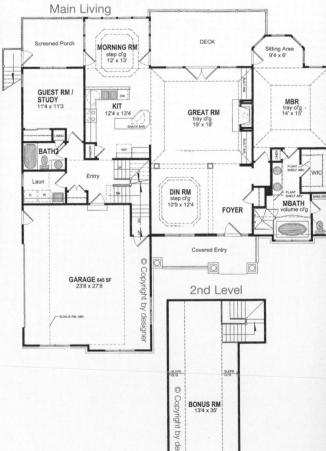

TRAFFIC PATTERNS

ONE OF THE MOST CRITICAL ELEMENTS OF A FLOOR PLAN PROVES TO BE THE TRAFFIC PATTERNS. In other words, how you travel from one room to another. The best way to determine if a plan has a logical traffic pattern is to simply imagine living in the house and walking from one area to another. For example, as you enter the home from either the front door or the side entrance, how can you walk to the kitchen? Do you have to "crisscross" through the family room? What if you want to move from the living area to your master bedroom?

The various rooms need to be arranged so that the flow of traffic throughout the house is logical. Ideally, you should be able to move from one area to another without crossing through any room. Instead, designated areas, often called Galleries, are created to direct traffic through the home

Over the last ten years or so, residential designers have made tremendous progress in offering "open" floor plans. By eliminating long hallways, unnecessary walls, and expanding ceiling heights, we have seen much more exciting living spaces. However, this "openness" has often been carried to the extreme. For instance, there is still a need for a hallway that offers privacy for bedrooms or bathrooms.

Excerpted from *Home Plan Buyer's Guide,*
an upcoming book by **Larry W. Garnett**

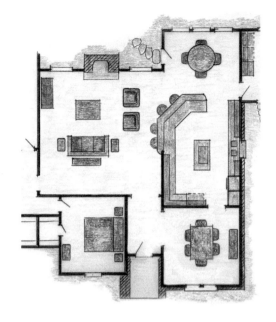

A designated Gallery provides better traffic flow throughout the home. Note how the family room is "defined" by the use of columns. Also, by adjusting the fireplace and media center locations, furniture placement functions much better.

GALLERY

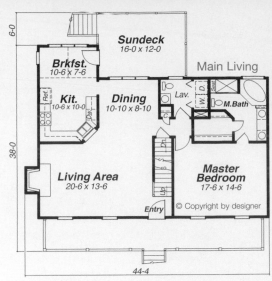

Main Living

Sundeck 16-0 x 12-0

Brkfst. 10-6 x 7-6

Kit. 10-6 x 10-0

Dining 10-10 x 8-10

Lav.

W.D.

M.Bath

Living Area 20-6 x 13-6

Master Bedroom 17-6 x 14-6

Entry

© Copyright by designer

44-4

38-0

6-0

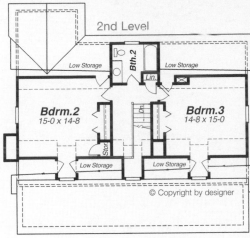

2nd Level

Low Storage   Bth.2   Low Storage

Lin.

Bdrm.2 15-0 x 14-8

Bdrm.3 14-8 x 15-0

Stor.

Low Storage   Low Storage

© Copyright by designer

Plan ID	71033	Price Code: C

Total Living Area	1,870 sq.ft.
Main Living	1,159 sq.ft.
2nd Level	711 sq.ft.
Bedrooms	3
Bathrooms	2.5
Dimensions	44'-4" x 38'-0"
Garage Type	Two-car garage
Foundation	Basement, Crawlspace*, Slab*

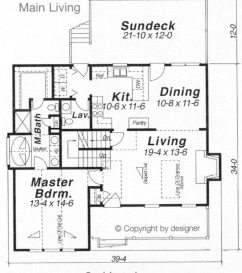

Main Living

Sundeck 21-10 x 12-0

Ref.   DW

Kit. 10-6 x 11-6

Dining 10-8 x 11-6

W.D.

M.Bath

Lav.

Pantry

Living 19-4 x 13-6

Master Bdrm. 13-4 x 14-6

Up

© Copyright by designer

39-4

34-0

12-0

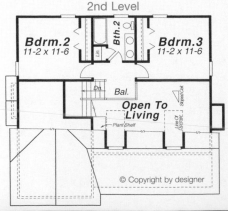

2nd Level

Bdrm.2 11-2 x 11-6

Bth.2

Bdrm.3 11-2 x 11-6

Lin.

Dn.

Bal.

Open To Living

Plant Shelf

© Copyright by designer

Plan ID	71023	Price Code: B

Total Living Area	1,553 sq.ft.
Main Living	1,055 sq.ft.
2nd Level	498 sq.ft.
Bedrooms	3
Bathrooms	2.5
Dimensions	39'-4" x 34'-0"
Garage Type	Two-car garage
Foundation	Basement, Crawlspace, Slab

ORDER NOW 1-800-235-5700 or at www.familyhomeplans.com

Plan ID **71028** Price Code: C

Total Living Area	1,765 sq.ft.
Main Living	1,210 sq.ft.
2nd Level	555 sq.ft.
Bedrooms	3
Bathrooms	2.5
Dimensions	43'-4" x 37'-0"
Garage Type	Two-car garage
Foundation	Basement, Crawlspace*, Slab*

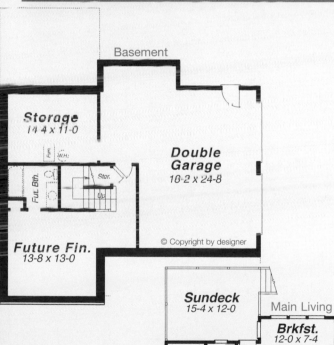

Basement

Storage
14-4 x 11-0

Double Garage
18-2 x 24-8

Future Fin.
13-8 x 13-0

© Copyright by designer

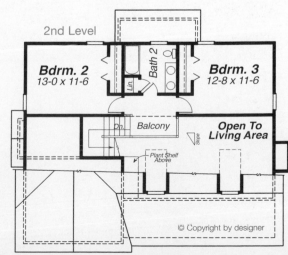

Main Living

Sundeck
15-4 x 12-0

Brkfst.
12-0 x 7-4

Kit.
12-0 x 8-0

Dining
12-0 x 11-10

Living
21-4 x 13-6

Master Bdrm.
15-4 x 13-6

M. Bath

Lav.

37-0

43-4

© Copyright by designer

2nd Level

Bdrm. 2
13-0 x 11-6

Bath 2

Bdrm. 3
12-8 x 11-6

Balcony

Open To Living Area

Plant Shelf Above

© Copyright by designer

Main Living

13-8 X 12-8

13-0 X 17-0

20-0 X 14-0

36-0

© Copyright by designer

◄ 36-0 ►

Plan ID	65246	Price Code: B

Total Living Area	1,625 sq.ft.
Main Living	1,108 sq.ft.
2nd Level	517 sq.ft.
Bedrooms	3
Bathrooms	2
Dimensions	36'-0" x 36'-0"
Foundation	Basement

2nd Level

9-10 X 11-8

12-0 X 11-8

© Copyright by designer

Main Living

11-0 X 10-0

11-2 X 11-0

40-0

11-4 X 13-0

11-8 X 12-0

13-4 X 17-0

© Copyright by designer

◄ 38-0 ►

Plan ID	65556	Price Code: C

Total Living Area	1,955 sq.ft.
Main Living	1,291 sq.ft.
2nd Level	664 sq.ft.
Bedrooms	3, 4
Bathrooms	2.5
Dimensions	38'-0" x 40'-0"
Foundation	Basement

2nd Level

11-0 X 14-0

© Copyright by designer

13-4 X 17-0

Plan ID **64988** Price Code: B

Total Living Area	1,680 sq.ft.
Main Living	1,148 sq.ft.
2nd Level	532 sq.ft.
Bedrooms	3
Bathrooms	2
Dimensions	36'-8" x 40' 8"
Foundation	Basement

Main Living

▲
40-8
▼

12-4 X 11-0

12-0 X 10-8

15-8 X 15-2

12-0 X 13-0

© Copyright by designer

◄ 36-8 ►

2nd Level

© Copyright by designer

9-6 X 11-4

12-8 X 11-2

Plan ID 64978 Price Code: C

Total Living Area	1,838 sq.ft.
Main Living	1,838 sq.ft.
Bedrooms	3
Bathrooms	2
Dimensions	36'-0" x 76'-0"
Garage Type	Two-car garage
Foundation	Slab

Main Living

PORCH

16-0 x 11-0

11-0 x 10-0

11-0 x 10-8

15-8 x 12-4

19-0 x 18-0

15-8 x 13-8

© Copyright by designer

2-CAR GARAGE
19-8 x 19-4

76-0

36-0

Plan ID 64977 Price Code: C

Total Living Area	1,779 sq.ft.
Main Living	1,779 sq.ft.
Bedrooms	3
Bathrooms	2
Dimensions	38'-0" x 78'-0"
Garage Type	Two-car garage
Foundation	Slab

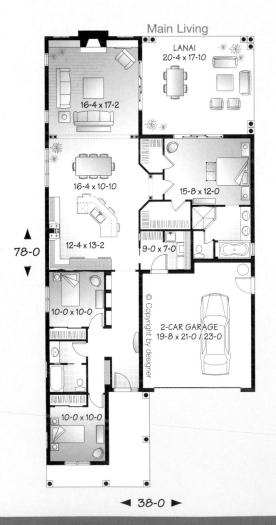

Main Living

LANAI
20-4 x 17-10

16-4 x 17-2

16-4 x 10-10

15-8 x 12-0

12-4 x 13-2

9-0 x 7-0

10-0 x 10-0

2-CAR GARAGE
19-8 x 21-0 / 23-0

© Copyright by designer

10-0 x 10-0

78-0

38-0

Plan ID 64986 Price Code: C

Total Living Area	1,816 sq.ft.
Main Living	1,816 sq.ft.
Bedrooms	3
Bathrooms	2
Dimensions	54'-8" x 57'-8"
Garage Type	Two-car garage
Foundation	Slab

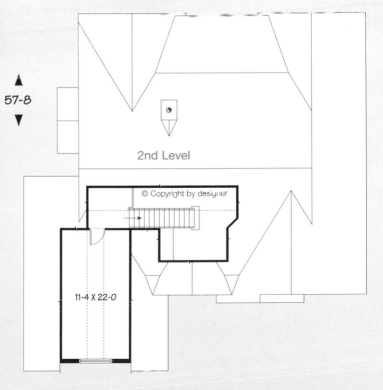

Main Living

14-0 X 12-4

14-0 X 14-4

14-0 / 17-8 X 14-6

15-4 X 19-0

8-8 X 7-6

10-8 X 11-6

10-0 X 11-4

57-8

2-CAR GARAGE
20-4 X 21-8

© Copyright by designer

54-8

2nd Level

© Copyright by designer

11-4 X 22-0

FRONT ELEVATION

Plan ID	65012	Price Code: C

Total Living Area	1,953 sq.ft.
Main Living	1,301 sq.ft.
2nd Level	652 sq.ft.
Bedrooms	3
Bathrooms	2.5
Dimensions	58'-0" x 55'-0"
Garage Type	Two-car garage
Foundation	1/2 Basement / 1/2 Crawlspace

Main Living

© Copyright by designer

2-CAR GARAGE
23-0 x 26-0

11-8 x 15-0

12-0 x 15-0

11-8 x 11-0

8-4 x 7-4

11-8 x 11-8

8-0 x 9-0

55-0

58-0

2nd Level

© Copyright by designer

BONUS ROOM
23-0 X 14-8

12-0 X 11-4

11-8 X 11-4

11-8 X 11-2

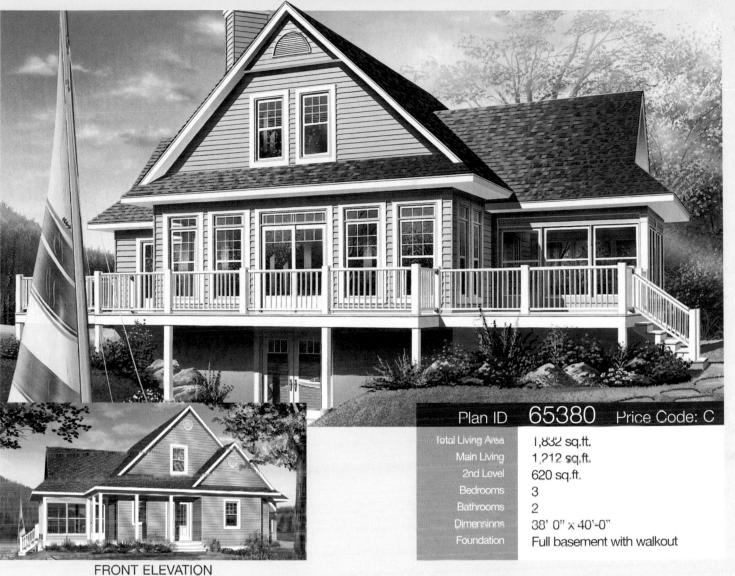

FRONT ELEVATION

Plan ID	65380	Price Code: C
Total Living Area	1,832 sq.ft.	
Main Living	1,212 sq.ft.	
2nd Level	620 sq.ft.	
Bedrooms	3	
Bathrooms	2	
Dimensions	38' 0" x 40'-0"	
Foundation	Full basement with walkout	

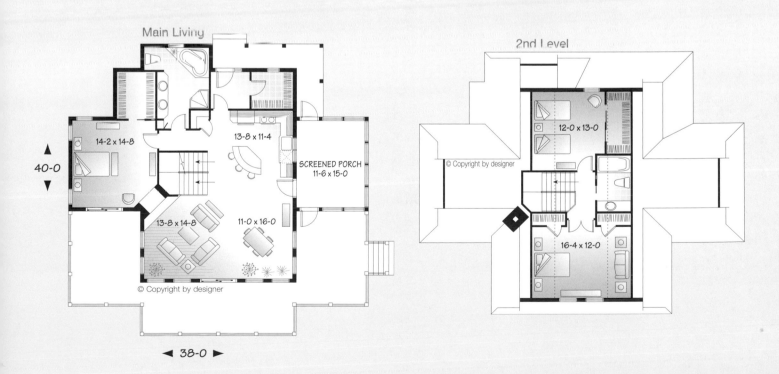

Main Living

14-2 x 14-8

13-8 x 11-4

SCREENED PORCH
11-6 x 15-0

40-0

13-8 x 14-8

11-0 x 16-0

© Copyright by designer

38-0

2nd Level

12-0 x 13-0

© Copyright by designer

16-4 x 12-0

Contemporary *Comforts* Inside

The design of this plan combines a traditional / European exterior with a contemporary floor plan. One of my favorite design features is the glass block wall in the gallery. Upon entering the home, one would notice the contorted flames of an inviting fire beyond – a very dramatic effect. I believe you'll also appreciate the way in which the three-sided fireplace and entertainment center are used to separate the great room, dining and kitchen area (see illustration). Skylights introduce even more natural light into the space. As in plan #24802 (pages 256-257), the "peripheral vision," of the kitchen and breakfast areas are enhanced through window placement. Throughout the home, we were very conscious of traffic patterns. Notice how the gallery transitions from the public to private spaces. Also, take note of the master bedroom's walk-in closet with two doors — one in the master bedroom and one in the vaulted master bath. This simple door placement adds so much to the livability of the house. We include a bonus room in a design whenever possible, and the one in this design offers unlimited possibilities.

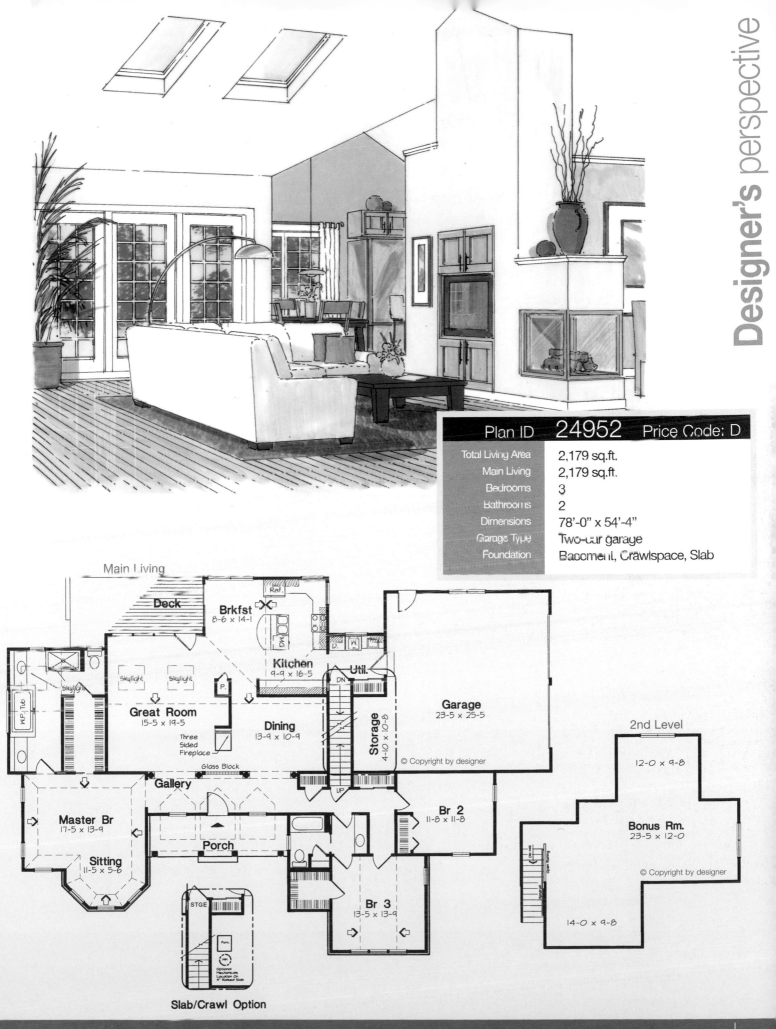

Plan ID **24952** **Price Code: D**

Total Living Area	2,179 sq.ft.
Main Living	2,179 sq.ft.
Bedrooms	3
Bathrooms	2
Dimensions	78'-0" x 54'-4"
Garage Type	Two-car garage
Foundation	Basement, Crawlspace, Slab

Main Living

Deck

Brkfst
8-6 x 14-1

Ref.

Kitchen
9-9 x 16-5

Util.

Skylight   Skylight

P.

Great Room
15-5 x 19-5

Dining
13-9 x 10-9

Storage
4-10 x 10-8

Garage
23-5 x 25-5

Three Sided Fireplace

© Copyright by designer

Glass Block

Gallery

Master Br
17-5 x 13-9

Porch

Br 2
11-8 x 11-8

2nd Level

12-0 x 9-8

Sitting
11-5 x 5-6

Bonus Rm.
23-5 x 12-0

© Copyright by designer

Br 3
13-5 x 13-9

14-0 x 9-8

STGE

Furn.

Optional Mechanicals Location On 4" Raised Slab

Slab/Crawl Option

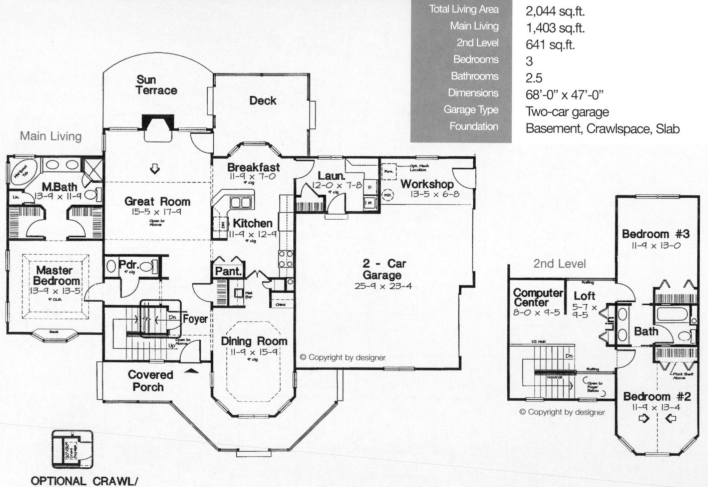

Main Living

Plan ID 24736 **Price Code: D**

Total Living Area	2,044 sq.ft.
Main Living	1,403 sq.ft.
2nd Level	641 sq.ft.
Bedrooms	3
Bathrooms	2.5
Dimensions	68'-0" x 47'-0"
Garage Type	Two-car garage
Foundation	Basement, Crawlspace, Slab

Sun Terrace

Deck

M.Bath
13-9 x 11-9

Great Room
15-5 x 17-9
Open to Above

Breakfast
11-9 x 7-0
4' clg.

Laun.
12-0 x 7-8
4' clg.

Workshop
13-5 x 6-8

Opt. Mech. Location

Kitchen
11-9 x 12-9
4' clg.

Master Bedroom
13-9 x 13-5
4' clg.

Pdr.
4' clg.

Pant.

Dn Foyer

2 - Car Garage
25-9 x 23-4

Up Open to Foyer Below

Dining Room
11-9 x 15-9
4' clg.

Covered Porch

© Copyright by designer

2nd Level

Computer Center
8-0 x 9-5

Loft
5-7 x 9-5

Bedroom #3
11-9 x 13-0

Bath

1/2 Hall

Dn

Handrail

Open to Foyer Below

Plant Shelf Above

Bedroom #2
11-9 x 13-4

© Copyright by designer

OPTIONAL CRAWL/
SLAB PLAN

Plan ID **24703**   Price Code: E

Total Living Area	2,465 sq.ft.
Main Living	1,749 sq.ft.
2nd Level	716 sq.ft.
Bedrooms	3
Bathrooms	2.5
Dimensions	73'-0" x 53'-4"
Garage Type	Two-car garage
Foundation	Basement, Crawlspace, Slab

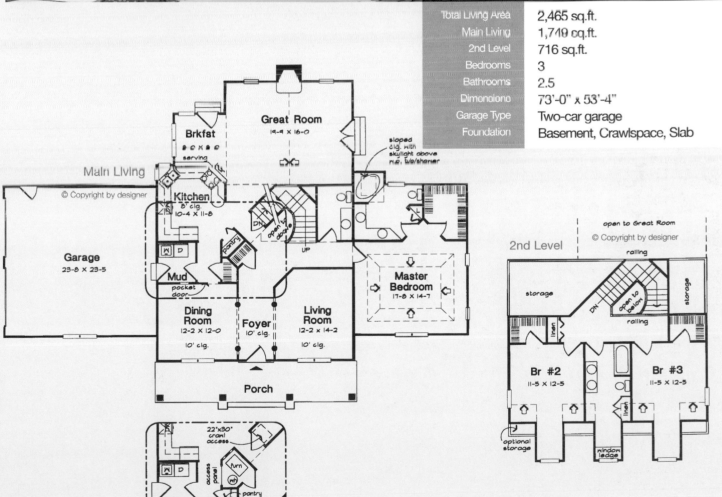

Main Living

© Copyright by designer

Great Room
19-9 X 16-0

Brkfst

serving

sloped clg. with skylight above
m.e. tub/shower

Kitchen
8' clg.
10-4 X 11-8

Garage
23-8 X 23-5

Mud
pocket door

pantry

DN

open to below

UP

Master Bedroom
17-8 X 14-7

Dining Room
12-2 X 12-0
10' clg.

Foyer
10' clg.

Living Room
12-2 X 14-2
10' clg.

Porch

2nd Level

open to Great Room

© Copyright by designer

railing

storage

storage

linen

DN

open to below

railing

Br #2
11-5 X 12-5

Br #3
11-5 X 12-5

linen

optional storage

window ledge

22"x30" crawl access

turn

access panel

pantry

Alternate Foundation Plan

This home, as shown on the photographs, is a modified version of the original plan #20368 and may differ from the actual blueprints.

Airy, Open *Elegance*

If open space suits your taste, here's a sturdy stucco classic to seriously consider. First impressions are revealed in the vaulted foyer. To the left, a soaring living room is brightened by a beautiful arched window. To the right, furnishings are showcased in the formal dining room. At the top of the stairs, a loft provides grand views of the airy family room below, which is separated from the kitchen/dinette by a two-sided fireplace. While upstairs, be sure to notice how bedrooms #2 and #3 share the bath and enjoy their own walk-in closets. On the main floor, the master suite features a garden spa, walk-in closet and access to a private deck.

Personal preference inspired the homeowners to utilize additional brick on the front elevation of this home. ▲

First impressions inside reveal a vaulted foyer and second-level loft. ▶

A beautiful round-top window allows beautiful views and plenty of natural light in the living room. ▶

A restful retreat is found in the master bath's garden spa. ▼

Plan ID	20368	Price Code: E
Total Living Area	2,372 sq.ft.	
Main Living	1,752 sq.ft.	
2nd Level	620 sq.ft.	
Bedrooms	3	
Bathrooms	2.5	
Dimensions	64'-0" x 52'-0"	
Garage Type	Three-car garage	
Foundation	Basement, Crawlspace, Slab	

Main Living

Deck

Family Rm
15-6 x 19-2
vaulted

MBr
15 x 13-2
pan vault

spa

Balcony above

Dinette/Kitchen
22 x 13-8
bench

D W
L

UP DN

desk

ov

pantry

Living Rm
13 x 13-8
vaulted

Foyer
vaulted

Dining Rm
11 x 13-8

Garage
21-4 x 31-4

© Copyright by designer

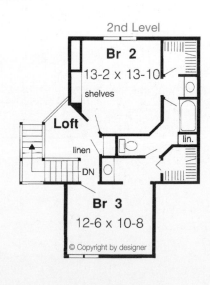

2nd Level

Br 2
13-2 x 13-10
shelves

Loft
linen
DN

lin.

Br 3
12-6 x 10-8

© Copyright by designer

Plan ID **20193** Price Code: D

Total Living Area	2,250 sq.ft.
Main Living	2,250 sq.ft.
Bedrooms	3
Bathrooms	2.5
Dimensions	68'-0" x 65'-0"
Garage Type	Two-car garage
Foundation	Basement, Crawlspace + Slab

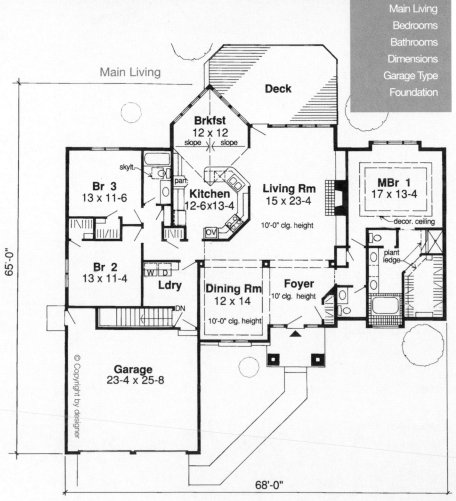

Main Living

Deck

Brkfst
12 x 12
slope · slope

skylt.

pan.

Br 3
13 x 11-6

Kitchen
12-6 x 13-4

Living Rm
15 x 23-4
10'-0" clg. height

MBr 1
17 x 13-4

decor. ceiling

ov

plant ledge

Br 2
13 x 11-4

W D

Ldry

Dining Rm
12 x 14
10'-0" clg. height

Foyer
10' clg. height

DN

65'-0"

© Copyright by designer

Garage
23-4 x 25-8

68'-0"

Plan ID 24959 Price Code: E

Total Living Area	2,464 sq.ft.
Main Living	2,464 sq.ft.
Bedrooms	3
Bathrooms	2.5
Dimensions	76'-6" x 67'-10"
Garage Type	Two-car garage
Foundation	Basement, Crawlspace, Slab

Main Living

TERRACE (Optional)

hot tub

COV PORCH

BREAKFAST 9'0" x 12'0"

KITCHEN 17'0" x 9'0"

snack bar

MASTER BR 23'6 x 15'6

butler's pantry

GREAT ROOM 16'0 x 19'6

opt. built-in

opt. built-in

BR #2 15'6 x 13'0

M.B.

make up

glass block

w.l.c.

PWD

LND

MUD RM.

1/2 wall

cl

dn

step

niche

open dormer above

niche

linen

B.

open dormer above

FOYER

step

© Copyright by designer

DINING 13'6 x 13'6

step step

TWO CAR GARAGE 30'0 x 22'6

storage

BR #3 15'6 x 13'6

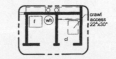

f wh

crawl access 22"x30"

cl

OPTIONAL CRAWL / SLAB PLAN

Plan ID	**24557**	Price Code: D
Total Living Area	2,110 sq.ft.	
Main Living	2,110 sq.ft.	
Bedrooms	3	
Bathrooms	2.5	
Dimensions	70'-0" x 56'-0"	
Garage Type	Three-car garage	
Foundation	Basement, Crawlspace, Slab	

Main Living

© Copyright by designer

Plan ID	20234	Price Code: E

Total Living Area	2,257 sq.ft.
Main Living	1,540 sq.ft.
2nd Level	717 sq.ft.
Bedrooms	4
Bathrooms	2.5
Dimensions	57'-0" x 56'-4"
Garage Type	Two-car garage
Foundation	Basement, Crawlspace, Slab

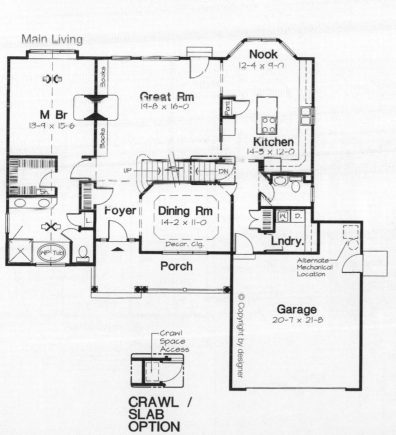

Main Living

Nook
12-4 x 9-0

Great Rm
19-8 x 16-0

M Br
13-9 x 15-6

Kitchen
14-5 x 12-0

Foyer

Dining Rm
14-2 x 11-0
Decor. Clg.

Lndry.

Porch

UP   DN

Alternate Mechanical Location

Garage
20-7 x 21-8

Crawl Space Access

CRAWL / SLAB OPTION

2nd Level

Open to Below

Br 3
12-0 x 12-0

DN

Linen

Br 2
13-0 x 12-0

Stor. Linen

Br 4
13-6 x 10-8

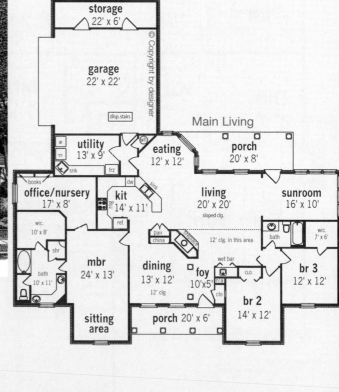

Main Living

Bfst.
11⁰ x 10⁴

COVERED DECK

Mbr.
14⁴ x 19²
11'-0" CEILING

Grt. Rm.
19⁰ x 18
CATHEDRAL CEILING

K
11⁸ x 14⁰

Suite
12⁰ x 14¹⁰
11'-0" CEILING

Gar.
12⁴ x 22⁴

Din.
12⁰ x 12⁸
11'-0" CEILING

DN

SHOE RACK

COVERED PORCH

© Copyright by designer

Gar.
24⁰ x 24⁰

Plan ID	44069	Price Code: D

Total Living Area	2,159 sq.ft.
Main Living	2,159 sq.ft.
Bedrooms	2
Bathrooms	2.5
Dimensions	71'-0" x 64'-4"
Garage Type	Three-car garage
Foundation	Basement, Crawlspace*, Slab*

storage
22' x 6'

garage
22' x 22'

disp. stairs

© Copyright by designer

Main Living

utility
13' x 9'

eating
12' x 12'

porch
20' x 8'

books

office/nursery
17' x 8'

wic.
10' x 8'

kit
14' x 11'

living
20' x 20'
sloped clg.

sunroom
16' x 10'

bath

wic.
7' x 6'

bath
10' x 11'

shr

mbr
24' x 13'

dining
13' x 12'
12' clg

pan
china

wet bar

12' clg. in this area

foy
10'x5'

clo

CLO.

br 3
12' x 12'

sitting
area

porch 20' x 6'

br 2
14' x 12'

Plan ID	65678	Price Code: E

Total Living Area	2,328 sq.ft.
Main Living	2,328 sq.ft.
Bedrooms	4
Bathrooms	2
Dimensions	68'-0" x 72'-0"
Garage Type	Two-car garage
Foundation	Basement, Crawlspace, Slab

Plan ID **65686** Price Code: D

Total Living Area	2,085 sq.ft.
Main Living	2,085 sq.ft.
Bedrooms	3
Bathrooms	2.5
Dimensions	64'-0" x 76'-0"
Garage Type	Three-car garage
Foundation	Slab

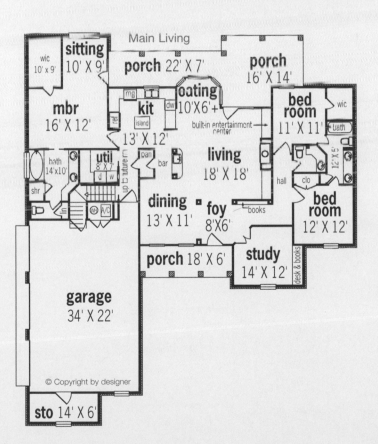

Main Living

sitting 10' X 9'
wic 10' x 9'
porch 22' X 7'
porch 16' X 14'
eating 10'X 6'+
mbr 16' X 12'
kit 13' X 12'
built-in entertainment center
bed room 11' X 11'
wic
bath
util 8' X 7'
pan
bar
living 18' X 18'
bath 14'x10'
shr
dining 13' X 11'
foy 8'X6'
books
hall
clo
bed room 12' X 12'
porch 18' X 6'
study 14' X 12'
desk & books
garage 34' X 22'
sto 14' X 6'
© Copyright by designer

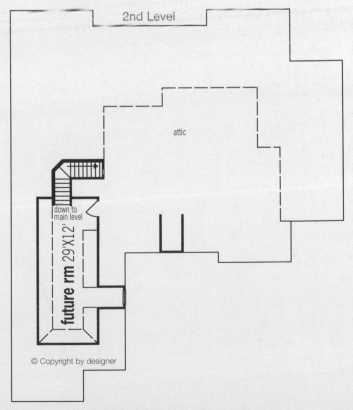

2nd Level

attic

down to main level
future rm 29'X12'
© Copyright by designer

Plan ID 65633	Price Code: E
Total Living Area	2,393 sq.ft.
Main Living	2,281 sq.ft.
2nd Level	112 sq.ft.
Bedrooms	3
Bathrooms	2.5
Dimensions	60'-0" x 71'-0"
Garage Type	Two-car garage
Foundation	Crawlspace, Slab

Main Living

© Copyright by designer

garage
22 x 22

deck
22 x 20

bath

sho

his clo   her clo

sto

bath   lin

screen porch
20 x 11

mbr
18 x 14

sitting

util   sink

d w

frz

up

fireplace

living
20 x 18

br 2
13 x 12

tv

kit

ref

clo

pass
thru   ov

a/c

wic

dr

wic

bath

eating
13 x 10

dining
12 x 12

foy
8 x 6

br 3
12 x 12

dr

china

porch
30 x 8

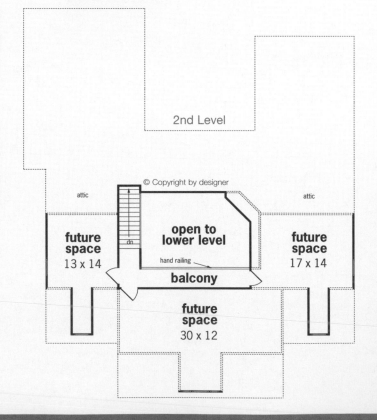

2nd Level

© Copyright by designer

attic

attic

future
space
13 x 14

open to
lower level

future
space
17 x 14

hand railing

dn

balcony

future
space
30 x 12

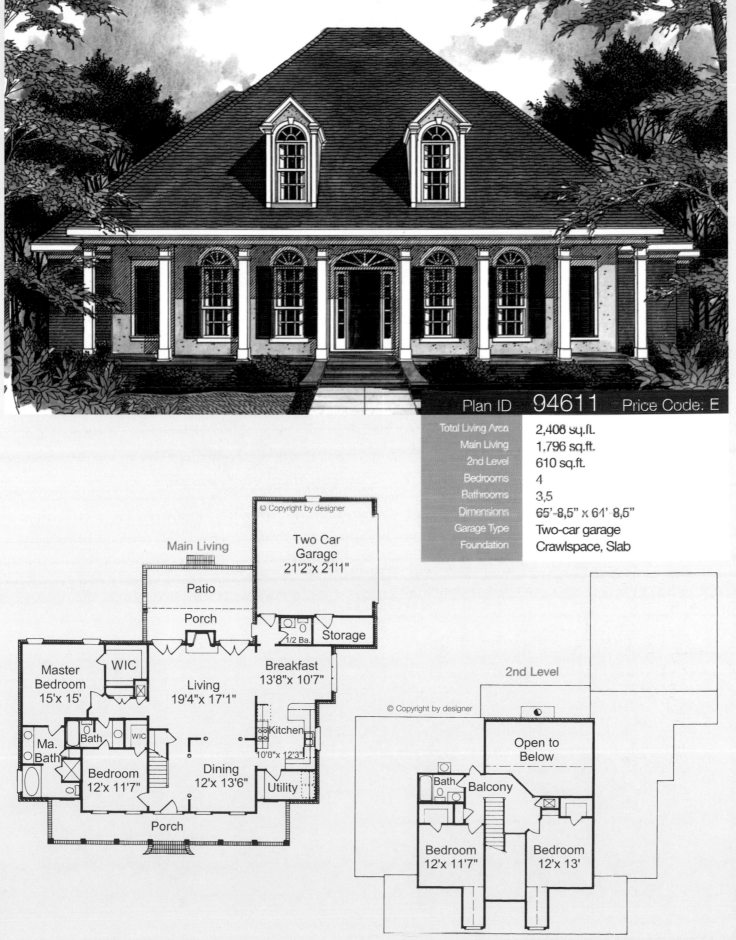

Plan ID **94611** Price Code: E

Total Living Area	2,406 sq. ft.
Main Living	1,796 sq. ft.
2nd Level	610 sq. ft.
Bedrooms	4
Bathrooms	3,5
Dimensions	65'-8,5" x 61'-8,5"
Garage Type	Two-car garage
Foundation	Crawlspace, Slab

Main Living

© Copyright by designer

Two Car Garage
21'2" x 21'1"

Patio

Porch

Storage

1/2 Ba.

Master Bedroom
15' x 15'

WIC

Breakfast
13'8" x 10'7"

Living
19'4" x 17'1"

Ma. Bath

Bath

WIC

Kitchen
10'8" x 12'3"

Bedroom
12' x 11'7"

Dining
12' x 13'6"

Utility

Porch

2nd Level

© Copyright by designer

Open to Below

Bath

Balcony

Bedroom
12' x 11'7"

Bedroom
12' x 13'

KITCHENS

IF THERE'S ONE LESSON WE SHOULD ALL HAVE LEARNED BY NOW, IT'S THE FACT THAT THE KITCHEN IS THE HUB OF THE HOME. If you still question the necessity of a large, open kitchen, just observe what happens the next time you have a group of people at your home. Invariably, everyone insists on gathering in the kitchen. Even if you place the food in the formal dining room, they will fill their plates and then attempt to return to the crowded kitchen!

While guests enjoy being in the kitchen socializing, the area must still function for food preparation. In addition to a center island with ample workspace, there should also be a counter space that can be utilized as an eating area. This allows people to either sit or stand at this "snack bar" while food continues to be prepared or served. If this counter surface is the same standard 3-ft. height, it still functions as a kitchen workstation.

Many homeowners want kitchens that open to the family room and dining areas. By creating this open situation, people tend to feel as though they are involved with the activities in the kitchen, even though they are actually in the family room or dining area. Additionally, the person preparing meals does not feel isolated and can remain involved in the conversations taking place in the family room.

While the traffic should not flow through the kitchen, there should a convenient and logical passage to the garage or service entrance for ease of unloading groceries. Somewhere along this service entrance passage, an area to drop the daily mail, keys, and cell phones will certainly be appreciated. Designing a practical storage for these items makes them less likely to end up on the kitchen counter.

Excerpted from *Home Plan Buyer's Guide,*
an upcoming book by **Larry W. Garnett**

This home, as shown on the photographs, is a modified version of the original plan #94670 and may differ from the actual blueprints.

Impressive, Front to Back

The design of this home's garage offers a practical, attractive solution for those who prefer the look a side-load garage, but are constrained by neighboring lots. Curb appeal is further enhanced by the grand arched entry. Once inside, immediate views to the dining room open to the living room, marked only by columns and a short wall. The living room features a corner fireplace and open views to the rear covered porch. The kitchen mingles seamlessly with the breakfast area, which offers access to the rear porch. The bedrooms form the right wing of the home's layout, with the master suite filling the rear and the other three forming a cul-de-sac around a full bath. This home is designed with a slab foundation.

Expansive windows bring the outdoors inside, in the sunny breakfast area. ▶

A handsome corner fireplace and views to the rear covered porch enhance the living room's ambiance. ▶

Open views from the living room also include the dining room and foyer. ▼

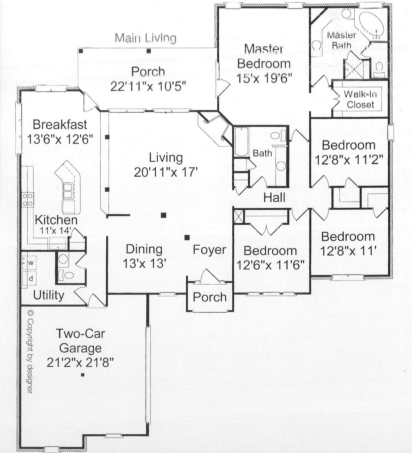

Plan ID	94670	Price Code: E
Total Living Area		2,471 sq.ft.
Main Living		2,471 sq.ft.
Bedrooms		4
Bathrooms		3
Dimensions		62'-10" x 75'-3"
Garage Type		Two-car garage
Foundation		Slab

Main Living

Porch 22'11"x 10'5"

Master Bedroom 15'x 19'6"

Master Bath

Walk-In Closet

Breakfast 13'6"x 12'6"

Living 20'11"x 17'

Bath

Bedroom 12'8"x 11'2"

Hall

Kitchen 11'x 14'

Dining 13'x 13'

Foyer

Bedroom 12'6"x 11'6"

Bedroom 12'8"x 11'

Utility

Porch

w d

© Copyright by designer

Two-Car Garage 21'2"x 21'8"

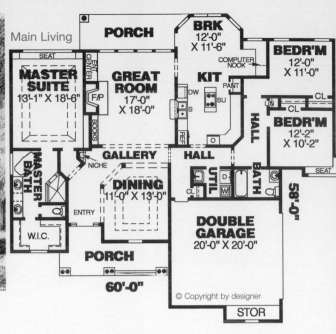

Plan ID 67027 Price Code: D

Total Living Area	2,028 sq.ft.
Main Living	2,028 sq.ft.
Bedrooms	3
Bathrooms	2
Dimensions	60'-0" x 58'-0"
Garage Type	Two-car garage
Foundation	Slab

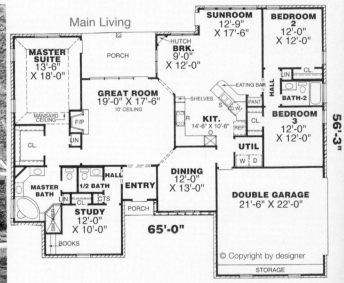

Plan ID 67043 Price Code: E

Total Living Area	2,350 sq.ft.
Main Living	2,350 sq.ft.
Bedrooms	3
Bathrooms	2.5
Dimensions	65'-0" x 56'-3"
Garage Type	Two-car garage
Foundation	Slab

Plan ID 67038 **Price Code:** D

Total Living Area	2,204 sq.ft.
Main Living	1,683 sq.ft.
2nd Level	521 sq.ft.
Bedrooms	3
Bathrooms	2.5
Dimensions	55' 0" x 49'-6"
Garage Type	Two-car garage
Foundation	Slab

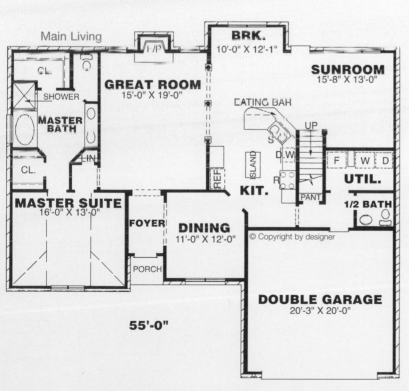

Main Living

CL.

SHOWER

MASTER BATH

GREAT ROOM
15'-0" X 19'-0"

BRK.
10'-0" X 12'-1"

SUNROOM
15'-8" X 13'-0"

EATING BAR

UP

D.W

CL.

LIN

REF

ISLAND

KIT.

F W D

UTIL.

MASTER SUITE
16'-0" X 13'-0"

FOYER

DINING
11'-0" X 12'-0"

PANT

1/2 BATH

© Copyright by designer

PORCH

DOUBLE GARAGE
20'-3" X 20'-0"

55'-0"

49'-6"

2nd Level

BEDROOM 2
12'-0" X 12'-7"

CL.

© Copyright by designer

BATH 2

DN

CL.

BEDROOM 3
11'-0" X 12'-0"

HALL

STOR

LIN

FUTURE PLAYROOM
11'-8" X 13'-5"

Plan ID 67028 Price Code: D

Total Living Area	2,036 sq.ft.
Main Living	2,036 sq.ft.
Bedrooms	3
Bathrooms	2
Dimensions	58'-10" x 59'-1"
Garage Type	Two-car garage
Foundation	Slab

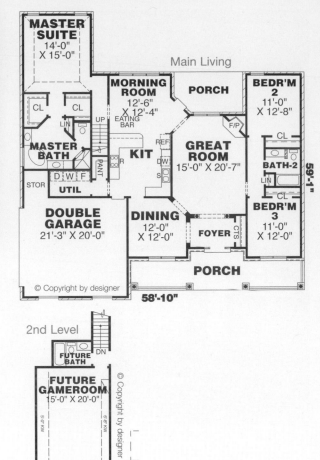

Plan ID 67002 Price Code: D

Total Living Area	2,185 sq.ft.
Main Living	2,185 sq.ft.
Bedrooms	3
Bathrooms	2
Dimensions	63'-6" x 65'-4"
Garage Type	Two-car garage
Foundation	Slab

ORDER NOW 1-800-235-5700 or at www.familyhomeplans.com

Plan ID 67045 **Price Code: D**

Total Living Area	2,120 sq. ft.
Main Living	2,126 sq. ft
Bedrooms	3
Bathrooms	2
Dimensions	72'-4" x 56'-0"
Garage Type	Two-car garage
Foundation	Slab

Main Living

BEDR'M-2
11'-2" X 12'-0"

GREAT ROOM
20'-0" X 16'-0"

BRK
10'-0"
X 10'-0"

HEARTH
ROOM
16'-0" X 12'-0"

F/P

EATING BAR

F/P

CL

BATH-2

BEDR'M
3
11'-0" X 11'-0"

CL

CTS

ENTRY

DINING
12'-4" X 13'-5"

KIT

ISLAND

REF

UP

DW

SU

PANT

MASTER
SUITE
13'-0" X 16'-0"

MASTER
BATH

CL

UTIL
D W

DOUBLE GARAGE
20'-0" X 20'-0"

PORCH

72'-4"

56'-0"

© Copyright by designer

2nd Level

CL

FUTURE
BEDR'M
11'-2" X 13'-0"

FUTURE
BATH

FUTURE
BEDR'M
11'-9" X 13'-0"

FUTURE
GAME ROOM
16'-0" X 13'-0"

DN

CL

11'-0" x 12'-8"

© Copyright by designer

Plan ID	94673	Price Code: D
Total Living Area		2,232 sq.ft.
Main Living		2,232 sq.ft.
Bedrooms		3
Bathrooms		2
Dimensions		57'-6" x 37'-10"
Garage Type		Two-car garage
Foundation		Slab

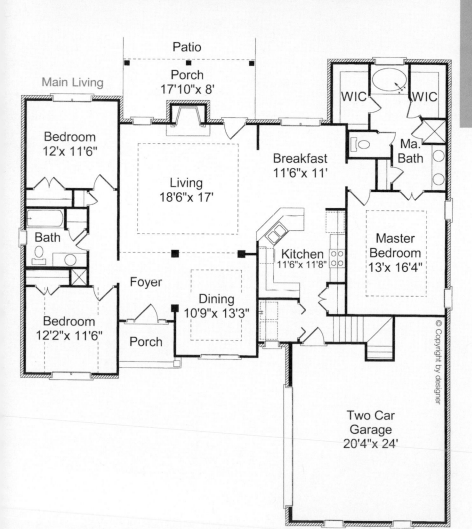

Main Living

Patio

Porch
17'10"x 8'

Bedroom
12'x 11'6"

Breakfast
11'6"x 11'

WIC

WIC

Ma.
Bath

Bath

Living
18'6"x 17'

Kitchen
11'6"x 11'8"

Master
Bedroom
13'x 16'4"

Foyer

Dining
10'9"x 13'3"

Bedroom
12'2"x 11'6"

Porch

© Copyright by designer

Two Car
Garage
20'4"x 24'

2nd Level

Gameroom
21'8"x 16'

© Copyright by designer

Plan ID **40013** Price Code: D

Total Living Area	2,046 sq.ft.
Main Living	2,046 sq.ft.
Bedrooms	3
Bathrooms	2.5
Dimensions	68'-2" x 57'-4"
Garage Type	Two car garage
Foundation	Basement, Crawlspace, Slab

Main Living

Porch
32-2x8-0

Breakfast
11-8x10-6

Master
Bedroom
14-0x17-6

Bath
9-0x15-3

Bedroom
11-10x11-6

Greatroom
17-6x17-6

Kitchen
11-8x14-11

Laundry
11-6x7-6

Storage
11-6x7-10

Bath

Bedroom
11-10x11-6

Foyer

Dining
13-0x11-6

1/2 Bath

Garage
23-4x21-8

© Copyright by designer

Porch
36-4x8-0

68-2

57-4

Basement Stair
Location

Down

linen   shelving

Raised

Laundry
12-0x9-6

Storage
11-0x9-10

*Basement option adds
45 sq. ft. to living area.

Garage
23-4x21-6

© Copyright by designer

Plan ID 40020   Price Code: D

Total Living Area	2,197 sq.ft.
Main Living	2,197 sq.ft.
Bedrooms	3
Bathrooms	2.5
Dimensions	72'-10" x 56'-6"
Garage Type	Two-car garage
Foundation	Basement, Crawlspace, Slab

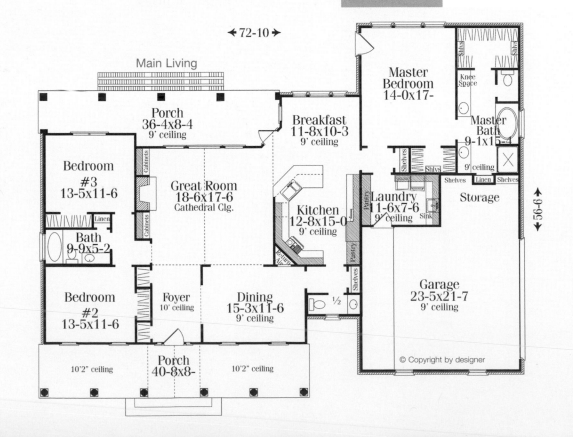

← 72-10 →

Main Living

Porch
36-4x8-4
9' ceiling

Breakfast
11-8x10-3
9' ceiling

Master Bedroom
14-0x17-

Knee Space

Master Bath
9-1x15-

Bedroom #3
13-5x11-6

Great Room
18-6x17-6
Cathedral Clg.

Kitchen
12-8x15-0
9' ceiling

Laundry
11-6x7-6
9' ceiling

Storage

Linen

Bath
9-9x5-2

Bedroom #2
13-5x11-6

Foyer
10' ceiling

Dining
15-3x11-6
9' ceiling

½

Garage
23-5x21-7
9' ceiling

Porch
40-8x8-
10'2" ceiling   10'2" ceiling

56-6

© Copyright by designer

Plan ID 40018 Price Code: D

Total Living Area	2,122 sq. ft.
Main Living	2,122 sq. ft.
Bedrooms	3
Bathrooms	2.5
Dimensions	69'-0" x 67'-0"
Garage Type	Two-car garage
Foundation	Basement, Crawlspace, Slab

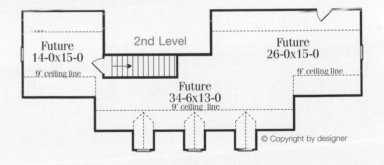

Main Living

61'-0"

Br 3
11-0x12-0

Br 4 /
Study
10-8x12-0

Patio

Garage
22-10x20-1

© Copyright by designer

Great Room
20-1x19-5
vaulted clg

plant shelf

Br 2
11-0x10-0

51'-0"

D
W

R
P

Kit/Dining
20-0x18-11

Dn

Entry

MBr
17-4x14-0
vaulted clg

Porch

Porch depth 6-0

Plan ID 69019   Price Code: D

Total Living Area	2,029 sq.ft.
Main Living	2,029 sq.ft.
Bedrooms	4
Bathrooms	2
Dimensions	61'-0" x 51'-0"
Garage Type	Two-car garage
Foundation	Basement

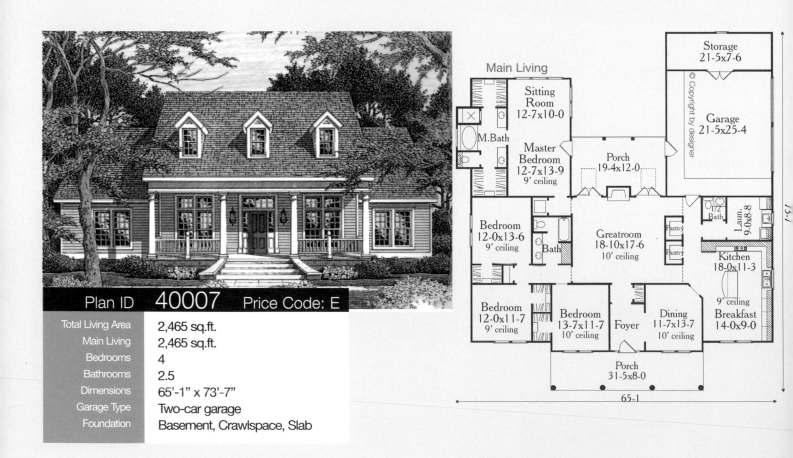

Main Living

Storage
21-5x7-6

Sitting
Room
12-7x10-0

© Copyright by designer

Garage
21-5x25-4

M.Bath

Master
Bedroom
12-7x13-9
9' ceiling

Porch
19-4x12-0

Bedroom
12-0x13-6
9' ceiling

Bath

Greatroom
18-10x17-6
10' ceiling

Pantry

1/2
Bath

Laun.
9-0x8-8

Pantry

Kitchen
18-0x11-3
9' ceiling

Bedroom
12-0x11-7
9' ceiling

Bedroom
13-7x11-7
10' ceiling

Foyer

Dining
11-7x13-7
10' ceiling

Breakfast
14-0x9-0

Porch
31-5x8-0

65-1

Plan ID 40007   Price Code: E

Total Living Area	2,465 sq.ft.
Main Living	2,465 sq.ft.
Bedrooms	4
Bathrooms	2.5
Dimensions	65'-1" x 73'-7"
Garage Type	Two-car garage
Foundation	Basement, Crawlspace, Slab

REAR ELEVATION

Plan ID **40019**   Price Code: D

Total Living Area	2,085 sq.ft.
Main Living	2,085 sq.ft.
Bedrooms	3
Bathrooms	2.5
Dimensions	65'-11" x 67'-9"
Garage Type	Two car garage
Foundation	Basement, Crawlspace, Slab

Main Living

Storage
21-6x6-0

Brick Patio

Garage
21-6x21-3

© Copyright by designer

M.Bath
16-1x13-1
9' ceiling

Porch
25-3x10-0
10' ceiling

Sitting
9-0x8-0
9' ceiling

½ Bath

Laun.
7-3x6-6
Shelves

Master Bedroom
16-1x15-0
9' ceiling

Bath 2

Greatroom
17-0x18-3
10' ceiling

Kitchen
14-10x12-10
9' ceiling

2nd Level

© Copyright by designer

Future
11-2x12-5
8' ceiling line

Step Down

Future
10-9x12-5
8' ceiling line

Step Down

Bedroom 2
11-3x11-6
9' ceiling

Bedroom 3
11-6x12-3
10' ceiling

Foyer

Dining
12-9x11-0
10' ceiling

Pantry

Breakfast
10-0x9-6
9' ceiling

Future
35-0x19-6
8' ceiling line

Porch
36-2x6-8

Arched Barrel Ceiling

Plan ID 68148 Price Code: D

Total Living Area	2,144 sq.ft.
Main Living	2,144 sq.ft.
Bedrooms	4
Bathrooms	2
Dimensions	67'-0" x 52'-0"
Garage Type	Two-car garage
Foundation	Basement*, Crawlspace*, Slab

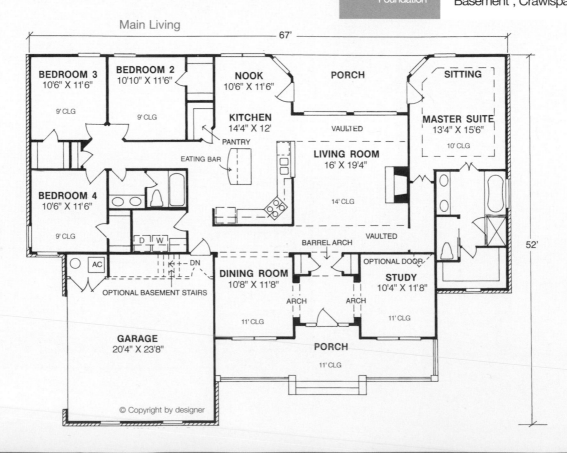

Main Living

BEDROOM 3 10'6" X 11'6" 9' CLG

BEDROOM 2 10'10" X 11'6" 9' CLG

NOOK 10'6" X 11'6"

PORCH

SITTING

KITCHEN 14'4" X 12

PANTRY

EATING BAR

VAULTED

MASTER SUITE 13'4" X 15'6" 10' CLG

LIVING ROOM 16' X 19'4"

14' CLG

BEDROOM 4 10'6" X 11'6" 9' CLG

D W

AC

BARREL ARCH

VAULTED

OPTIONAL DOOR

OPTIONAL BASEMENT STAIRS

DINING ROOM 10'8" X 11'8" 11' CLG

STUDY 10'4" X 11'8" 11' CLG

ARCH ARCH

GARAGE 20'4" X 23'8"

PORCH 11' CLG

67'

52'

© Copyright by designer

Plan ID 68162   Price Code: E

Total Living Area	2,252 sq.ft.
Main Living	1,736 sq.ft.
2nd Level	516 sq.ft.
Bedrooms	4
Bathrooms	3
Dimensions	80' 0" x 59' 0"
Garage Type	Two-car garage
Foundation	Basement*, Crawlspace*, Slab

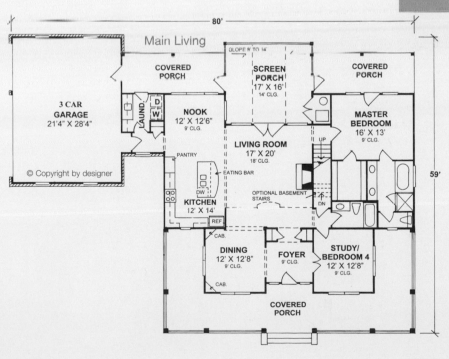

Main Living

2nd Level

This home, as shown on the photographs, is a modified version of the original plan #69510 and may differ from the actual blueprints.

Zoned for *Privacy*

The H-shaped floor plan allows for very private zones within this home. The secondary bedrooms are effectively separated from the master suite, which offers a generous sitting area in the bedroom and pampering amenities in the bath. Upon entering the home, the gallery offers stunning views into the elegantly appointed volume great room with its fireplace, built-in shelves and pair of sliding glass doors that open to a backyard terrace.

Modifications to this home included removal of a dormer and the substitution of siding on the exterior. The originally designed brick façade is shown above. ▲

The private master bedroom offers a comfortable sitting area and special ceiling treatments. ▶

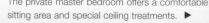

Views from the gallery, into the great room, provide elegant first impressions. ▲

Plan ID	69510	Price Code: D
Total Living Area	2,018 sq.ft.	
Main Living	2,018 sq.ft.	
Bedrooms	3	
Bathrooms	2	
Dimensions	64' 0" x 57'-0"	
Garage Type	Two-car garage	
Foundation	Basement, Crawlspace, Slab, Walkout Basement*	

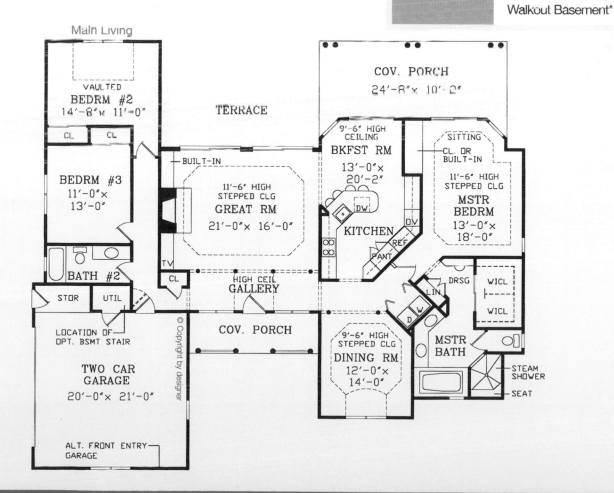

Main Living

VAULTED
BEDRM #2
14'-8" x 11'-0"

TERRACE

COV. PORCH
24'-8" x 10'-2"

CL   CL

BUILT-IN

9'-6" HIGH CEILING
BKFST RM
13'-0" x 20'-2"

SITTING
CL. OR BUILT-IN

BEDRM #3
11'-0" x 13'-0"

11'-6" HIGH STEPPED CLG
GREAT RM
21'-0" x 16'-0"

DW

11'-6" HIGH STEPPED CLG
MSTR BEDRM
13'-0" x 18'-0"

KITCHEN

OV

REF

BATH #2

TV

CL

PANT

DRSG   WICL

STOR   UTIL

HIGH CEIL
GALLERY

LIN   W

WICL

LOCATION OF OPT. BSMT STAIR

COV. PORCH

D   W

MSTR BATH

TWO CAR GARAGE
20'-0" x 21'-0"

9'-6" HIGH STEPPED CLG
DINING RM
12'-0" x 14'-0"

STEAM SHOWER

SEAT

ALT. FRONT ENTRY GARAGE

© Copyright by designer

Plan ID	**69512**	Price Code: E

Total Living Area	2,282 sq.ft.
Main Living	2,282 sq.ft.
Bedrooms	3
Bathrooms	2.5
Dimensions	60'-0" x 57'-0"
Garage Type	Two-car garage
Foundation	Basement, Crawlspace, Slab

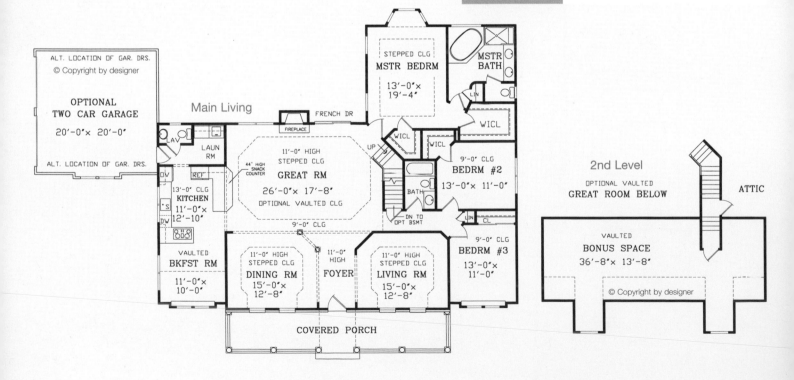

Plan ID **96865** Price Code: F

Total Living Area	2,302 sq.ft.
Main Living	1,570 sq.ft.
2nd Level	732 sq.ft.
Bedrooms	4
Bathrooms	2.5
Dimensions	70' 8" x 53'-0"
Garage Type	Two-car garage
Foundation	Basement, Crawlspace, Slab

Main Living

70'-8"

1 BAY GARAGE
22' 0"x13'-0"

9' OVERHEAD DOOR

SHOP/
STORAGE
9'-3"x16'-9"

WISE BENCH

53'-0"

9' OVERHEAD DOOR   9' OVERHEAD DOOR

2 BAY GARAGE
22'-0"x23'-0"

STEPS

COVERED PORCH

48" DIAM

10'-0"

LNDRY

KITCHEN
15'-6"x11'-8"
(9' CLG)
ISLAND

PNTRY

COATS

PWDR

FRENCH
DOORS

FORMAL DINING
10'-8"x11'-0"
(9' CLG)

DESK

COATS

FOYER
(9' CLG)

DN
UP

UP

GREAT ROOM
21'-5"x15'-1"
(9' CLG)

OFFICE/
GUEST ROOM
10'-8"x11'-0"
(9' CLG)

SHWR
TILE   JACC

MASTER
BATH
(9' CLG)

W.I.C.

MASTER BDRM
14'-0"x18'-0"
(10' TRAY CLG)

8'-0"

8'-0"

8'-0"

COVERED PORCH

STEPS

© Copyright by designer

2nd Level

© Copyright by designer

BONUS ROOM
21'-5"x18'-0"
(FUTURE)

8' CLG
SLOPED CLG

8' CLG
SLOPED CLG

6'-8"±
KNEEWALL

6'-8"±
KNEEWALL

COMPUTER
AREA

STORAGE

4'-0"± KNEEWALL

SLOPED CLG   8' CLG   SLOPED CLG

4'-0"± KNEEWALL

HOME
ENTERTAINMENT
AREA

FAMILY
ROOM
10'-8"x24'-5"
(VAULTED)

BATH

TUB/SHWR

STRG/
LINEN

LINEN

8' CLG

RIDGE

1st Floor
Plant Shelf

OPEN RAILING

RIDGE

DN

BEDROOM #2
11'-0"x10'-8"

DN

OPEN TO BELOW
(VAULTED)

BEDROOM #3
10'-8"x11'-0"

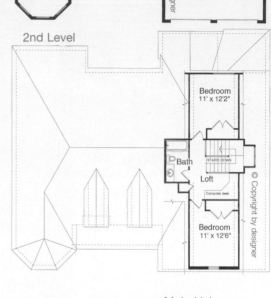

Main Living

Master Bedroom 14'4" x 14'8"

Great Room 18'1" x 18'11"

Breakfast 11'2" x 11'8"

Porch

Kitchen 15'5" x 11'2"

Laun.

STAIRS UP

DOWN

Dining Room 11' x 13'

Foyer

Porch

Two-car Garage 22' x 21'

WALK-IN CLOSET

Library 11'4" x 12'2"

© Copyright by designer

2nd Level

Bedroom 11' x 12'2"

Bath

STAIRS DOWN

Loft

Computer desk

Bedroom 11' x 12'6"

© Copyright by designer

Plan ID 50012   Price Code: E

Total Living Area	2,449 sq.ft.
Main Living	1,925 sq.ft.
2nd Level	524 sq.ft.
Bedrooms	3
Bathrooms	2.5
Dimensions	56'-4" x 53'-4"
Garage Type	Two-car garage
Foundation	Basement

Main Living

Deck

Breakfast 11' x 9'

Great Room 16'6" x 17'2"

Master Bedroom 14' x 17'10"

slope ceiling

slope ceiling

Hall

Kitchen 13'2" x 12'7"

Laun.

wood rail

pantry

stairs up

walk-in closet

Two-car Garage 23'9" x 20'0"

Dining Room 11'2" x 15'4"

Foyer

Bath

46'8"

© Copyright by designer

54'8"

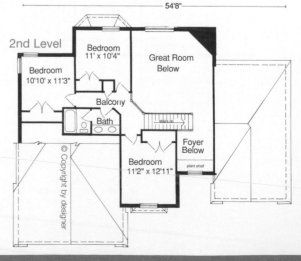

2nd Level

Bedroom 10'10" x 11'3"

Bedroom 11' x 10'4"

Great Room Below

Balcony

Bath

stairs dn

Foyer Below

Bedroom 11'2" x 12'11"

plant shelf

© Copyright by designer

Plan ID 92631   Price Code: D

Total Living Area	2,157 sq.ft.
Main Living	1,511 sq.ft.
2nd Level	646 sq.ft.
Bedrooms	4
Bathrooms	2.5
Dimensions	54'-8" x 46'-8"
Garage Type	Two-car garage
Foundation	Basement

ORDER NOW 1-800-235-5700 or at www.familyhomeplans.com

Plan ID 97710 Price Code: D

Total Living Area	2,198 sq.ft.
Main Living	1,706 sq.ft.
2nd Level	492 sq.ft.
Bedrooms	3
Bathrooms	2.5
Dimensions	59'-4" x 65'-0"
Garage Type	Two-car garage
Foundation	Basement

Main Living

Breakfast 9' x 10'
Kitchen 8'4" x 15'4"
Great Room 16'10" x 21'
Dressing
walk-in closet
Dining Room 13'8" x 11'8"
Hall
Foyer
Master Bedroom 14' x 17'4"
Bath
Porch
Laun.
Two-car Garage 21' x 29'8"
© Copyright by designer
59'4"
65'

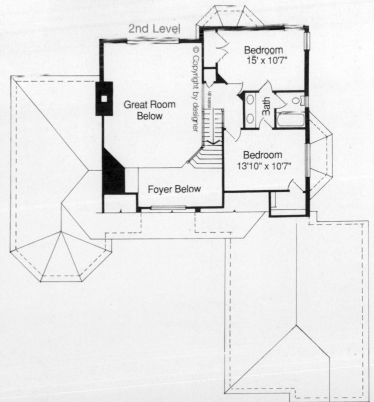

2nd Level

Great Room Below
Bedroom 15' x 10'7"
Bath
Bedroom 13'10" x 10'7"
Foyer Below
© Copyright by designer

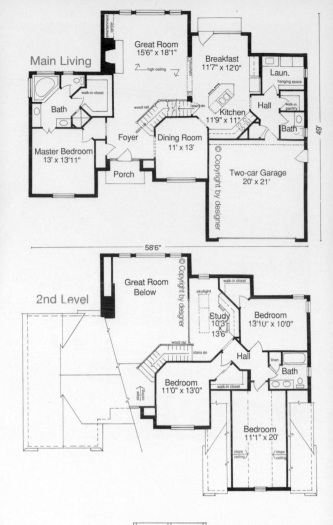

Plan ID 92643   Price Code: D

Total Living Area	2,209 sq.ft.
Main Living	1,542 sq.ft.
2nd Level	667 sq.ft.
Bedrooms	3
Bathrooms	2.5
Dimensions	58'-6" x 49'-0"
Garage Type	Two-car garage
Foundation	Basement

Main Living

Great Room 15'6" x 18'1"
Breakfast 11'7" x 12'0"
Laun.
Bath
Kitchen 11'9" x 11'
Hall
Bath
Master Bedroom 13' x 13'11"
Foyer
Dining Room 11' x 13'
Porch
Two-car Garage 20' x 21'

58'6"
49'

2nd Level

Great Room Below
Study 10'3" x 13'6"
Bedroom 13'10" x 10'0"
Bedroom 11'0" x 13'0"
Hall
Bath
Bedroom 11'1" x 20'

Plan ID 92697   Price Code: D

Total Living Area	2,017 sq.ft.
Main Living	1,432 sq.ft.
2nd Level	585 sq.ft.
Bedrooms	3
Bathrooms	2.5
Dimensions	58'-0" x 44'-4"
Garage Type	Two-car garage
Foundation	Basement

Main Living

Porch
Breakfast 12'1" x 11'7"
Great Room 20' x 15'4"
Laun.
Kitchen 11'10" x 12'10"
Bath
Two-car Garage 21' x 20'
Dining Room 11'10" x 11'6"
Foyer
Master Bedroom 12' x 15'
Porch

2nd Level

Bedroom 12'2" x 12'
Great Room Below
Bedroom 12'2" x 11'10"
Balcony

Plan ID 50023 Price Code: E

Total Living Area	2,332 sq.ft.
Main Living	1,680 sq ft
2nd Level	652 sq.ft.
Bedrooms	4
Bathrooms	2.5
Dimensions	58'-8" x 46'-8"
Garage Type	Two-car garage
Foundation	Basement

Main Living

Breakfast 11' x 9'

Great Room 18'7" x 17'2"

Dressing

Bath

Kitchen 13'2" x 12'6"

WALK IN CLOSET

Laun.

PANTRY

STAIRS DOWN

OPEN WOOD RAIL

STAIRS UP

46'-8"

Two Car Garage 22' x 23'9"

Dining Room 11'2"x 15'

Foyer

Master Bedroom 13'10" x 18'6"

Porch

SLOPED

SLOPED

SOFFIT

© Copyright by designer

58'-8"

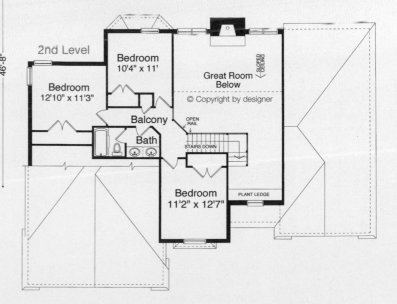

2nd Level

Bedroom 10'4" x 11'

Bedroom 12'10" x 11'3"

Great Room Below

SLOPED CEILING

© Copyright by designer

Balcony

OPEN RAIL

Bath

STAIRS DOWN

Bedroom 11'2" x 12'7"

PLANT LEDGE

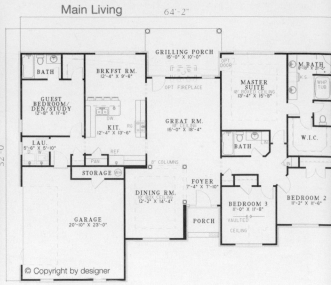

Main Living 64'-2"

Plan ID 62317 Price Code: C

Total Living Area	2,022 sq.ft.
Main Living	2,022 sq.ft.
Bedrooms	4
Bathrooms	2
Dimensions	64'-2" x 52'-0"
Garage Type	Two-car garage
Foundation	Crawlspace, Slab

Main Living 52'-6"

2nd Level

Plan ID 62136 Price Code: E

Total Living Area	2,413 sq.ft.
Main Living	2,413 sq.ft.
Bedrooms	3
Bathrooms	2
Dimensions	52'-6" x 79'-6"
Garage Type	Two-car garage
Foundation	Crawlspace, Slab

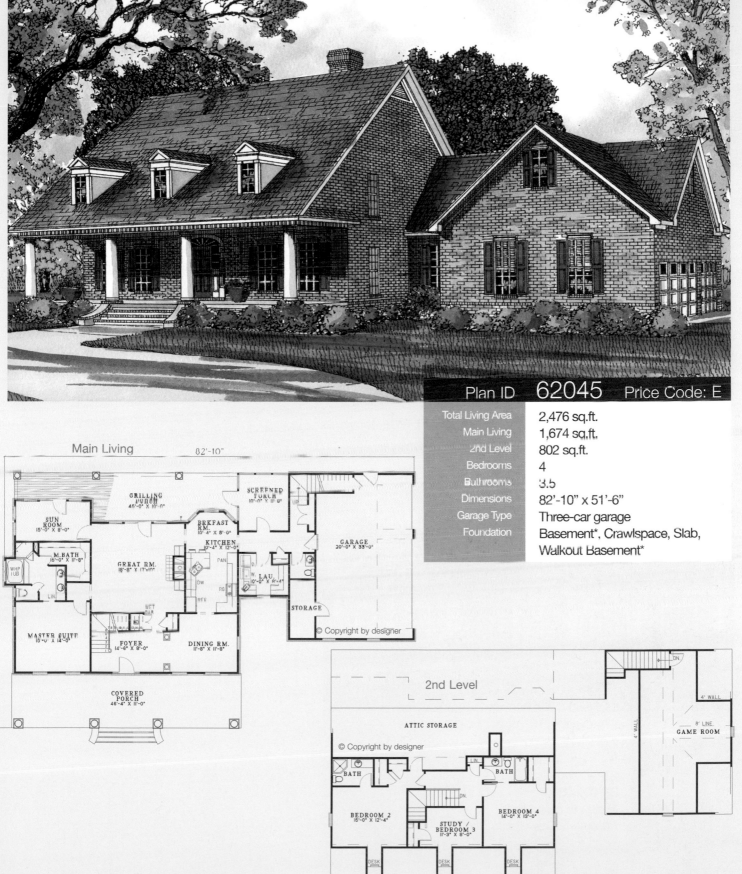

Plan ID 62045 Price Code: E

Total Living Area	2,476 sq.ft.
Main Living	1,674 sq.ft.
2nd Level	802 sq.ft.
Bedrooms	4
Bathrooms	3.5
Dimensions	82'-10" x 51'-6"
Garage Type	Three-car garage
Foundation	Basement*, Crawlspace, Slab, Walkout Basement*

Main Living 82'-10"

51'-6"

GRILLING PORCH 45'-0" X 10'-0"

SCREENED PORCH 10'-0" X 11'-0"

SUN ROOM 15'-0" X 8'-0"

M. BATH 16'-0" X 11'-8"

BRKFAST RM. 10'-4" X 8'-0"

KITCHEN 10'-4" X 12'-0"

GARAGE 20'-0" X 33'-0"

GREAT RM. 18'-8" X 17'-10"

WHP TUB

W. LAU. 10'-0" X 8'-4"

STORAGE

MASTER SUITE 18'-0" X 14'-0"

WET BAR

FOYER 14'-6" X 8'-0"

DINING RM. 11'-8" X 11'-8"

© Copyright by designer

COVERED PORCH 46'-4" X 11'-0"

2nd Level

ATTIC STORAGE

© Copyright by designer

GAME ROOM

4' WALL

8' LINE

4' WALL

BATH

BATH

BEDROOM 2 15'-0" X 12'-4"

STUDY / BEDROOM 3 11'-3" X 8'-0"

BEDROOM 4 14'-0" X 13'-0"

DESK DESK DESK

Plan ID 71042 Price Code: E

Total Living Area	2,322 sq.ft.
Basement	1,128 sq.ft.
Main Living	1,194 sq.ft.
Bedrooms	3
Bathrooms	2.5
Dimensions	59'-0" x 34'-0"
Foundation	Basement

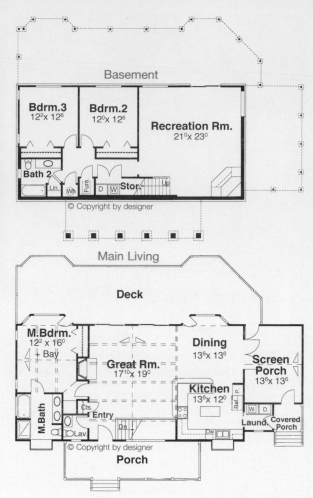

Plan ID 92463 Price Code: D

Total Living Area	2,071 sq.ft.
Main Living	2,071 sq.ft.
Bedrooms	3
Bathrooms	2.5
Dimensions	63'-0" x 63'-0"
Garage Type	Three-car garage
Foundation	Basement, Crawlspace, Slab

ORDER NOW 1-800-235-5700 or at **www.familyhomeplans.com**

Plan ID 92443 Price Code: D

Total Living Area	2,184 sq.ft.
Main Living	2,184 sq.ft.
Bedrooms	3
Bathrooms	3
Dimensions	71' 2" x 58'-1"
Garage Type	Two-car garage
Foundation	Basement, Slab

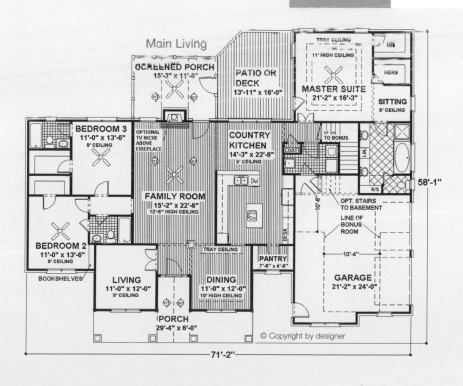

Main Living

SCREENED PORCH 15'-2" x 11'-6"

PATIO OR DECK 13'-11" x 16'-0"

TRAY CEILING
11' HIGH CEILING
MASTER SUITE 21'-2" x 16'-3"

HIS

HERS

SITTING 9' CEILING

BEDROOM 3 11'-0" x 13'-6" 9' CEILING

OPTIONAL TV NICHE ABOVE FIREPLACE

COUNTRY KITCHEN 14'-3" x 22'-6" 9' CEILING

UP TO BONUS

COATS

DW

FAMILY ROOM 15'-2" x 22'-6" 12'-6" HIGH CEILING

K/S

LIN

K/S

10'-6"

OPT. STAIRS TO BASEMENT

LINE OF BONUS ROOM

BEDROOM 2 11'-0" x 13'-6" 9' CEILING

TRAY CEILING

10'-4"

BOOKSHELVES

PANTRY 7'-6" x 4'-6"

GARAGE 21'-2" x 24'-0"

LIVING 11'-0" x 12'-0" 9' CEILING

DINING 11'-0" x 12'-0" 10' HIGH CEILING

DESK

PORCH 29'-4" x 6'-0"

© Copyright by designer

58'-1"

71'-2"

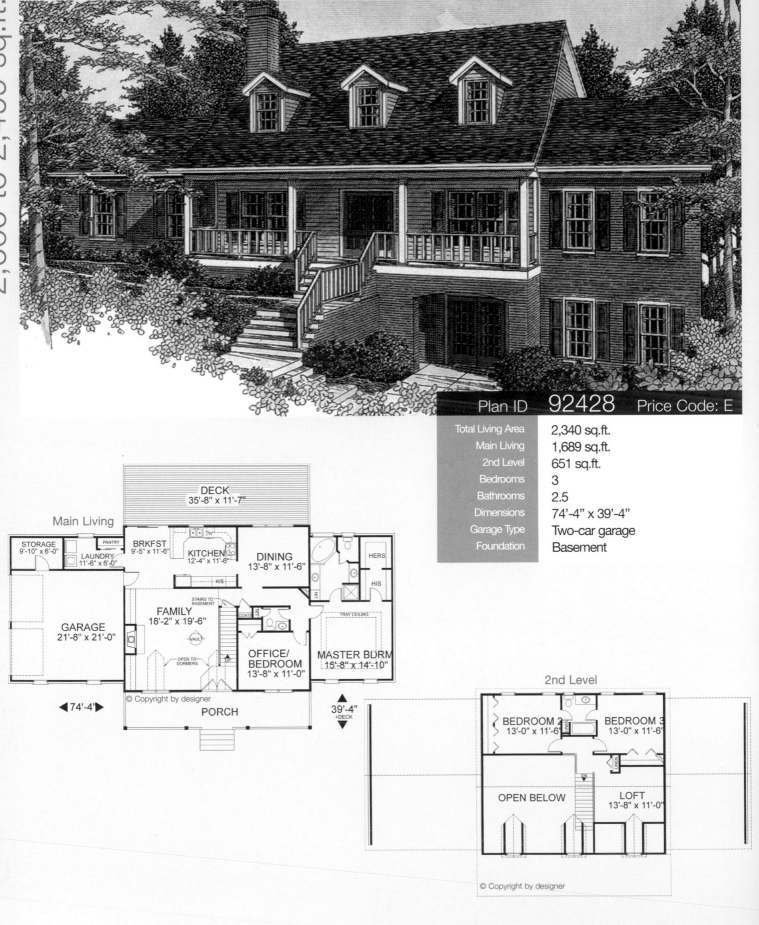

Plan ID	**92428**	Price Code: E
Total Living Area	2,340 sq.ft.	
Main Living	1,689 sq.ft.	
2nd Level	651 sq.ft.	
Bedrooms	3	
Bathrooms	2.5	
Dimensions	74'-4" x 39'-4"	
Garage Type	Two-car garage	
Foundation	Basement	

Main Living

DECK
35'-8" x 11'-7"

STORAGE
9'-10" x 6'-0"

PANTRY

BRKFST
9'-5" x 11'-6"

KITCHEN
12'-4" x 11'-6"

DINING
13'-8" x 11'-6"

LAUNDRY
11'-6" x 6'-0"

HERS

HIS

K/S

LIN

GARAGE
21'-8" x 21'-0"

FAMILY
18'-2" x 19'-6"

STAIRS TO BASEMENT

COATS

LIN

TRAY CEILING

VAULT

OPEN TO DORMERS

UP

OFFICE/
BEDROOM
13'-8" x 11'-0"

MASTER BDRM
15'-8" x 14'-10"

© Copyright by designer

◄ 74'-4' ►

PORCH

39'-4"
+DECK

2nd Level

BEDROOM 2
13'-0" x 11'-6"

LINEN

BEDROOM 3
13'-0" x 11'-6'

LINEN

OPEN BELOW

DN

LOFT
13'-8" x 11'-0"

© Copyright by designer

Designing for PRIVACY

WE ALL SEEM TO APPRECIATE THE OPPORTUNITY TO FIND A PLACE TO ENJOY SOME PEACE AND QUIET. Unfortunately, as we "open up" our floor plans, these secluded areas are more and more difficult to find. The solution does not involve building more walls and returning to long hallways. The idea of a kitchen merging with the dining room and family space appeals to most homeowners. However, a short hallway, or "buffer zone" leading to the master sleeping area certainly functions better than opening directly into the family room or foyer.

Secondary bedrooms also require a certain amount of seclusion. Ideally, they should be located away from the master suite. While perhaps not as important for children's rooms, the idea of secluded and quiet bedrooms becomes very important for homeowners anticipating the secondary bedrooms to be used by their guests.

Designing homes with privacy in mind really just requires a logical, yet critical analysis of the plan. While sound can usually be controlled with insulation, visual privacy becomes a much more challenging detail. Remember that hallways are not always a bad design element. Often, a short hall that requires turning a corner before seeing the bedroom entrance can create the perception of seclusion.

Excerpted from *Home Plan Buyer's Guide*, an upcoming book by **Larry W. Garnett**

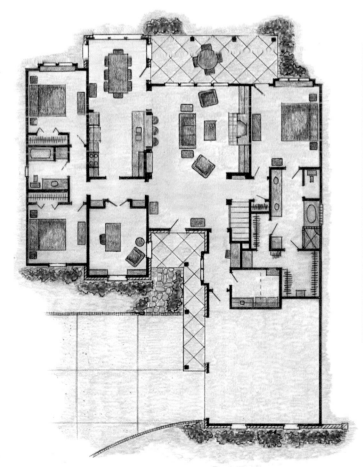

A short hallway leading to the master bedroom from the foyer is the key to maintaining privacy in this plan. Note also the home theater above the garage. This location allows the surround sound system to be enjoyed by those watching a movie while not disturbing others in the home.

HOME THEATER

Plan ID 59070 Price Code: C

Total Living Area	2,000 sq.ft.
Main Living	2,000 sq.ft.
Bedrooms	4
Bathrooms	2.5
Dimensions	68'-0" x 55'-8"
Garage Type	Two-car garage
Foundation	Basement, Crawlspace, Slab

Plan ID 59073 Price Code: D

Total Living Area	2,200 sq.ft.
Main Living	2,200 sq.ft.
Bedrooms	3
Bathrooms	3.5
Dimensions	78'-0" x 58'-6"
Garage Type	Two-car garage
Foundation	Crawlspace, Slab

Plan 59074

Main Living

Main Living
- Optional Deck 16-8 x 13
- Rear Porch 11-8 x 9
- Lounge/Office 7-10 x 12-4
- Master Bedroom 13-8 x 16-8 (CLEAR)
- Master Bath 9-6 x 12-8
- Jet Tub
- Rear Porch 16-8 x 6-2
- Breakfast 11-4 x 14-6
- Bedroom 3 12-4 x 13-6 9' CLG. HT. (TYP.)
- Clos.
- Hall Bath
- Hall
- Great Room 16-8 x 19-4 (CLEAR) 12' CLG. HT.
- Kitchen 11-4 x 14-8
- Entry
- Closet 9-6 x 7-8
- Storage
- Storage
- Bedroom 2 12-4 x 13-6
- Foyer 14-4 x 5-8
- Half Columns
- Dining 11-4 x 13-8
- Front Porch 14-4 x 5
- Utility 8 x 9-10
- Three Car Garage 23-4 x 36-8

NOTE: DASHED WALLS INDICATE OPTIONAL WALLS IF BASEMENT OPTION IS CHOSEN.

© Copyright by designer

2nd Level

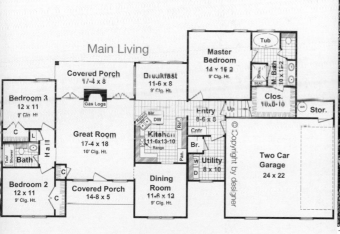

- BONUS ROOM 8' CLG. HT. 13-8 x 36-8 (CLEAR)
- ATTIC ACCESS

© Copyright by designer

Plan ID	59074	Price Code: E

Total Living Area	2,251 sq.ft.
Main Living	2,251 sq.ft.
Bedrooms	3
Bathrooms	2.5
Dimensions	73'-8" x 58'-4"
Garage Type	Three-car garage
Foundation	Basement, Crawlspace, Slab

Plan 59026

Main Living
- Covered Porch 17-4 x 8
- Breakfast 11-6 x 8 9' Clg. Ht.
- Master Bedroom 14 x 16-2 9' Clg. Ht.
- M. Bath 10 x 12
- Tub
- Bedroom 3 12 x 11 9' Clg. Ht.
- Gas Logs
- Great Room 17-4 x 18 10' Clg. Ht.
- Kitchen 11-6 x 13-10 Range
- Entry 8-6 x 8
- Clos. 10x8-10
- Stor.
- Bath
- Hall
- Bedroom 2 12 x 11 9' Clg. Ht.
- Covered Porch 14-8 x 5
- Dining Room 11-6 x 12 9' Clg. Ht.
- Utility 8 x 10
- Two Car Garage 24 x 22

© Copyright by designer

2nd Level

- Down
- Closet
- Optional Bath
- Living Area 14-4 x 16-6 (13-8 x 16-0 Clear) 8' Clg. Ht.
- Attic Access

© Copyright by designer

Plan ID	59026	Price Code: D

Total Living Area	2,024 sq.ft.
Main Living	1,638 sq.ft.
2nd Level	386 sq.ft.
Bedrooms	3
Bathrooms	2
Dimensions	72'-10" x 41'-0"
Garage Type	Two-car garage
Foundation	Basement, Crawlspace, Slab

Main Living

2nd Level

Plan ID	41009	Price Code: D

Total Living Area	2,105 sq.ft.
Main Living	1,531 sq.ft.
2nd Level	574 sq.ft.
Bedrooms	3
Bathrooms	2.5
Dimensions	63'-0" x 45'-0"
Foundation	Basement, Crawlspace

Main Living

2nd Level

Plan ID	41010	Price Code: D

Total Living Area	2,099 sq.ft.
Main Living	1,528 sq.ft.
2nd Level	571 sq.ft.
Bedrooms	3
Bathrooms	2.5
Dimensions	63'-0" x 45'-0"
Foundation	Basement, Crawlspace

Plan ID 41012 Price Code: E

Total Living Area	2,276 sq.ft.
Main Living	1,664 sq.ft.
2nd Level	612 sq.ft.
Bedrooms	3
Bathrooms	2.5
Dimensions	66'-0" x 39'-0"
Foundation	Basement, Crawlspace

Main Living

66'-0"

Deck
14'-0" x 9'-4"

Kitchen
19'-9" x 12'-6"

Utility

Pantry

Porch
38'-0" x 7'-0"

Dining Room
13'-6" x 11'-0"

Sitting Rm.
13'-6" x 13'-0"

Living Room
13'-2" x 18'-2"

Master Bedroom
13'-2" x 15'-4"

Foyer
10'-0" x 8'-6"

39'-0"

© Copyright by designer

2nd Level

Bedroom
11'-0" x 15'-0"

Bedroom
11'-0" x 15'-0"

Balcony

© Copyright by designer

Plan ID 77103 Price Code: E

Total Living Area	2,440 sq.ft.
Main Living	1,780 sq.ft.
2nd Level	690 sq.ft.
Bedrooms	4
Bathrooms	2.5
Dimensions	51'-0" x 71'-0"
Garage Type	Two-car garage
Foundation	Basement, Crawlspace, Slab

Main Living

SLOPE CLG. UP TO 10'-0"
MASTER SUITE
18'-3" X 13'-0"

BATH 1

GLASS SHR.

OPEN ABOVE
FAMILY RM.
16'-0" X 19'-11"

PORCH

NOOK
11'-7" x 9'-10"

LINE OF
UPPER FLOOR

RAISED BAR

STAIR UP

STOR.

KITCH.
13'-0"X 12'-6"

PANT.

CATHEDRAL CLG.
LIVING RM.
12'-1" X 14'-0"

ENTRY

DINING RM.
13'-2" X 12'-5"

SHELF

UTIL.

P.

STORAGE

© Copyright by designer

GARAGE
19'-3"X 20'-2"

2nd Level

© Copyright by designer

OPEN ABOVE
FAMILY ROOM

BED RM.2
11'-8" X 11'-8"

STAIR DOWN

WOOD RAIL

LINEN

B.3

OPEN ABOVE ENTRY

STOR.

BED RM.3
10'-9" X 10'-8"

STOR.

BED RM.4
10'-0" x 10'-0"

SLOPE CLG. UP TO 10'-0"

ORDER NOW 1-800-235-5700 or at www.familyhomeplans.com

Plan ID **77135** Price Code: C

Total Living Area	2,000 sq. ft.
Main Living	1,440 sq. ft.
2nd Level	560 sq. ft.
Bedrooms	3
Bathrooms	2.5
Dimensions	47'-6" x 49'-6"
Garage Type	Two-car garage
Foundation	Basement, Crawlspace, Slab

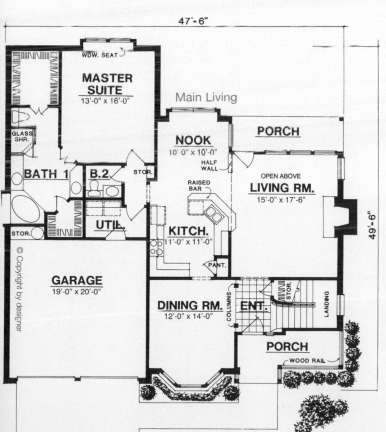

Main Living

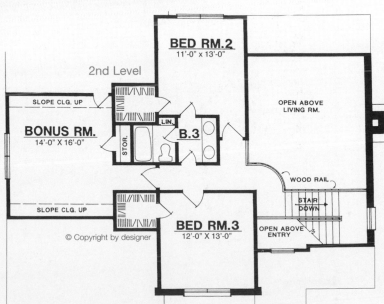

2nd Level

Plan ID **77087** Price Code: E

Total Living Area	2,297 sq.ft.
Main Living	1,752 sq.ft.
2nd Level	545 sq.ft.
Bedrooms	3
Bathrooms	3
Dimensions	61'-0" x 57'-4"
Garage Type	Two-car garage
Foundation	Basement, Crawlspace, Slab

Plan ID **77095** Price Code: **E**

Total Living Area	2,333 sq. ft.
Main Living	2,333 sq. ft.
Bedrooms	4
Bathrooms	2.5
Dimensions	77' 1" x 57'-0"
Garage Type	Two-car garage
Foundation	Basement, Crawlspace, Slab

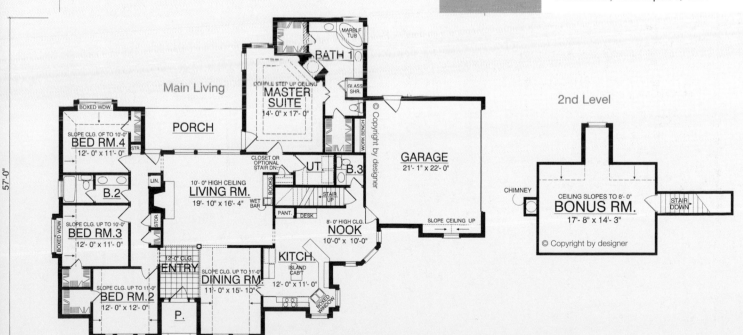

Main Living

77'-1"

57'-0"

BOXED WDW.

SLOPE CLG. OF TO 10'-0"
BED RM.4
12'-0" x 11'-0"

STR

LIN.

B.2

BOXED WDW

SLOPE CLG. UP TO 10'-0"
BED RM.3
12'-0" x 11'-0"

STOR

12'-0" CLG.
ENTRY

SLOPE CLG. UP TO 11'-0"
BED RM.2
12'-0" x 12'-0"

P.

SLOPE CLG. UP TO 11'-0"
DINING RM.
11'-0" x 15'-10"

BOXED WINDOW

PORCH

MARBLE TUB

BATH 1

DOUBLE STEP UP CEILING
MASTER SUITE
14'-0" x 17'-0"

GLASS SHR.

BOXED WINDOW

CLOSET OR OPTIONAL STAIR DN.

10'-0" HIGH CEILING
LIVING RM.
19'-10" x 16'-4"

BOOKS

WET BAR

PANT.

DESK

UT.

STAIR UP

B.3

GARAGE
21'-1" x 22'-0"

© Copyright by designer

SLOPE CEILING UP

8'-0" HIGH CLG.
NOOK
10'-0" x 10'-0"

KITCH.
ISLAND CAB'T

2nd Level

CHIMNEY

CEILING SLOPES TO 8'-0"
BONUS RM.
17'-8" x 14'-3"

STAIR DOWN

© Copyright by designer

Plan ID 77080 Price Code: D

Total Living Area	2,143 sq.ft.
Main Living	1,535 sq.ft.
2nd Level	585 sq.ft.
Bedrooms	4
Bathrooms	3
Dimensions	54'-6" x 41'-10"
Garage Type	Two-car garage
Foundation	Basement, Crawlspace, Slab

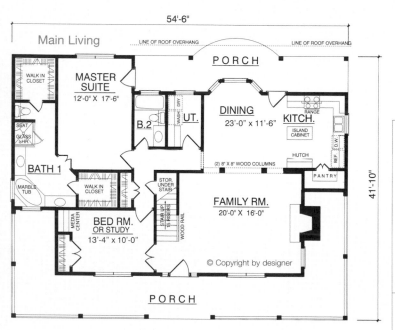

Main Living

54'-6"

LINE OF ROOF OVERHANG   LINE OF ROOF OVERHANG

PORCH

WALK IN CLOSET

MASTER SUITE
12'-0" X 17'-6"

B.2

UT.

WASH./DRY

DINING
23'-0" X 11'-6"

KITCH.

RANGE

ISLAND CABINET

SEAT GLASS SHR.

BATH 1

MARBLE TUB

WALK IN CLOSET

STOR. UNDER STAIR

STAIR UP 15 RISERS

WOOD RAIL

(2) 8" X 8" WOOD COLUMNS

HUTCH

REF. D.W.

PANTRY

MEDIA CENTER

BED RM. OR STUDY
13'-4" X 10'-0"

FAMILY RM.
20'-0" X 16'-0"

© Copyright by designer

PORCH

41'-10"

2nd Level

BENCH WITH STORAGE

BOOKS   STUDY AREA   BOOKS

BED RM.2
12'-0" x 12'-10"

STOR.

W. I. CLOS.

STAIR DOWN

B.3

1/2 WALL

LINEN

BED RM.3
11'-10" x 12'-10"

ATTIC ACCESS

STAINED GLASS

© Copyright by designer

ORDER NOW 1-800-235-5700 or at www.familyhomeplans.com

Plan ID	**59092**	Price Code: D
Total Living Area	2,250 sq.ft.	
Main Living	2,250 sq.ft.	
Bedrooms	4	
Bathrooms	3	
Dimensions	66'-8" x 70'-8"	
Garage Type	Two-car garage	
Foundation	Crawlspace, Slab	

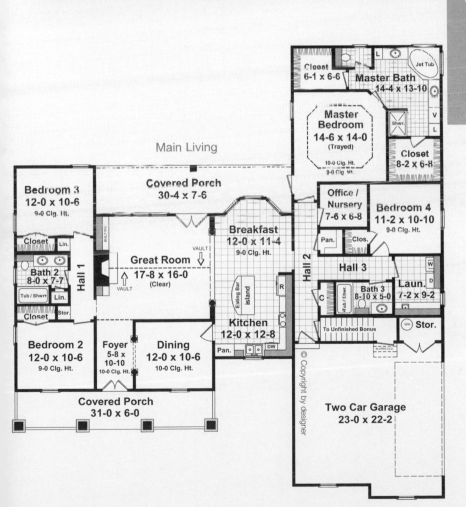

Main Living

Closet
6-1 x 6-6

L

Jet Tub

Master Bath
14-4 x 13-10

Shwr.

V

L

Master Bedroom
14-6 x 14-0
(Trayed)
10-0 Clg. Ht.
9-0 Clg. Ht.

Closet
8-2 x 6-8

Bedroom 3
12-0 x 10-6
9-0 Clg. Ht.

Covered Porch
30-4 x 7-6

Closet
Lin.

Bath 2
8-0 x 7-7

Hall 1

Tub / Shwr.
Lin.

Closet
Stor.

BUILT-INS

VAULT

Great Room
17-8 x 16-0
(Clear)

VAULT

Breakfast
12-0 x 11-4
9-0 Clg. Ht.

Eating Bar
Island

R

Pan.

Clos.

Office / Nursery
7-6 x 6-8

Bedroom 4
11-2 x 10-10
9-0 Clg. Ht.

Hall 2

Hall 3

W

C

Tub / Shwr.

Bath 3
8-10 x 5-0

Laun.
7-2 x 9-2

Bedroom 2
12-0 x 10-6
9-0 Clg. Ht.

Foyer
5-8 x 10-10
10-0 Clg. Ht.

Dining
12-0 x 10-6
10-0 Clg. Ht.

Kitchen
12-0 x 12-8

Pan.

DW

To Unfinished Bonus

WH

Stor.

SLOPED CLG.

Covered Porch
31-0 x 6-0

Two Car Garage
23-0 x 22-2

© Copyright by designer

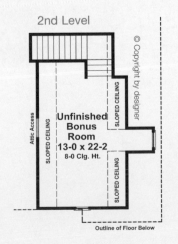

2nd Level

Attic Access

SLOPED CEILING

SLOPED CEILING

SLOPED CEILING

SLOPED CEILING

Unfinished Bonus Room
13-0 x 22-2
8-0 Clg. Ht.

Outline of Floor Below

© Copyright by designer

Plan ID 79156 Price Code: D

Total Living Area	2,069 sq.ft.
Main Living	2,069 sq.ft.
Bedrooms	3
Bathrooms	2
Dimensions	57'-8" x 68'-10"
Garage Type	Two-car garage
Foundation	Crawlspace, Slab

Plan ID 79000 Price Code: D

Total Living Area	2,079 sq.ft.
Main Living	2,079 sq.ft.
Bedrooms	3
Bathrooms	2
Dimensions	61'-6" x 59'-0"
Garage Type	Two-car garage
Foundation	Crawlspace, Slab

Plan ID **63365** **Price Code: D**

Total Living Area	2,140 sq. ft.
Main Living	2,140 sq. ft.
Bedrooms	4
Bathrooms	3
Dimensions	62'-4" x 51'-0"
Garage Type	Two-car garage
Foundation	Slab

Main Living

Bedroom 2
10⁸ · 11¹⁰

Bath 3

Covered Porch

Master Bedroom
16¹⁰ · 13⁰

w.i.c.

Nook

Bedroom 3
12⁰ · 11⁰

Family
19⁰ · 15¹⁰

Kitchen

Laun.

Master Bath

© Copyright by designer

Bath 2

Living
10¹⁰ · 12⁸

Foyer

Dining
10¹⁰ · 12⁸

2 Car Garage

Bedroom 4
12⁰ · 11⁰

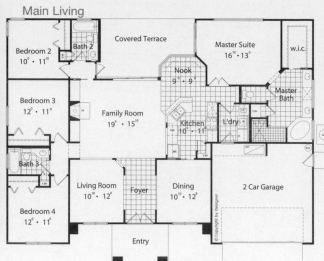

Main Living

Plan ID 63364 Price Code: D

Total Living Area	2,089 sq.ft.
Main Living	2,089 sq.ft.
Bedrooms	4
Bathrooms	3
Dimensions	61'-8" x 21'-10"
Garage Type	Two-car garage
Foundation	Slab

Main Living

Plan ID 63050 Price Code: D

Total Living Area	2,041 sq.ft.
Main Living	2,041 sq.ft.
Bedrooms	4
Bathrooms	2
Dimensions	60'-4" x 56'-0"
Garage Type	Two-car garage
Foundation	Slab

| Plan ID | 63005 | Price Code: E |

Total Living Area	2,362 sq. ft.
Main Living	2,362 sq. ft.
Bedrooms	4
Bathrooms	3
Dimensions	65'-8" x 70'-4"
Garage Type	Two-car garage
Foundation	Slab

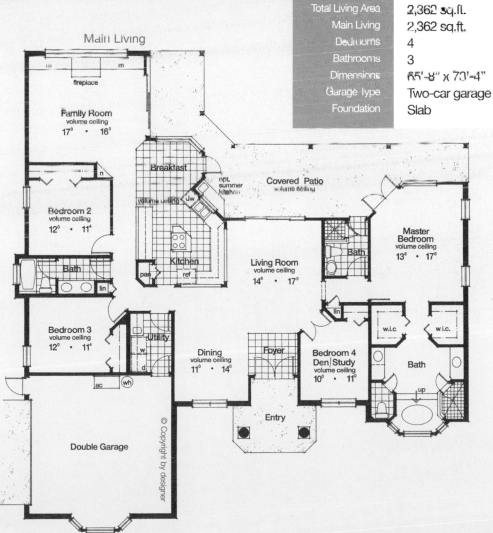

Plan ID 94173 Price Code: E

Total Living Area	2,421 sq.ft.
Main Living	1,884 sq.ft.
2nd Level	537 sq.ft.
Bedrooms	3
Bathrooms	2.5
Dimensions	60'-0" x 53'-6"
Garage Type	Two-car garage
Foundation	Basement

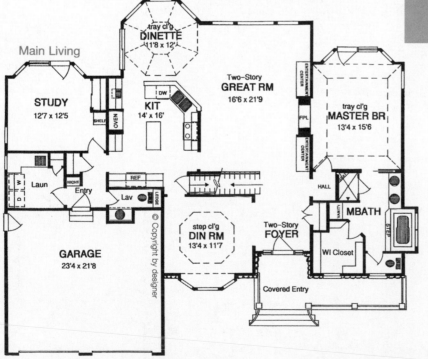

Main Living

DINETTE
tray cl'g
11'8 x 12'

STUDY
12'7 x 12'5

KIT
14' x 16'

Two-Story
GREAT RM
16'6 x 21'9

MASTER BR
tray cl'g
13'4 x 15'6

Laun

Entry

Lav

step cl'g
DIN RM
13'4 x 11'7

Two-Story
FOYER

MBATH

HALL

WI Closet

GARAGE
23'4 x 21'8

Covered Entry

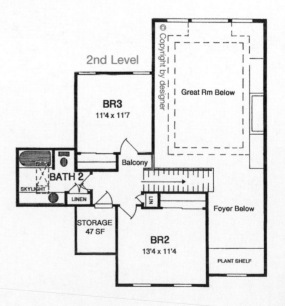

2nd Level

BR3
11'4 x 11'7

Great Rm Below

BATH 2

Balcony

LINEN

STORAGE
47 SF

BR2
13'4 x 11'4

Foyer Below

PLANT SHELF

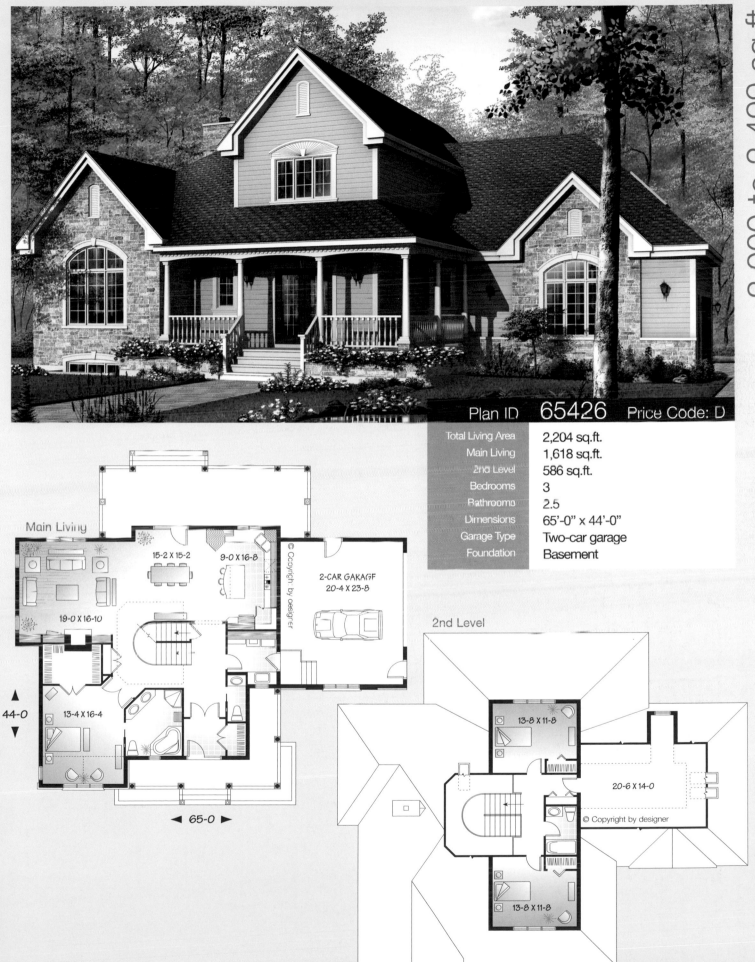

Plan ID **65426** Price Code: **D**

Total Living Area	2,204 sq.ft.
Main Living	1,618 sq.ft.
2nd Level	586 sq.ft.
Bedrooms	3
Bathrooms	2.5
Dimensions	65'-0" x 44'-0"
Garage Type	Two-car garage
Foundation	Basement

Main Living

15-2 X 15-2   9-0 X 16-8

© Copyright by designer

2-CAR GARAGE
20-4 X 23-8

19-0 X 16-10

13-4 X 16-4

44-0

◄ 65-0 ►

2nd Level

13-8 X 11-8

20-6 X 14-0

© Copyright by designer

13-8 X 11-8

FRONT ELEVATION

Plan ID	65368	Price Code: D
Total Living Area	2,111 sq.ft.	
Main Living	1,545 sq.ft.	
2nd Level	566 sq.ft.	
Bedrooms	3	
Bathrooms	2.5	
Dimensions	56'-0" x 53'-2"	
Garage Type	Two-car garage	
Foundation	1/2 Basement / 1/2 Crawlspace	

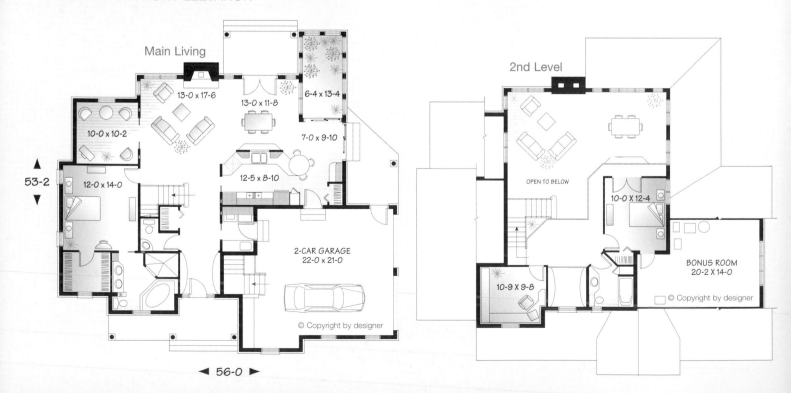

Main Living

13-0 x 17-6
13-0 x 11-8
6-4 x 13-4
10-0 x 10-2
7-0 x 9-10
12-0 x 14-0
12-5 x 8-10
53-2
2-CAR GARAGE
22-0 x 21-0
© Copyright by designer
56-0

2nd Level

OPEN TO BELOW
10-0 X 12-4
10-9 X 9-8
BONUS ROOM
20-2 X 14-0
© Copyright by designer

ORDER NOW 1-800-235-5700 or at www.familyhomeplans.com

Plan ID **65143** Price Code: **E**

Total Living Area	2,265 sq.ft.
Main Living	1,371 sq.ft.
2nd Level	894 sq.ft.
Bedrooms	4
Bathrooms	3.5
Dimensions	58' 0" x 50'-4"
Garage Type	Two-car garage
Foundation	Basement

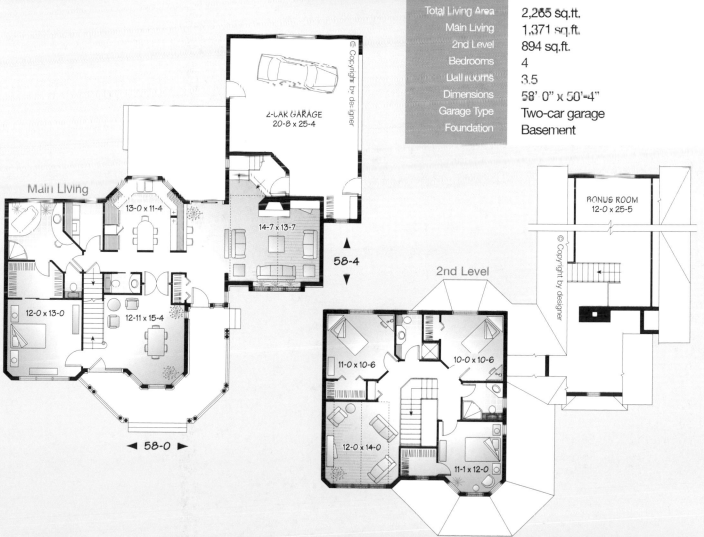

Main Living

2-CAR GARAGE
20-8 x 25-4

14-7 x 13-7

13-0 x 11-4

12-0 x 13-0

12-11 x 15-4

58-4

58-0

BONUS ROOM
12-0 x 25-5

2nd Level

11-0 x 10-6

10-0 x 10-6

12-0 x 14-0

11-1 x 12-0

© Copyright by designer

Main Living

		10-10 X 12-0	10-10 X 12-0	
11-0 X 12-0				
				13-0 X 5-4
		27-4 X 18-8		
13-0 X 13-8				12-0 X 15-4

© Copyright by designer

42-0

◄ 54-0 ►

Plan ID 64982 Price Code: D

Total Living Area	2,146 sq.ft.
Main Living	2,146 sq.ft.
Bedrooms	4
Bathrooms	3
Dimensions	54'-0" x 42'-0"
Foundation	Crawlspace

Main Living

LANAI 14-0 x 14-0	13-8 x 16-4
	12-0 x 10-0
22-0 x 24-0	12-0 x 10-0
16-4 x 15-8	14-8 x 8-8
11-0 x 13-0	2-CAR GARAGE 19-8 x 21-0

© Copyright by designer

76-0

◄ 38-0 ►

Plan ID 64979 Price Code: D

Total Living Area	2,122 sq.ft.
Main Living	2,122 sq.ft.
Bedrooms	3
Bathrooms	2.5
Dimensions	38'-0" x 76'-0"
Garage Type	Two-car garage
Foundation	Slab

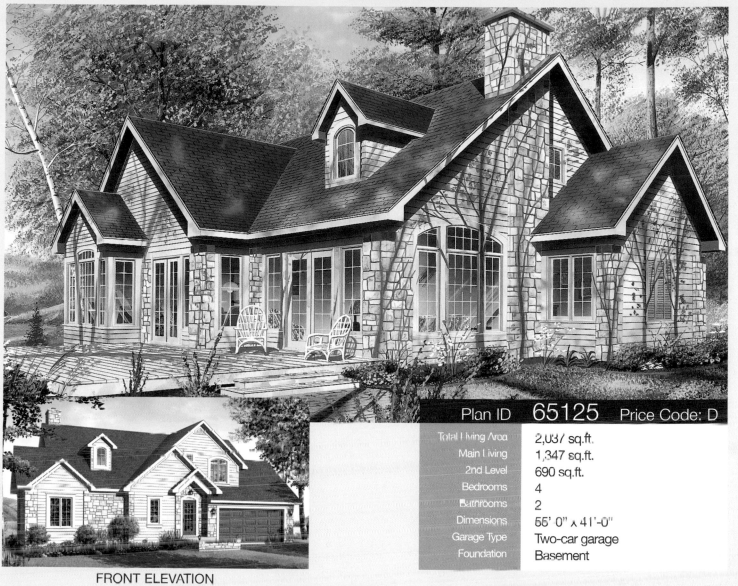

FRONT ELEVATION

Plan ID **65125** Price Code: D

Total Living Area	2,037 sq.ft.
Main Living	1,347 sq.ft.
2nd Level	690 sq.ft.
Bedrooms	4
Bathrooms	2
Dimensions	55'-0" x 41'-0"
Garage Type	Two-car garage
Foundation	Basement

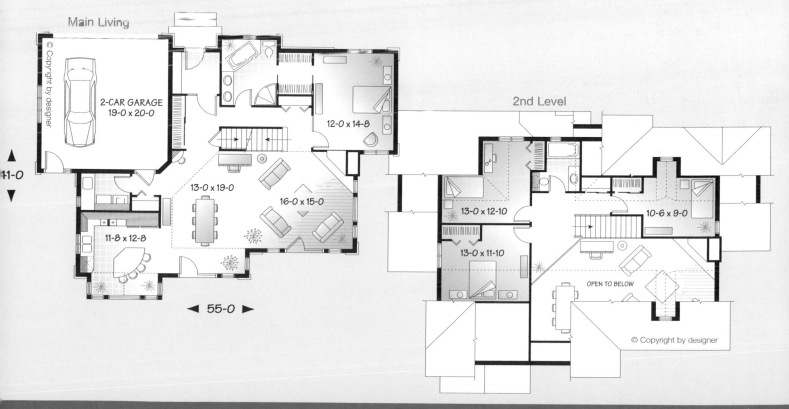

Main Living

© Copyright by designer

2-CAR GARAGE
19-0 x 20-0

12-0 x 14-8

13-0 x 19-0

16-0 x 15-0

11-8 x 12-8

41-0

55-0

2nd Level

13-0 x 12-10

13-0 x 11-10

10-6 x 9-0

OPEN TO BELOW

© Copyright by designer

Sophisticated Charm

The charming gazebo on the front porch offers just a hint of this home's tasteful design throughout. Stepping inside from the sprawling front porch, a 2-story foyer leads to the vaulted great room, complete with corner fireplace, skylights and views to the rear. The kitchen and breakfast areas are open to the great room, their space subtly defined by columns and ceiling height. A sensible utility core contains the laundry area, pantry, closet and serving counter for the adjacent dining room. The generously sized master suite offers privacy from secondary bedrooms and includes his and her walk-in closets. Upstairs, an abundant unfinished loft provides unlimited possibilities for future use.

Brick and stone modifications to the exterior enhance this home's stately character. ▲

ORDER NOW 1-800-235-5700 or at www.familyhomeplans.com

The kitchen boasts an abundance of counter and work space with its generously sized island. ▶

A second-level balcony overlooks the skylit, vaulted great room with its corner fireplace. ▼

Plan ID	69520	Price Code: G
Total Living Area		2,874 sq.ft.
Main Living		2,116 sq.ft.
2nd Level		728 sq.ft.
Bedrooms		4
Bathrooms		3
Dimensions		72'-0" x 47'-0"
Garage Type		Three-car garage
Foundation		Basement, Crawlspace, Slab

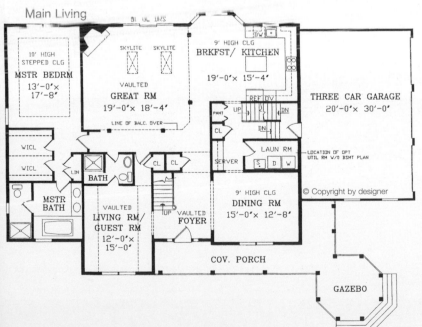

Main Living

10' HIGH STEPPED CLG
MSTR BEDRM 13'-0" x 17'-8"

SKYLITE SKYLITE

VAULTED GREAT RM 19'-0" x 18'-4"

LINE OF BALC. OVER

9' HIGH CLG BRKFST/ KITCHEN 19'-0" x 15'-4"

THREE CAR GARAGE 20'-0" x 30'-0"

WICL

REF UV

PANT

UP

DN

CL

DN

WICL

LIN

BATH

CL CL

LAUN RM

SERVER S D W

LOCATION OF OPT UTIL RM W/O BSMT PLAN

© Copyright by designer

MSTR BATH

VAULTED LIVING RM/ GUEST RM 12'-0" x 15'-0"

UP

VAULTED FOYER

9' HIGH CLG DINING RM 15'-0" x 12'-8"

COV. PORCH

GAZEBO

2nd Level

BEDRM #2 15'-0" x 13'-4"

UPPER GREAT RM

WICL

LIN

DN

VAULTED UNFIN. LOFT 19'-0" x 16'-0"

RAIL

BALCONY

UNFIN ATTIC

DN

DN

BATH

UPPER FOYER

VAULTED BEDRM #3 15'-0" x 13'-0"

CL

© Copyright by designer

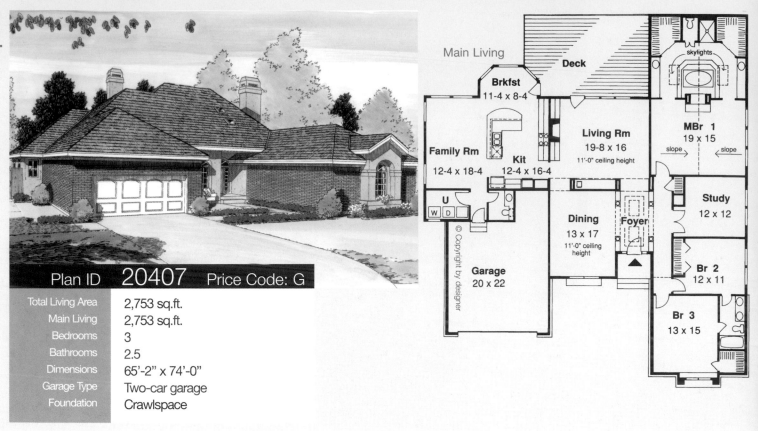

Main Living

Deck

Brkfst
11-4 x 8-4

Family Rm
12-4 x 18-4

Kit
12-4 x 16-4

Living Rm
19-8 x 16
11'-0" ceiling height

MBr 1
19 x 15

slope   slope

skylights

Study
12 x 12

Br 2
12 x 11

U
W D

Dining
13 x 17
11'-0" ceiling height

Foyer

Garage
20 x 22

Br 3
13 x 15

© Copyright by designer

Plan ID 20407   Price Code: G

Total Living Area	2,753 sq.ft.
Main Living	2,753 sq.ft.
Bedrooms	3
Bathrooms	2.5
Dimensions	65'-2" x 74'-0"
Garage Type	Two-car garage
Foundation	Crawlspace

Main Living   64'-0"

Deck

Hearth Rm
19-4 x 15-5

slope   slope

Kitchen
11-4 x 13

desk

Living Rm
16 x 21-4
10' ceiling height

MBr 1
15-4 x 15-6
vaulted

Ldry
D W

pan.

DN   UP

10' clg. ht.

plant ledge
above

12'
ceiling
height

Garage
21-4 x 21-8

Dining Rm
13 x 11-8
decor. ceiling

Foy

plant ledge
12'
ceiling
height

48'-6"

© Copyright by designer

Plan ID 20173   Price Code: F

Total Living Area	2,511 sq.ft.
Main Living	1,973 sq.ft.
2nd Level	538 sq.ft.
Bedrooms	4
Bathrooms	2.5
Dimensions	64'-0" x 48'-6"
Garage Type	Two-car garage
Foundation	Basement

Br 3
11 x 13

2nd Level

Opt Br 4
10 x 10-8

linen

DN

skyl't

© Copyright by designer

Br 2
13 x 11-8

foyer
below

Plan ID **24953** Price Code: F

Total Living Area	2,614 sq.ft.
Main Living	2,614 sq.ft
Bedrooms	3
Bathrooms	2.5
Dimensions	82'-0" x 61'-4"
Garage Type	Two-car garage
Foundation	Basement, Crawlspace, Slab

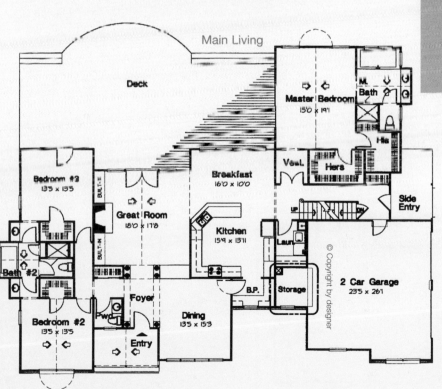

Main Living

Deck

Master Bedroom
15'0 x 19'1

M. Bath

His

Veal.

Hers

Bedroom #3
13'5 x 13'5

Breakfast
16'0 x 10'0

Great Room
18'0 x 17'8

Side Entry

Kitchen
15'4 x 13'11

BUILT-IN

Laun.

Bath #2

UP DN

Foyer

Pwd.

Dining
13'5 x 15'3

B.P.

Storage

2 Car Garage
23'5 x 26'1

© Copyright by designer

Bedroom #2
13'5 x 13'5

Entry

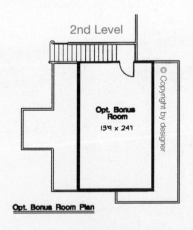

2nd Level

Opt. Bonus Room
13'4 x 24'1

© Copyright by designer

Opt. Bonus Room Plan

FURN H

Opt. Mech.

Slab/Crawl Option

Plan ID 20233 Price Code: G

Total Living Area	2,768 sq.ft.
Main Living	1,895 sq.ft.
2nd Level	873 sq.ft.
Bedrooms	4
Bathrooms	2.5
Dimensions	66'-4.5" x 49'-11"
Garage Type	Two-car garage
Foundation	Basement, Crawlspace, Slab, Basement + Crawlspace

Main Living

66'-4 1/2"

49'-11"

Great Room
14-6 x 21-1

Nook
11-6 x 12-5

Kitchen
12-1 x 14-2

Master Bedroom
14-6 x 21-1

Open To Below

Line of Loft Above

Pwd

Desk

Shlvs

Ref

Slope   Slope

Whirlpool Tub

Master Bath
9-3 x 12-3

Den/Parlor
12-0 x 12-0

Foyer

Dn

Butler's Pantry

Laun

Stor

Open To Below

Dining
13-9 x 12-0

Shlvs

Garage
24-3 x 20-3

© Copyright by designer

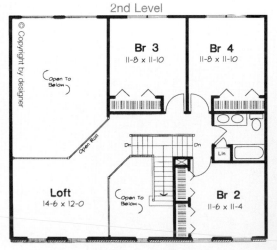

2nd Level

© Copyright by designer

Br 3
11-8 x 11-10

Br 4
11-8 x 11-10

Open To Below

Open Roll

Loft
14-6 x 12-0

Open To Below

Dn

Dn

Lin

Br 2
11-6 x 11-4

Plan ID **24702**   Price Code: G

Total Living Area	2,859 sq. ft.
Main Living	1,939 sq. ft
2nd Level	920 sq. ft.
Bedrooms	4
Bathrooms	2.5
Dimensions	62'-8" x 63'-6"
Garage Type	Three-car garage
Foundation	Basement, Crawlspace, Slab

Main Living

MBr 14-10 x 15-1

Family Rm 16-8 x 19-10

Breakfast 10-6 x 9-0

Kitchen 14-4 x 13-6

Lndry

Library/Parlor 12-6 x 13-6

Foyer

Dining 12-6 x 13-4

3 Car Garage 21-8 x 33-0

© Copyright by designer

2nd Level

Br 2 15-0 x 11-8

Balcony

Br 4 11-0 x 13-6

Attic Storage

Br 3 12-8 x 13-4

Attic Storage

Open to Below

© Copyright by designer

Plan ID **62195** **Price Code: F**

Total Living Area	2,553 sq.ft.
Main Living	2,553 sq.ft.
Bedrooms	4
Bathrooms	3
Dimensions	66'-2" x 81'-0"
Garage Type	Three-car garage
Foundation	Basement, Crawlspace, Slab

Plan ID **71004** Price Code: G

Total Living Area	2,753 sq.ft.
Main Living	1,622 sq.ft.
2nd Level	1,131 sq.ft.
Bedrooms	4
Bathrooms	3.5
Dimensions	39'-6" x 76'-0"
Garage Type	Two-car garage
Foundation	Crawlspace

Main Living

Double Garage
21^4 x 23^8

Sundeck

© Copyright by designer

Brkfst.
11^8 x 13^6

Laund.
W. D.
Lav.

Stepped Ceil.

Master Bdrm.
19^4 x 13^2

Kit.
13^6 x 11^0
Dw.
Ov. Ref.

Pantry
Butler's Pantry

M.Bath

Up

Dining
13^6 x 11^6

Living
19^6 x 19^6

Entry

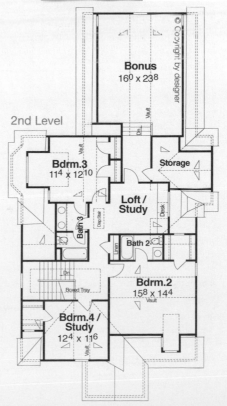

© Copyright by designer

Bonus
16^0 x 23^8

2nd Level

Bdrm.3
11^4 x 12^{10}

Storage

Loft /
Study

Bath 3

Bath 2

Boxed Tray

Bdrm.2
15^8 x 14^4

Bdrm.4 /
Study
12^4 x 11^6

MASTER BATHS

THE MASTER BATH HAS BEEN THE FOCUS OF ATTENTION FOR A NUMBER OF YEARS. In fact, it's not unusual to actually allot more square footage to the bath than the bedroom itself. They're what you might call "Wow! Rooms" – areas where a person's first reaction is simply, "Wow!" But, just how functional are these areas? Do they satisfy the homeowner's requirements day in and day out? Although it's difficult to answer these questions precisely, we do know this: an increasing number of individuals who have lived in a home with one of these ultra-extravagant baths specifically request a more functional design for their next master bath.

For the last few years, the master tub has been the focal point of bath design. Often the sizes small swimming pools, these areas have been adorned with Roman columns and extravagant marble finishes. In general, today's homeowners prefer a more reasonable size tub, but may still enjoy the whirlpool option. Rather than allocate the area and expense for a large tub, they appreciate the functionality of a spacious shower. In fact, one of the most requested items is a large, "door-less" shower.

A master bath cannot truly function as a dressing area without having ample clothes storage. When designed properly, the need for clothes storage in

the bedroom itself becomes unnecessary. While functional layouts and practical dressing area details form the basic elements of exceptional bath design, even the most thoughtful creation will be incomplete without careful attention to the materials, products, and colors used. Quite often, the services of a qualified interior design professional will determine the ultimate success of a master bath.

Excerpted from *Home Plan Buyer's Guide*, an upcoming book by **Larry W. Garnett**

Although a spectacular view can offer an opportunity to use expansive glass in the master bath, the view from the master bedroom remains a priority. To provide plenty of natural light in the bath without compromising privacy, consider using glass block instead of large windows.

Plan ID 94644 **Price Code: G**

Total Living Area	2,898 sq.ft.
Main Living	2,135 sq.ft.
2nd Level	763 sq.ft.
Bedrooms	5
Bathrooms	3
Dimensions	62'-6" x 70'-0"
Garage Type	Two-car garage
Foundation	Crawlspace

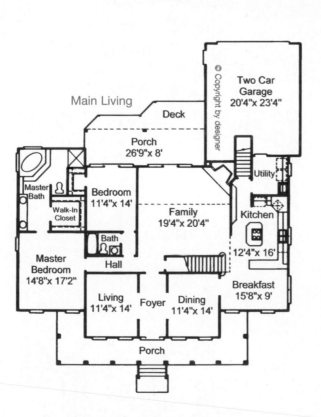

Main Living

Two Car Garage 20'4"x 23'4"

© Copyright by designer

Deck

Porch 26'9"x 8'

Utility

Master Bath

Bedroom 11'4"x 14'

Family 19'4"x 20'4"

Kitchen 12'4"x 16'

Walk-In Closet

Bath

Master Bedroom 14'8"x 17'2"

Hall

Living 11'4"x 14'

Foyer

Dining 11'4"x 14'

Breakfast 15'8"x 9'

Porch

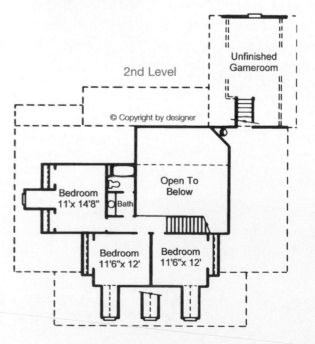

2nd Level

Unfinished Gameroom

© Copyright by designer

Open To Below

Bedroom 11'x 14'8"

Bath

Bedroom 11'6"x 12'

Bedroom 11'6"x 12'

ORDER NOW 1-800-235-5700 or at www.familyhomeplans.com

Plan ID **94663**   Price Code: F

Total Living Area	2,665 sq.ft.
Main Living	1,916 sq.ft.
2nd Level	749 sq.ft.
Bedrooms	4
Bathrooms	3
Dimensions	62'-0" x 63' 8.5"
Garage Type	Two-car garage
Foundation	Crawlspace, Slab

Main Living

© Copyright by designer

Two Car Garage
21'4"x 21'4"

Patio

Porch

Utility
12'2"x 7'6"

WIC

Master Bedroom
18'x 14'2"

Living
20'2"x 20'

Breakfast
14'2"x 9'6"

Master Bath

Bath

Kitchen
12'2"x 12'

Dining
11'6"x 15'

Bedroom
11'6"x 11'4"

Porch

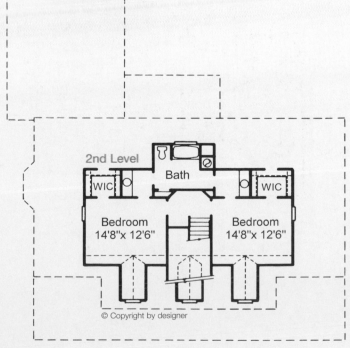

2nd Level

WIC   Bath   WIC

Bedroom
14'8"x 12'6"

Bedroom
14'8"x 12'6"

© Copyright by designer

Plan ID 65673   Price Code: F

Total Living Area	2,542 sq.ft.
Main Living	1,510 sq.ft.
2nd Level	1,032 sq.ft.
Bedrooms	3
Bathrooms	3.5
Dimensions	52'-0" x 74'-0"
Garage Type	Two-car garage
Foundation	Basement, Crawlspace, Slab

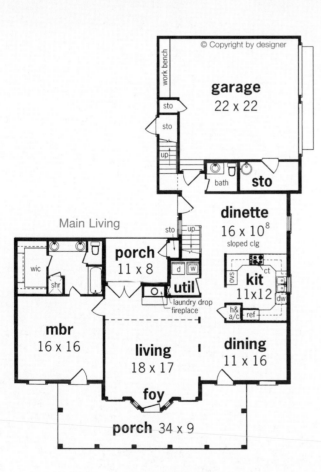

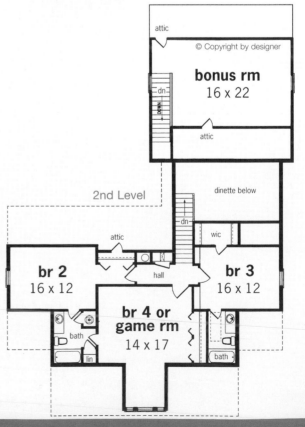

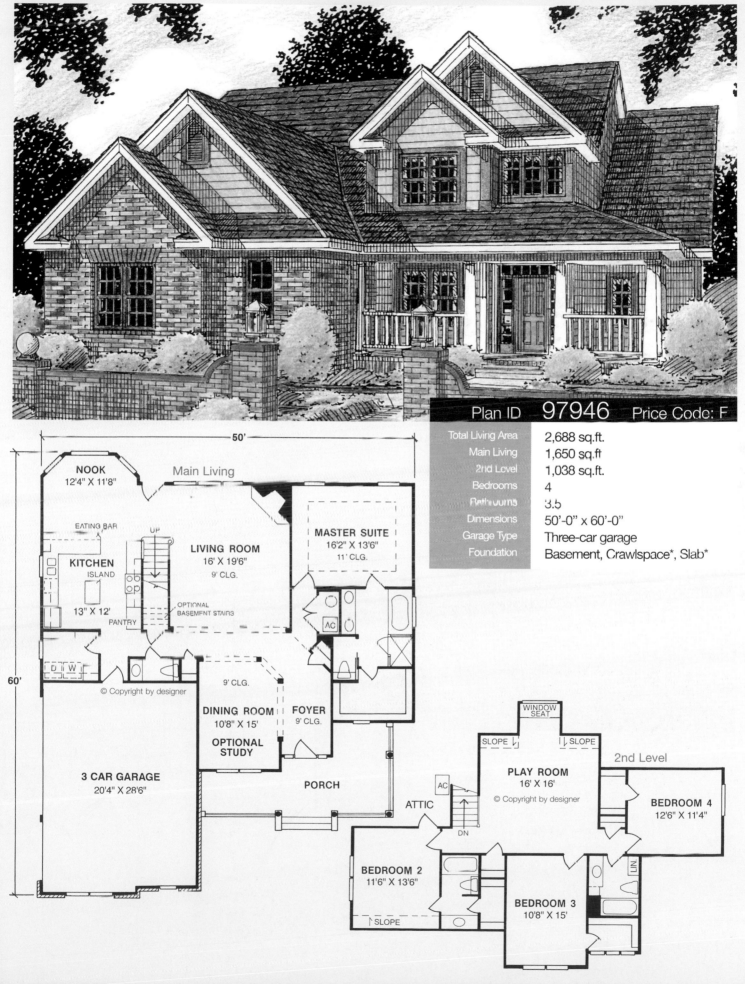

Plan ID 97946 — Price Code: F

Total Living Area	2,688 sq.ft.
Main Living	1,650 sq.ft
2nd Level	1,038 sq.ft.
Bedrooms	4
Bathrooms	3.5
Dimensions	50'-0" x 60'-0"
Garage Type	Three-car garage
Foundation	Basement, Crawlspace*, Slab*

Main Living

NOOK 12'4" X 11'8"

EATING BAR

KITCHEN ISLAND 13" X 12'

PANTRY

UP

LIVING ROOM 16' X 19'6" 9' CLG.

OPTIONAL BASEMENT STAIRS

MASTER SUITE 16'2" X 13'6" 11' CLG.

AC

D W

9' CLG.

DINING ROOM 10'8" X 15'

OPTIONAL STUDY

FOYER 9' CLG.

3 CAR GARAGE 20'4" X 28'6"

PORCH

© Copyright by designer

2nd Level

WINDOW SEAT

SLOPE   SLOPE

PLAY ROOM 16' X 16'

© Copyright by designer

BEDROOM 4 12'6" X 11'4"

ATTIC

AC

DN

BEDROOM 2 11'6" X 13'6"

SLOPE

BEDROOM 3 10'8" X 15'

LIN

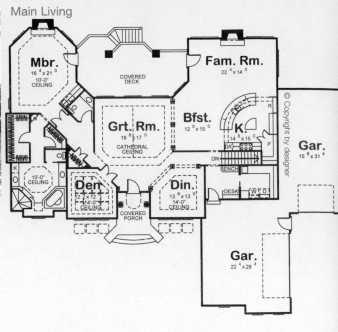

Main Living

Plan ID 44042 Price Code: F

Total Living Area	2,613 sq.ft.
Main Living	2,613 sq.ft.
Bedrooms	1
Bathrooms	1.5
Dimensions	85'-0" x 73'-0"
Garage Type	Three-car garage
Foundation	Basement, Crawlspace*, Slab*

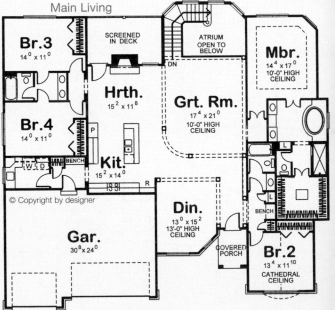

Main Living

Plan ID 44067 Price Code: G

Total Living Area	2,788 sq.ft.
Main Living	2,788 sq.ft.
Bedrooms	4
Bathrooms	3
Dimensions	67'-0" x 63'-0"
Garage Type	Three-car garage
Foundation	Basement, Crawlspace*, Slab*

Plan ID 44039 Price Code: G

Total Living Area	2,843 sq.ft.
Main Living	1,936 sq.ft.
2nd Level	907 sq.ft.
Bedrooms	4
Bathrooms	3.5
Dimensions	75'-0" x 64'-0"
Garage Type	Three-car garage
Foundation	Basement, Crawlspace*, Slab*

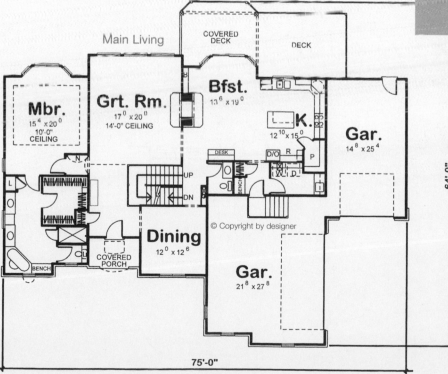

Main Living

COVERED DECK

DECK

Mbr. 15⁴ x 20⁰ 10'-0" CEILING

Grt. Rm. 17⁰ x 20⁰ 14'-0" CEILING

Bfst. 13⁶ x 19⁰

K. 12¹⁰ x 15⁰

Gar. 14⁸ x 25⁴

DESK

UP

DN

Dining 12⁰ x 12⁶

COVERED PORCH

BENCH

Gar. 21⁸ x 27⁸

© Copyright by designer

75'-0"

64'-0"

2nd Level

SEAT

SEAT

Br.3 13⁶ x 13⁰

Br.4 12⁶ x 13⁰

DN

Br.2 12⁰ x 12⁶ 10'-0" CEILING

Unfin. Stor. 21⁸ x 24¹⁰ ADDS 318 SQ.FT.

© Copyright by designer

Plan ID 97486 Price Code: F

Total Living Area	2,517 sq.ft.
Main Living	2,517 sq.ft.
Bedrooms	3
Bathrooms	2.5
Dimensions	77'-0" x 59'-0"
Garage Type	Two-car garage
Foundation	Basement, Crawlspace*, Slab*

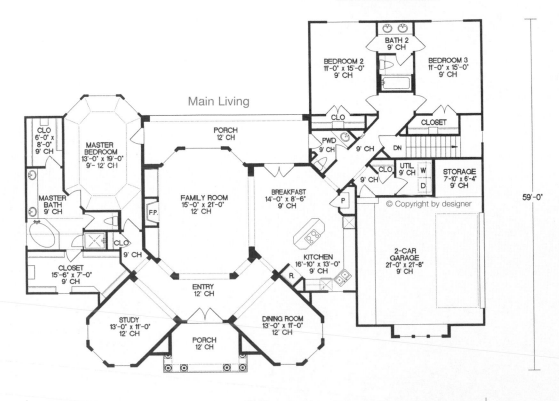

Plan ID 99473 Price Code: F

Total Living Area	2,039 sq.ft.
Main Living	2,087 sq ft
2nd Level	552 sq.ft.
Bedrooms	4
Bathrooms	3.5
Dimensions	68'-7" x 57'-4"
Garage Type	Three-car garage
Foundation	Basement*, Slab

Main Living

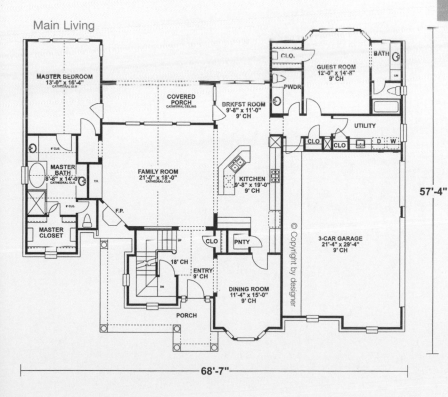

2nd Level

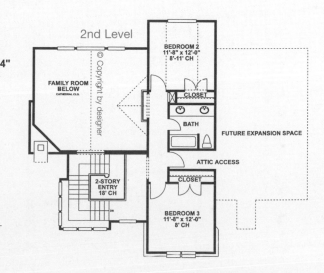

Plan ID **69005** Price Code: G

Total Living Area	2,806 sq.ft.
Basement	548 sq.ft.
Main Living	1,473 sq.ft.
2nd Level	785 sq.ft.
Bedrooms	4
Bathrooms	2.5
Dimensions	54'-8" x 51'-0"
Garage Type	Two-car garage
Foundation	Basement

54'-8"

51'-0"

Main Living

Atrium below

Deck

Dn

Great Rm
18-0x19-10

Dining
10-2x13-3

Kit
11-0x
13-3

vaulted

vaulted

Bar

W
D

P

MBr
14-0x16-9

Foyer

Up

Garage
21-4x21-4

Porch

© Copyright by designer

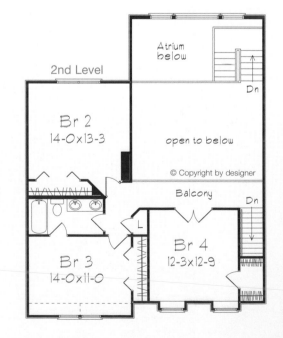

2nd Level

Atrium below

Dn

Br 2
14-0x13-3

open to below

© Copyright by designer

Balcony

Dn

L

Br 3
14-0x11-0

Br 4
12-3x12-9

Plan ID 24989 Price Code: F

Total Living Area	2,502 sq. ft.
Main Living	1,782 sq. ft.
2nd Level	810 sq. ft.
Bedrooms	3
Bathrooms	2.5
Dimensions	84'-0" x 35'-0"
Garage Type	Two-car garage
Foundation	Basement, Crawlspace, Slab, Basement + Crawlspace

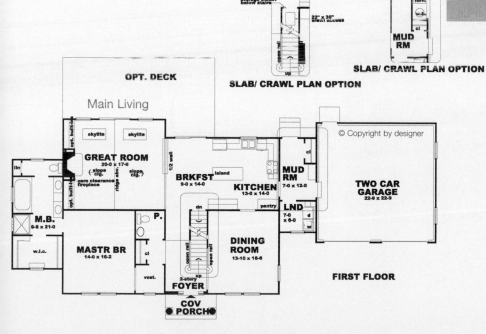

SLAB/ CRAWL PLAN OPTION

SLAB/ CRAWL PLAN OPTION

MUD RM

OPT. DECK

Main Living

© Copyright by designer

GREAT ROOM
20-0 x 17-6

BRKFST
9-0 x 14-0

island

KITCHEN
13-0 x 14-0

MUD RM
7-0 x 12-0

TWO CAR GARAGE
22-8 x 22-9

pantry

LND
7-0 x 6-0

M.B.
9-8 x 21-0

MASTR BR
14-0 x 18-2

DINING ROOM
13-10 x 16-6

FOYER

COV PORCH

FIRST FLOOR

2nd Level

B.
8-0 x 9-10

BEDRM #2
12-0 x 16-6

BEDRM #3
13-10 x 17-0

© Copyright by designer

Plan ID 69011   Price Code: F

Total Living Area	2,723 sq.ft.
Main Living	2,723 sq.ft.
Bedrooms	3
Bathrooms	2.5
Dimensions	79'-0" x 64'-2"
Garage Type	Three-car garage
Foundation	Basement

Main Living

79'-0"

Patio

MBr
16-7x16-0
vaulted

Brk
14-4x11-0

Hearth Rm
15-8x14-0
vaulted

Br 2
12-0x11-0

Great Rm
17-11x23-8
vaulted

Kitchen
14-4x12-8

Br 3
12-0x11-5

Foyer

Dining
12-0x15-0
tray clg

Br 4 /
Study
14-4x11-0
vaulted

Porch

Garage
21-4x29-4

64'-2"

© Copyright by designer

Plan ID 69003   Price Code: F

Total Living Area	2,597 sq.ft.
Main Living	1,742 sq.ft.
2nd Level	855 sq.ft.
Bedrooms	4
Bathrooms	3.5
Dimensions	61'-4" x 48'-0"
Garage Type	Two-car garage
Foundation	Basement, Crawlspace, Slab

Main Living

61'-4"

Screened
Porch
vaulted

Deck

Great Rm
17-0x17-0
vaulted

Hearth Rm
15-8x13-0

Kitchen
14-0x13-0

48'-0"

Dining
12-0x15-9

Entry

MBr
18-4x17-5
vaulted

Garage
21-4x21-4

© Copyright by designer

2nd Level

Br 2
12-11x11-0

open to below

Br 3
12-0x13-4

Br 4
13-0x10-3

open to below

© Copyright by designer

Plan ID 94994 Price Code: G

Total Living Area	2,957 sq.ft.
Main Living	2,063 sq.ft.
2nd Level	894 sq.ft.
Bedrooms	4
Bathrooms	4
Dimensions	72'-8" x 51'-4"
Garage Type	Three-car garage
Foundation	Basement, Crawlspace*, Slab*

Main Living

Brst. 8'-8" CLG. 15⁰ x 11⁴
Kit. 13⁰ x 10⁹
Grt. rm. 16⁰ x 20⁸
Den 11⁸ x 13⁴
WET BAR
12'-0" CEILING
Gar. 20⁸ x 31⁴
Din. 12⁰ x 14⁰
E.
Liv. 12⁰ x 15⁰
Mbr. 13⁰ x 16³
10'-0" CEILING
CVRD. STOOP
UP DN
CATHEDRAL CEILING
TRAPS
DESK
w/p
© Copyright by designer

51'-4"
72'-8"

2nd Level

Br. 2 13⁰ x 12³
Br. 3 12⁰ x 13⁰
Br. 4 12⁰ x 13⁰
OPEN TO BELOW
DISPLAY
BOOKS
LIN.
LIN.
DN
TRAPS
© Copyright by designer

Plan ID **69007** Price Code: G

Total Living Area	2,828 sq.ft.
Main Living	2,006 sq.ft.
2nd Level	822 sq.ft.
Bedrooms	5
Bathrooms	3.5
Dimensions	70'-6" x 55'-6"
Garage Type	Two-car garage
Foundation	Basement

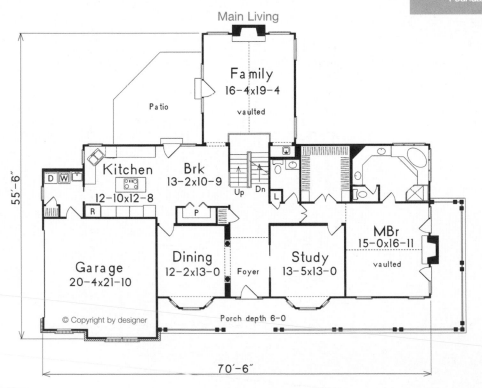

Main Living

Family
16-4x19-4
vaulted

Patio

Kitchen
12-10x12-8

Brk
13-2x10-9

Up Dn

Garage
20-4x21-10

Dining
12-2x13-0

Foyer

Study
13-5x13-0

MBr
15-0x16-11
vaulted

© Copyright by designer

Porch depth 6-0

55'-6"

70'-6"

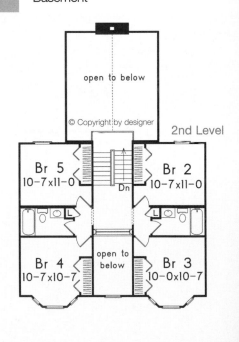

2nd Level

open to below

© Copyright by designer

Br 5
10-7x11-0

Br 2
10-7x11-0

Dn

Br 4
10-7x10-7

open to below

Br 3
10-0x10-7

Plan ID 69000 Price Code: G

Total Living Area	2,874 sq.ft.
Main Living	2,874 sq.ft.
Bedrooms	4
Bathrooms	2.5
Dimensions	83'-0" x 50'-4"
Garage Type	Two-car garage
Foundation	Basement

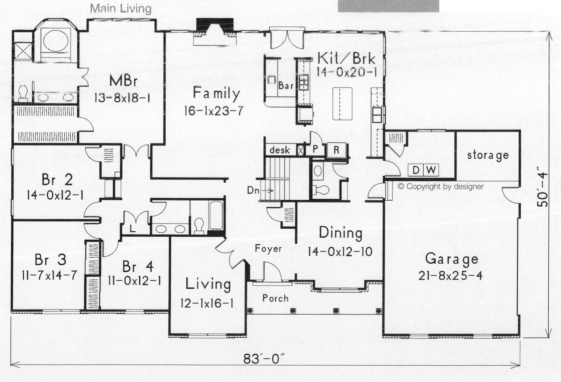

Plan ID 96827   Price Code: F

Total Living Area	2,571 sq.ft.
Main Living	1,658 sq.ft.
2nd Level	913 sq.ft.
Bedrooms	5
Bathrooms	2.5
Dimensions	63'-0" x 63'-0"
Garage Type	Two-car garage
Foundation	Basement, Crawlspace, Slab

Plan ID 96839 Price Code: F

Total Living Area	2,599 sq. ft.
Main Living	1,602 sq. ft.
2nd Level	997 sq.ft.
Bedrooms	5
Bathrooms	2.5
Dimensions	71'-8" x 57'-0"
Garage Type	Three-car garage
Foundation	Basement, Crawlspace, Slab

Main Living

71'-8"

SINGLE BAY GARAGE 21'-0"x14'-0" (9'-6" CLG)

8' WIDE COVERED PORCH

9' OVERHEAD DOOR

SHOP/STORAGE 11'-10"x16'-10" (9'-6" CLG)

WORK BENCH

LNDRY

COATS

PWDR

STORAGE SHELVES

KITCHEN 12'-3"x13'-1" (9' CLG)

PNTRY

DESK

FRENCH DOORS

FORMAL DINING 12'-0"x12'-0" (9' CLG)

NOOK

GREAT ROOM 24'-5"x18'-1" (9' CLG)

DN UP

COATS

UP

FOYER 12'-1"x9'-1" (9' CLG)

COMPUTER DESK

CLOSE

CLOSE

OFFICE/ HOME SCHOOL/ BEDROOM #5 12'-0"x11'-0" (9' CLG)

MSTR BATH (9' CLG)

W.I.C.

MASTER BDRM 12'-6"x17'-4" (10' TRAY CLG)

FP

57'-0"

STEPS

TWIN BAY GARAGE 21'-0"x22'-0" (9'-6" CLG)

9' OVERHEAD DOOR

9' OVERHEAD DOOR

© Copyright by designer

8' WIDE COVERED PORCH

STEPS

Optional

UP

DN

FOYER (9' CLG)

2nd Level

© Copyright by designer

BONUS ROOM (UNFINISHED) 20'-5"x18'-0" (8' CLG)

BEDROOM #4 12'-0"x13'-1" (8' CLG)

BATH

LINEN

LINEN

TUB/SHWR

BEDROOM #3 12'-0"x13'-1" (8' CLG)

8' CLG

REC ROOM 24'-5"x13'-5"

DN

VAULTED AREA

STORAGE (UNFINISHED) 9'-8"x20'-6"

SLOPED CLG

8' CLG

SLOPED CLG

BEDROOM #2 12'-0"x11'-0" (8' CLG)

Plan ID **96823** Price Code: F

Total Living Area	2,645 sq.ft.
Main Living	1,658 sq.ft.
2nd Level	987 sq.ft.
Bedrooms	4
Bathrooms	3
Dimensions	85'-6" x 56'-0"
Garage Type	Two-car garage
Foundation	Basement

Main Living

OPTIONAL STAIRS TO BONUS ROOM OVER GARAGE

WORK BENCH · STORAGE UNDER STAIR

WORKSHOP/ STORAGE

GARAGE 23'-5"x29'-5"

GARAGE ENTRY

GARAGE FOYER

LNDRY

KITCHEN 11'-0"x13'-0" (9' CLG)

PANTRY

BATH

FORMAL DINING 11'-10"x13'-0" (9' CLG)

FOYER (9' CLG)

FRENCH DOORS

10' WIDE COVERED PORCH

NOOK

GREAT ROOM 23'-3"x14'-2" (9' CLG)

MASTER BATH (9' CLG)

SHOWER TILE

W.I.C.

MASTER BEDROOM 14'-0"x18'-2" (10' TRAY CLG)

OFFICE/GUEST/ HOME SCHOOL 11'-0"x13'-6" (9' CLG)

8' WIDE COVERED PORCH

8' WIDE COVERED PORCH

STEPS

© Copyright by designer

2nd Level

BEDROOM #4 11'-10"x13'-0"

LNDRY/SINKS

BATH

COMPUTER ROOM

FAMILY ROOM (10' TRAY CLG) 22'-1"x18'-3"

BEDROOM #3 11'-10"x12'-0"

BOOKS

© Copyright by designer

Bonus Room

OPTIONAL STAIRS TO BONUS ROOM OVER GARAGE

STORAGE

BONUS ROOM 14'-0"x26'-0"

7' CLG IN DORMER

8' FLAT CLG

SLOPED CLG

48" KNEEWALL

Plan ID 96825   **Price Code: G**

Total Living Area	2,705 sq. ft.
Main Living	1,787 sq. ft.
2nd Level	1,008 sq. ft.
Bedrooms	4
Bathrooms	3
Dimensions	64'-4" x 56'-4"
Garage Type	Two-car garage
Foundation	Basement, Crawlspace, Slab

Main Living

W.I.C.

MASTER BEDROOM
14'-0"x17'-0"
(11' TRAY)

JACC

SHWR

MASTER BATH

D | W | COATS

LNDRY /
1/2 BATH

W.I.C.

BENCH

COVERED PORCH
29'-0"x8'-0"

© Copyright by designer

NOOK
11'-3"x10'-0"
(9' CLG)

GREAT ROOM
28'-5"x19'-5"
(9' CLG)

F.P.

RAISED

KITCHEN
11'-5"x
11'-4"
(9' CLG)

PAN

FRIG

GARAGE
24'-0"x22'-0"
(9'-6" CLG)

MINI-VAN

WORK BENCH/STORAGE

DN

UP

BUILT-IN CABS

DINING ROOM
11'-0"x15'-8"
(9' CLG)

FOYER
9' CLG

PWDR

COATS

WRAP AROUND PORCH
25'-0"x8'-0"

2nd Level

60" KNEEWALL

FUTURE
(UNFINISHED)
18'-5"x18'-7"
(8' CLG)

60"
KNEEWALL

W.I.C.

BEDROOM #4
10'-10"x11'-0"
(8' CLG)

BEDROOM #3
10'-10"x11'-0"
(8' CLG)

STORAGE

TUB/SHWR

W.I.C.

LINEN/STORAGE

SHLVS | LIN

SHWR

W.I.C.

DN

BEDROOM #2
11'-0"x13'-0"
(8' CLG)

FAMILY ROOM
16'-1"x19'-1"
(VAULTED)

© Copyright by designer

Plan ID **59079** Price Code: F

Total Living Area	2,601 sq.ft.
Main Living	2,601 sq.ft.
Bedrooms	4
Bathrooms	3.5
Dimensions	84'-0" x 56'-4"
Garage Type	Two-car garage
Foundation	Crawlspace, Slab

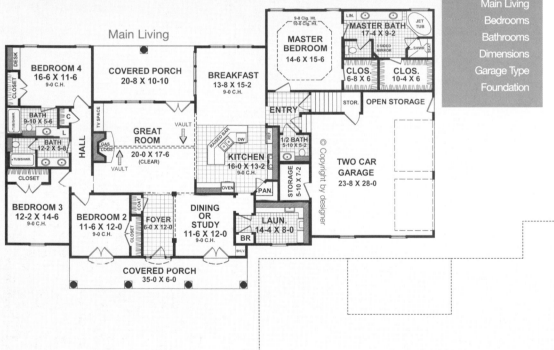

2nd Level

UNFINISHED BONUS ROOM
18'-8" X 18'-0"
(CLEAR)
8'-0" C.H.

ATTIC ACCESS

© Copyright by designer

Plan ID 50049 Price Code: F

Total Living Area	2,500 sq.ft.
Main Living	1,808 sq.ft.
2nd Level	698 sq.ft.
Bedrooms	3
Bathrooms	2.5
Dimensions	62'-8" x 49'-0"
Garage Type	Two-car garage
Foundation	Basement

Main Living

Master Bedroom 16'2" x 14'
SLOPE
Great Room 18'2" x 18'2" CARPET
10" DIA WOOD COLUMNS
Breakfast 11'10" x 9'9" HARDWOOD
Laun
VINYL
CERAMIC TILE
Kitchen 14'7" x 12' HARDWOOD
Mud Room
WALK-IN PANTRY
Dressing
WALK-IN CLOSET
Foyer
STAIRS UP
DOWN
Dining Room 12' x 13' CARPET
Bath HDWD
HDWD
Porch SLOPED CEILING
Two-Car Garage 20' x 21'

© Copyright by designer

2nd Level

SLOPED
Great Room Below
© Copyright by designer
Loft 10'4" x 17' Irreg.
WALK-IN CLOSET
Bedroom 13'10" x 10'8"
STAIRS DOWN
Hall
STAIRS UP
Foyer Below
Bedroom 12' x 13'
WALK-IN CLOSET
Bath
SLOPED
Bonus Room 11'1" x 17'9"

Personal Space

A deep, covered front porch shelters the entry of this stylish one-story home, designed with plenty of personal space. Once inside, the foyer lends immediate views to the formal dining room and library, which could serve as a home office. At the core of the home, the kitchen opens to the breakfast area and family room, which is located at the rear as a secluded retreat. The master suite, with his and her walk-in closets and bayed windows, enjoys effective separation from the secondary bedrooms, positioned on the opposite side of the home.

Outdoor living space abounds at the rear of this design, with a sprawling sundeck. The homeowners modified the original plan by adding a screened-in porch. ▶

The family room is light an bright, with a generous array of transom windows. ▶

The formal dining room is highlighted by special ceiling details and views to the rear sundeck. ▼

Plan ID	71119	Price Code: F
Total Living Area	2,614 sq.ft.	
Main Living	2,614 sq.ft.	
Bedrooms	3	
Bathrooms	2.5	
Dimensions	70'-10" x 70'-9"	
Garage Type	Two-car garage	
Foundation	Basement, Crawlspace, Slab	

Main Living

Bdrm.3 13-8 x 11-6
Bdrm.2 13-8 x 11-6
Familly 17-4 x 20-6
Brkfst. 10-0 x 12-8
Sundeck 38-5 x 24-0
Kitchen 17-8 x 12-2
Dining 13-10 x 13-0 w/ Bay
Master Bdrm. 13-4 x 19-6 w/ Bay
Foyer 6-0 x 15-8
Living/ Library 13-8 x 11-8
M.Bath
Double Garage 21-4 x 27-8
Bth. 2
Cab.
Pant.
Lin.
Lav.
Down
78-9
70-10
© Copyright by designer

2nd Level

Future Finish 1681 Sq. Ft.
Down
© Copyright by designer

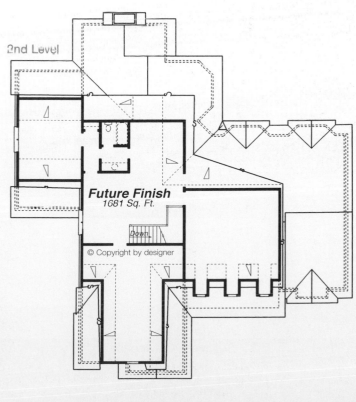

Plan ID 41002 Price Code: G

Total Living Area	2,977 sq.ft.
Main Living	2,121 sq.ft.
2nd Level	856 sq.ft.
Bedrooms	3
Bathrooms	2.5
Dimensions	64'-0" x 57'-0"
Garage Type	Two-car garage
Foundation	Basement, Crawlspace

Main Living

Screened Porch 21'-0" x 13'-6" (cathedral clg.)

Porch 41'-2" x 8'-0"

Kitchen 21'-6" x 13'-0"

Great Room 19'-6" x 15'-5" (cathedral clg.)

Master Bedroom 12'-6" x 15'-5"

Pantry Utility

Balcony above

© Copyright by designer

Foyer 8'-6" x 6'-0"

Bedroom 11'-4" x 12'-1"

Bedroom 13'-0" x 12'-1"

Garage 21'-2" x 23'-4"

2nd Level

Great Room below

Bonus Rm. 21'-2" x 13'-5"

Bonus Rm. 22'-2" x 13'-5"

© Copyright by designer

Plan ID 41001 Price Code: F

Total Living Area	2,525 sq.ft.
Main Living	1,850 sq.ft.
2nd Level	675 sq.ft.
Bedrooms	3
Bathrooms	3
Dimensions	65'-7" x 53'-0"
Garage Type	Two-car garage
Foundation	Basement, Crawlspace

Main Living

Breakfast 10'-5" x 10'-0"

Porch 36'-4" x 7'-4"

Sitting 10'-5" x 7'-3"

Kitchen 16'-5" x 9'-10"

Great Room 20'-10" x 16'-8" (cathedral clg.)

Master Bedroom 14'-6" x 16'-8"

Utility

Pantry

balcony above

© Copyright by designer

Dining Rm. 11'-0" x 16'-2"

Foyer 7'-5" x 13'-6"

Study 10'-7" x 12'-1"

Garage 14'-4" x 25'-1"

2nd Level

© Copyright by designer

open to Great Room below

Bonus Rm. 16'-1" x 12'-0"

Balcony

Bonus Rm. 14'-6" x 11'-7"

Bedroom 11'-3" x 16'-2"

Bedroom 14'-1" x 12'-11"

desk

Plan ID	79243	Price Code: F

Total Living Area	2,507 sq.ft.
Main Living	1,743 sq.ft.
2nd Level	764 sq.ft.
Bedrooms	4
Bathrooms	2.5
Dimensions	74'-0" x 50'-0"
Garage Type	Two-car garage
Foundation	Crawlspace, Slab

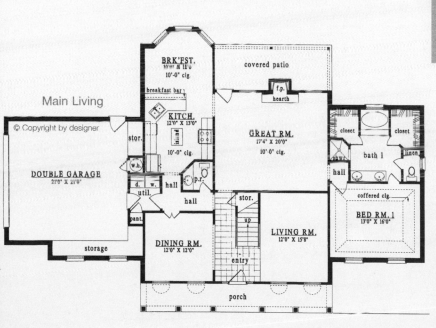

Main Living

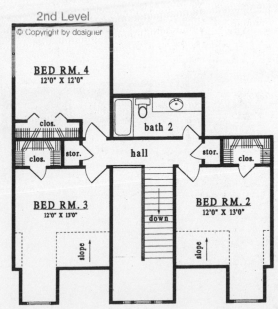

2nd Level

Plan ID 64980 **Price Code: G**

Total Living Area	2,992 sq.ft.
Main Living	1,654 sq.ft.
2nd Level	1,338 sq.ft.
Bedrooms	4
Bathrooms	3.5
Dimensions	72'-0" x 52'-0"
Garage Type	Three-car garage
Foundation	Basement

Main Living

52-0

© Copyright by designer

21-8 X 14-4

17-4 X 14-8

20-4 X 12-6

3-CAR GARAGE
20-8 X 20-0

11-0 X 12-0

10-0 X 6-0

12-8 X 13-0

72-0

2nd Level

18-0 X 14-4

10-8 X 14-6

12-8 X 16-0

10-8 X 13-4

© Copyright by designer

Plan ID 65126 Price Code: G

Total Living Area	2,802 sq.ft.
Main Living	2,219 sq.ft.
2nd Level	583 sq.ft.
Bedrooms	3
Bathrooms	2.5
Dimensions	91'-4" x 40'-8"
Garage Type	Three-car garage
Foundation	Crawlspace

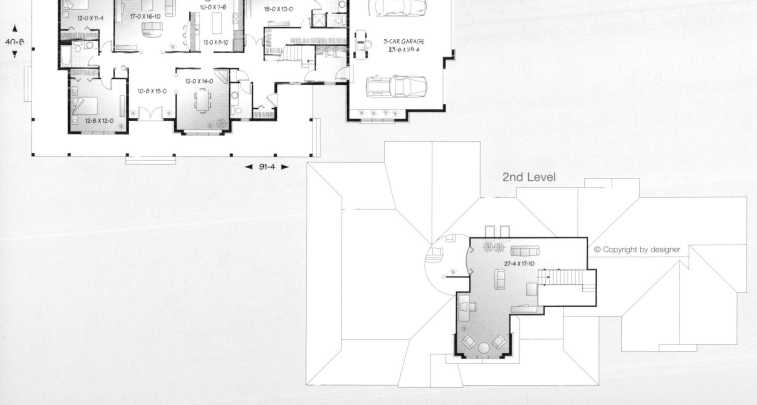

Main Living

40-8

12-0 X 11-4

17-0 X 16-10

10-0 X 7-6

15-0 X 13-0

12-0 X 8-10

© Copyright by designer

3-CAR GARAGE
23-8 X 29-4

10-8 X 15-0

12-0 X 14-0

12-8 X 12-0

91-4

2nd Level

27-4 X 17-10

© Copyright by designer

Main Living

© Copyright by designer

2nd Level

© Copyright by designer

Plan ID 94178   Price Code: F

Total Living Area	2,652 sq.ft.
Main Living	1,891 sq.ft.
2nd Level	761 sq.ft.
Bedrooms	3
Bathrooms	3
Dimensions	80'-8" x 57'-0"
Garage Type	Three-car garage
Foundation	Basement

Main Living

© Copyright by designer

2nd Level

© Copyright by designer

Plan ID 94177   Price Code: G

Total Living Area	2,792 sq.ft.
Main Living	2,069 sq.ft.
2nd Level	723 sq.ft.
Bedrooms	3
Bathrooms	2.5
Dimensions	60'-10" x 65'-6"
Garage Type	Two-car garage
Foundation	Basement

Plan ID	94175	Price Code: G
Total Living Area	2,797 sq.ft.	
Main Living	2,148 sq.ft.	
2nd Level	649 sq.ft.	
Bedrooms	3	
Bathrooms	2.5	
Dimensions	73'-4" x 63'-2"	
Garage Type	Three-car garage	
Foundation	Basement	

© Copyright by designer

© Copyright by designer

GARAGES

AS DEVELOPERS CONTINUE TO CARVE OUT SMALLER AND SMALLER LOTS, HOMEOWNERS AND BUILDERS FACE A DIFFICULT CHALLENGE OF CREATING IMPRESSIVE HOMES WITH OUTSTANDING CURB APPEAL. **When a 20 ft. wide garage with front-facing doors dominates a 38 ft. wide home, it often seems as though garages are being built with small homes attached.**

So, is there a solution? Unless the development allows for garages placed along a dedicated alley, the options are limited with a narrow lot. However, several design details can help "soften" the impact of garages. First, two single doors usually work better than one large door. If the budget allows, new doors that are reminiscent of intricately detailed carriage house doors are now available from several manufacturers. Careful attention to roof lines can also help. Essentially, try to draw attention to another portion of the house, such as the entry, while downplaying the garage itself.

Excerpted from *Home Plan Buyer's Guide,* an upcoming book by **Larry W. Garnett**

TO LEARN MORE ABOUT GARAGES, visit www.homeplanbuyersguide.com

Plan ID **94163**   Price Code: G

Total Living Area	2,843 sq.ft.
Main Living	2,155 sq.ft.
2nd Level	688 sq.ft.
Bedrooms	3
Bathrooms	2.5
Dimensions	69'-8" x 59' 10"
Garage Type	Two-car garage
Foundation	Basement

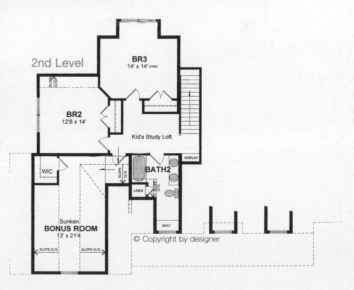

Main Living

Veranda (Optional) 646 sf

Screened Porch 143 sf

DIN 14' x 10'6

GREAT RM coffered clg 19'8 X 20'4

Sitting Area 9' x 5'

MBR 14'2 x 16'

KITCHEN 14' x 12'8

SNACK BAR

Laun

WIC

Mud Rm

BENCH

GARAGE 21'4 X 21'4

DIN RM 13'8 x 14'4

FOYER

LIBRARY 11'8 x 14'

Pdr MBATH

WIC

SHELVES

Covered Wood Porch 210 sf

© Copyright by designer

2nd Level

BR3 14' x 14' (max)

BR2 12'6 x 14'

Kid's Study Loft

WIC

BATH2

Sunken BONUS ROOM 13' x 21'4

SLOPE CL'G   SLOPE CL'G

© Copyright by designer

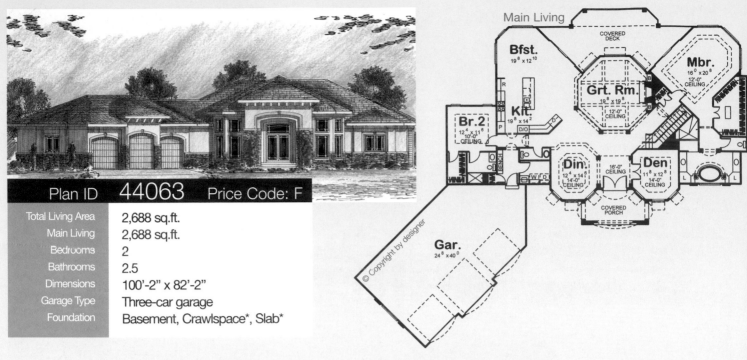

Main Living

Plan ID 44063 **Price Code: F**

Total Living Area	2,688 sq.ft.
Main Living	2,688 sq.ft.
Bedrooms	2
Bathrooms	2.5
Dimensions	100'-2" x 82'-2"
Garage Type	Three-car garage
Foundation	Basement, Crawlspace*, Slab*

Main Living

Plan ID 63011 **Price Code: F**

Total Living Area	2,660 sq.ft.
Main Living	2,660 sq.ft.
Bedrooms	3
Bathrooms	3
Dimensions	66'-4" x 74'-4"
Garage Type	Two-car garage
Foundation	Slab

Plan ID 63181   Price Code: G

Total Living Area	2,887 sq.ft.
Main Living	2,212 sq.ft
2nd Level	675 sq.ft.
Bedrooms	3
Bathrooms	3
Dimensions	70'-0" x 74'-1"
Garage Type	Two-car garage
Foundation	Slab

Main Living

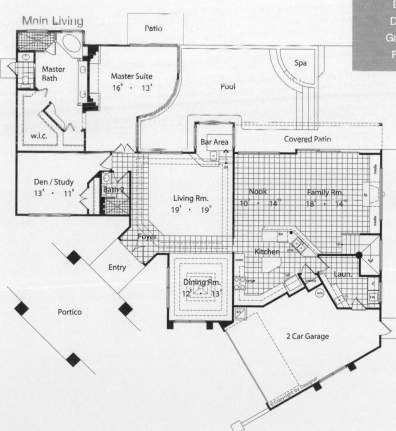

2nd Level

Plan ID 58900 Price Code: G

Total Living Area	2,797 sq.ft.
Main Living	2,797 sq.ft.
Bedrooms	3
Bathrooms	4
Dimensions	67'-6" x 88'-0"
Garage Type	Three-car garage
Foundation	Slab

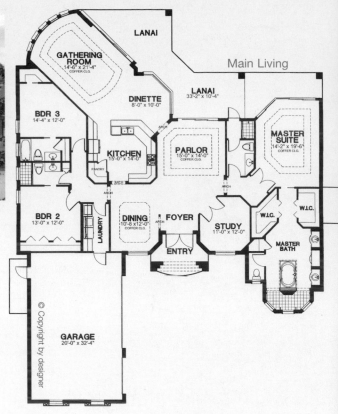

Main Living

Plan ID 58904 Price Code: G

Total Living Area	2,793 sq.ft.
Main Living	2,793 sq.ft.
Bedrooms	3
Bathrooms	4
Dimensions	68'-0" x 88'-0"
Garage Type	Two-car garage
Foundation	Slab

Main Living

REAR ELEVATION

Plan ID	64987	Price Code: G
Total Living Area		2,849 sq.ft.
Main Living		2,106 sq.ft.
2nd Level		743 sq.ft.
Bedrooms		3
Bathrooms		2.5
Dimensions		60'-0" x 56'-0"
Garage Type		Two-car garage
Foundation		Slab

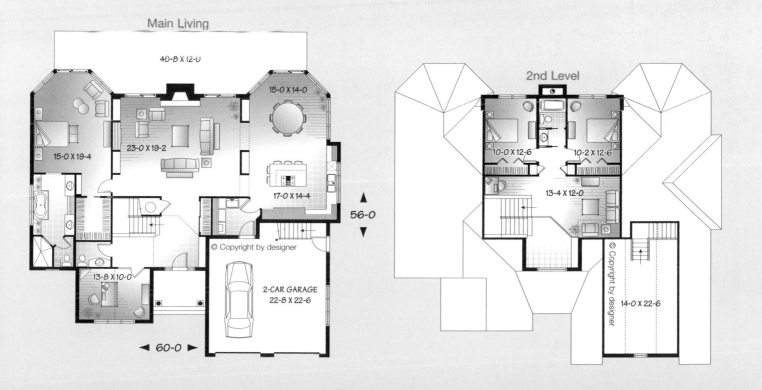

Main Living

40-8 X 12-0

15-0 X 14-0

23-0 X 19-2

15-0 X 19-4

17-0 X 14-4

56-0

13-8 X 10-0

© Copyright by designer

2-CAR GARAGE
22-8 X 22-6

60-0

2nd Level

10-0 X 12-6

10-2 X 12-6

13-4 X 12-0

© Copyright by designer

14-0 X 22-6

Designer's perspective

Open, Active, *Entertaining*

This plan was designed with the active family in mind. The living areas of the plan are basically open to each other – separated only by architectural elements, not solid walls. The living and dining rooms, for example, are defined from one another by columns and ceiling details. To accommodate those who work at home, bedroom #2 could also double as an office. In the master bedroom, take note of the window placement. To complement the main set of windows, we placed smaller windows just around the corner. This window arrangement makes all the difference in experiencing the room. I like to call it a room's "peripheral vision." We carried this same design concept into the kitchen area (see illustration). Notice that every wall, adjacent to a main window, has a smaller complimentary window or door. Looking at the illustration, you can imagine how comfortable this room must feel. The three-sided fireplace adds to the unrestricted flow of the room. The lower level includes the children's bedrooms and an openly configured recreation room and home theatre room.

Plan ID	24802	Price Code: L
Total Living Area		4,064 sq.ft.
Basement		1,598 sq.ft.
Main Living		2,466 sq.ft.
Bedrooms		4
Bathrooms		3
Dimensions		78' 0" x 52'-4"
Garage Type		Three-car garage
Foundation		Basement

Basement

Home Theater
24-0 x 17-0

built-ins

wet bar

W/H

furn.

UP

Utility
13-0 x 25-10

2-sided fireplace

Rec. Rm
20-8 x 15-0

Br 3
15-8 x 13-10

Br 4
13-0 x 12-4

Storage
18-11 x 8-6

Storage
22-2 x 15-10

© Copyright by designer

Main Living

whirlpool

Master Suite
15-0 x 16-0

Lin

shelves

Lin

Living Rm
20-2 x 18-10
11'-9" clg.

built-ins

oven

DW

Kitchen
15-6 x 17-0

Hearth Rm
15-6 x 12-0

Deck

3-sided fireplace

Brkfst
12-0 x 13-0

ref

Ldry

W

D

counter

pantry desk pantry bench

railing DN

Study / Br 2
13-0 x 12-0

railing

Foyer

columns

Dining Rm
13-0 x 11-2

Garage
31-8 x 21-8

© Copyright by designer

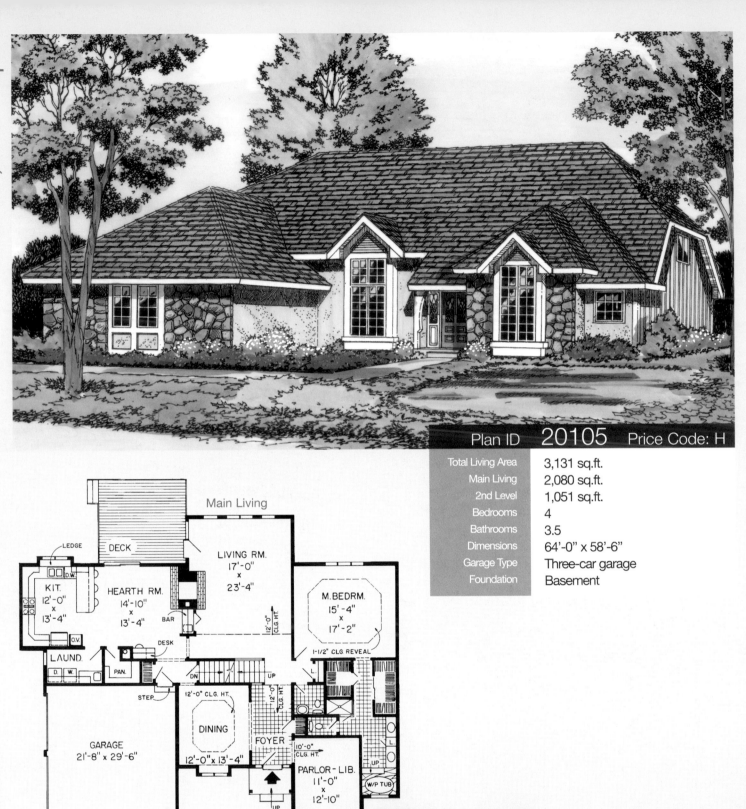

Plan ID **20105** Price Code: H

Total Living Area	3,131 sq.ft.
Main Living	2,080 sq.ft.
2nd Level	1,051 sq.ft.
Bedrooms	4
Bathrooms	3.5
Dimensions	64'-0" x 58'-6"
Garage Type	Three-car garage
Foundation	Basement

Main Living

LEDGE

DECK

KIT.
12'-0"
x
13'-4"

HEARTH RM.
14'-10"
x
13'-4"

BAR

LIVING RM.
17'-0"
x
23'-4"

M. BEDRM.
15'-4"
x
17'-2"

1-1/2" CLG REVEAL

O.V.

DESK

LAUND.

D. W.

PAN.

STEP

DN

UP

DINING
12'-0" x 13'-4"

12'-0" CLG. HT.

FOYER

10'-0"
CLG. HT.

UP

GARAGE
21'-8" x 29'-6"

PARLOR - LIB.
11'-0"
x
12'-10"

W/P TUB

UP

© Copyright by designer

BEDRM. 4
15'-10" x 11'-4"

2nd Level

SLOPE

BEDRM. 2
17'-2" x 11'-0"

© Copyright by designer

HALF
WALL

SHELVES

DN

BEDRM. 3
21'-4" x 11'-0"

SLOPE

TO ATTIC

Plan ID 24613   Price Code: I

Total Living Area	3,323 sq.ft.
Main Living	2,294 sq.ft.
2nd Level	1,029 sq.ft.
Bedrooms	4
Bathrooms	3.5
Dimensions	71'-0" x 73'-10"
Garage Type	Three-car garage
Foundation	Basement, Crawlspace, Slab

Main Living

Master Suite
17-0 x 14-4
pan vault

Great Rm
16-8 x 24-10

Dining Rm
13-0 x 15-2

Brkfst
12-6 x 12-6
vaulted clg

make-up

Kitchen
13-10 x 11-10
oven

skylights above

edge of bridge above

pantry

built-ins

Library
12-3 x 17-3

whirlpool

Foyer

Ldry

open above

Optional Mechanical Placement

3 Car Garage
22-11 x 31-8

© Copyright by designer

73'-10"

71'-0"

crawl access

UP

Alternate Foundation Option

2nd Level

Br 2
12-11 x 12-3

open to below

railing

DN

railing

window seat

Br 4
13-0 x 11-10

linen

Br 3
13-8 x 13-6
approx.

© Copyright by designer

Inviting Courtyard Entry

This design employs the concept of an entry courtyard, with the front door tucked out of view from the street. With this kind of arrangement, a person can really feel the inviting, yet sheltered nature of the plan. Once inside, you are treated to a view of the open, curved stairway leading to the lower living area. The ceiling in the living room rises to 12'-7" and is emphasized even more by the placement of an impressive colonnade. This is quite a nice design contrast to the sheltered entry. The living room shares a double-sided fireplace with the kitchen, breakfast and hearth room areas (see illustration). This arrangement is one of our favorites. The kitchen is where most people gather, and to have three different conversation zones is a wonderful feature when entertaining guests. Notice how the breakfast nook is placed in a gazebo type layout. With all the natural light pouring in from five sides, this room should certainly wake you up in the morning. Please note that bedroom #2 can easily double as a home office to accommodate those who work from home.

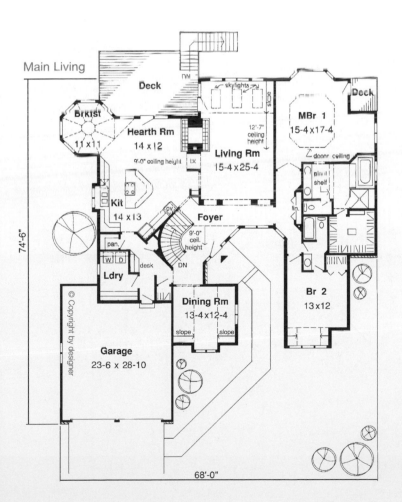

Main Living

Deck

DN

Brkfst
11 x 11

Hearth Rm
14 x 12

9'-0" ceiling height

skylights

slope

Living Rm
15-4 x 25-4

12'-7" ceiling height

MBr 1
15-4 x17-4

Deck

door ceiling

t.v.

Kit
14 x 13

plant shelf

lin.

Foyer

9'-0" ceil. height

DN

pan.

w d

desk

Ldry

DN

Dining Rm
13-4 x12-4

slope   slope

Br 2
13 x12

Garage
23-6 x 28-10

© Copyright by designer

74'-6"

68'-0"

Plan ID	**20166**	Price Code: L
Total Living Area	4,403 sq.ft.	
Basement	1,635 sq.ft.	
Main Living	2,768 sq.ft.	
Bedrooms	4	
Bathrooms	4	
Dimensions	68'-0" x 74'-6"	
Garage Type	Two-car garage	
Foundation	Basement	

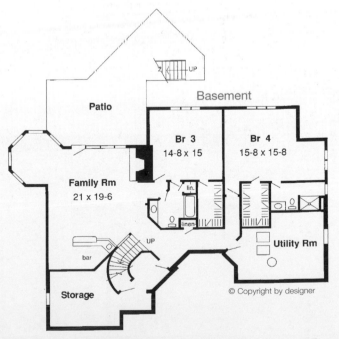

UP

Patio

Basement

Br 3
14-8 x 15

Br 4
15-8 x 15-8

Family Rm
21 x 19-6

lin.

linen

Utility Rm

bar

UP

Storage

© Copyright by designer

Plan ID 44051 Price Code: L

Total Living Area	4,212 sq.ft.
Main Living	3,245 sq.ft.
2nd Level	747 sq.ft.
Bedrooms	3
Bathrooms	3.5
Dimensions	85'-0" x 86'-0"
Garage Type	Three-car garage
Foundation	Basement, Crawlspace*, Slab*

Main Living

DECK

DECK

Mbr.
16⁰ x 20⁰
12'-0" CEILING

Atrium
28⁸ x 12⁰
OPEN TO BELOW

Hrth.
16⁰ x 14⁸

COVERED DECK

Sit.
12⁴ x 10⁰

Bfst.
19⁰ x 18⁰

Grt. Rm.
22⁰ x 21⁰
2 STORY CEILING

UP

© Copyright by designer

Kit.
19⁰ x 16⁰

BAR

Gar.
12⁰ x 40⁴

DRESSER

BENCH

Parlor
12⁴ x 11⁰
2 STORY CEILING

Din.
12⁸ x 15⁸

W D

COVERED PORCH

DN

Gar.
21⁴ x 36⁴

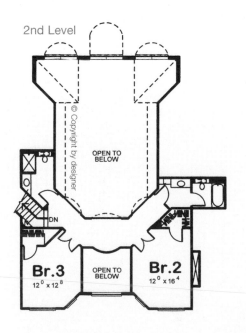

2nd Level

© Copyright by designer

OPEN TO BELOW

DN

Br.3
12⁰ x 12⁸

OPEN TO BELOW

Br.2
12⁰ x 16⁴

Plan ID 44068 Price Code: K

Total Living Area	3,887 sq.ft.
Main Living	2,872 sq.ft.
2nd Level	1,015 sq.ft.
Bedrooms	2
Bathrooms	2.5
Dimensions	116'-2" x 87'-8"
Garage Type	Three-car garage
Foundation	Basement, Crawlspace*, Slab*

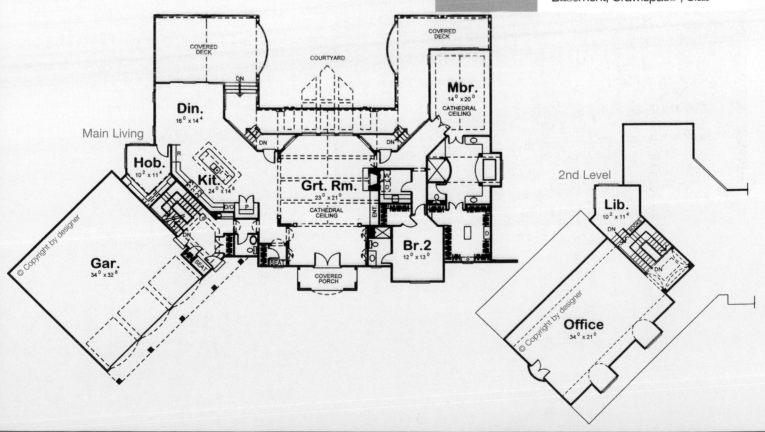

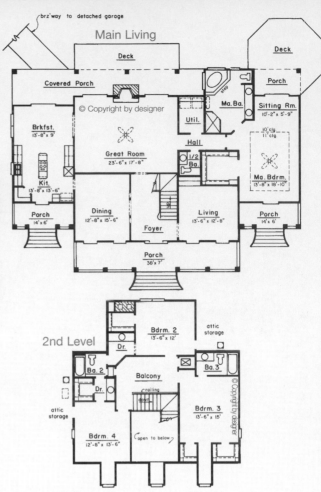

Plan ID 94622   Price Code: H

Total Living Area	3,149 sq.ft.
Main Living	2,033 sq.ft.
2nd Level	1,116 sq.ft.
Bedrooms	4
Bathrooms	3.5
Dimensions	66'-0" x 56'-0"
Garage Type	Two-car garage
Foundation	Crawlspace, Slab

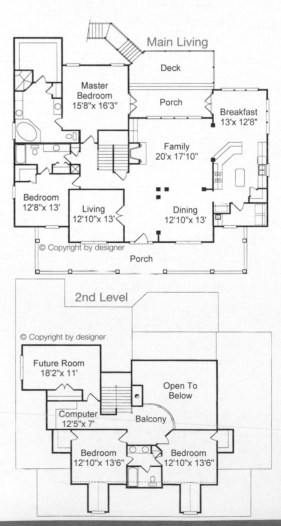

Plan ID 94666   Price Code: H

Total Living Area	3,194 sq.ft.
Main Living	2,391 sq.ft.
2nd Level	803 sq.ft.
Bedrooms	4
Bathrooms	3
Dimensions	61'-0" x 60'-4"
Garage Type	Two-car garage
Foundation	Post

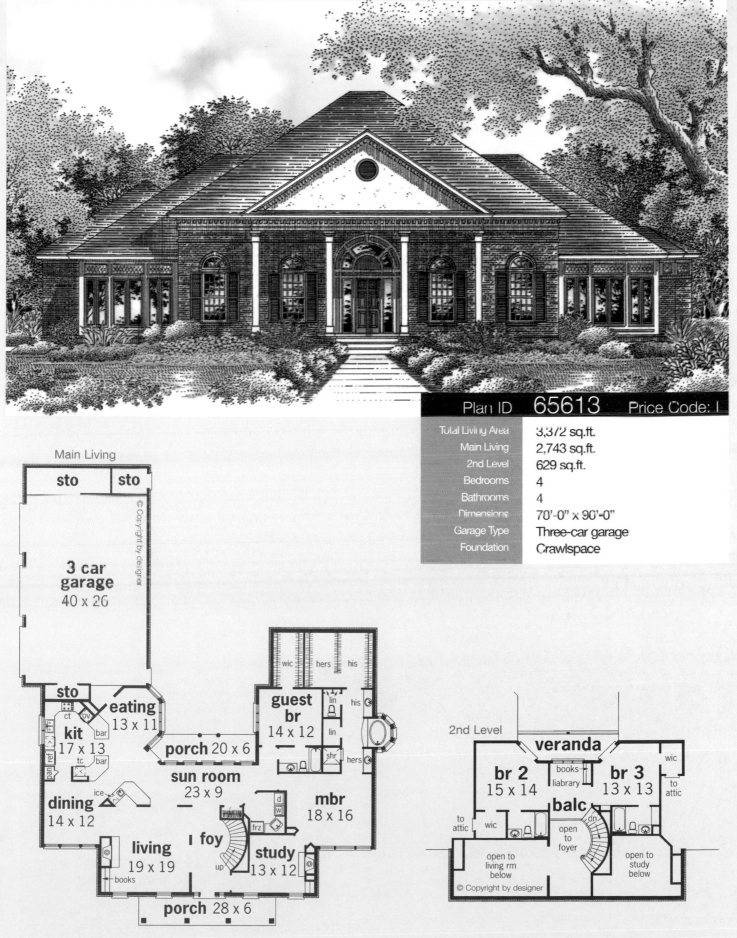

Plan ID	65613	Price Code: I
Total Living Area		3,372 sq. ft.
Main Living		2,743 sq. ft.
2nd Level		629 sq. ft.
Bedrooms		4
Bathrooms		4
Dimensions		70'-0" x 90'-0"
Garage Type		Three-car garage
Foundation		Crawlspace

Main Living

sto | sto

3 car garage 40 x 26

© Copyright by designer

sto

eating 13 x 11

kit 17 x 13

dining 14 x 12

porch 20 x 6

sun room 23 x 9

guest br 14 x 12

wic | hers | his

his

lin

lin

shr

hers

mbr 18 x 16

living 19 x 19

foy

study 13 x 12

up

porch 28 x 6

2nd Level

veranda

br 2 15 x 14

books library

br 3 13 x 13

wic

to attic

balc

open to foyer

dn

to attic

wic

open to living rm below

open to study below

© Copyright by designer

Pampering Guest Suite

An upper level guest suite with its own private covered balcony might make out-of-town guests hesitant to leave. On the main floor, the foyer opens to a beautifully configured dining area and parlor, defined by columns and rich ceiling details. The nearby kitchen encourages entertaining as it flows freely with the dinette and gathering room. To the rear of the home, a private study provides a secluded sanctuary for work at home. Privacy is also afforded to the bedrooms, with secondary quarters separated from the master. The master suite exudes luxury with spacious his and her walk-in closets, his and her vanities, soaking tub, and a beautifully showcased walk-in shower. A covered lanai wraps the rear of the home and is accessed by the main living areas and master bedroom.

The dining room, embellished with arches and columns, is brightened by a trio of arch-topped windows. ▶

Luxurious views onto the covered balcony, from the upper level guest suite. ◄

The gathering room enjoys both a corner entertainment center, as well as open access to the covered lanai. ▼

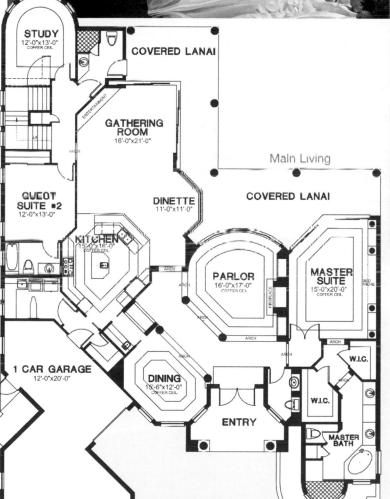

STUDY
12'-0"x13'-0"
COFFER CEIL.

COVERED LANAI

GATHERING ROOM
16'-0"x21'-0"

Main Living

GUEST SUITE #2
12'-0"x13'-0"

DINETTE
11'-0"x11'-0"

COVERED LANAI

KITCHEN
15'-0"x16'-0"
COFFER CEIL.

PARLOR
16'-0"x17'-0"
COFFER CEIL.

MASTER SUITE
15'-0"x20'-0"
COFFER CEIL.

1 CAR GARAGE
12'-0"x20'-0"

DINING
15'-6"x12'-0"
COFFER CEIL.

ENTRY

W.I.C.

W.I.C.

MASTER BATH

2 CAR GARAGE
22'-0"x25'-0"

© Copyright by designer

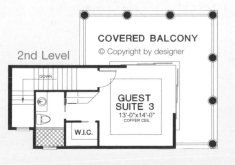

Plan ID **58906** Price Code: I

Total Living Area	3,341 sq.ft.
Main Living	2,999 sq.ft.
2nd Level	342 sq.ft.
Bedrooms	3
Bathrooms	4.5
Dimensions	65'-0" x 108'-0"
Garage Type	Three-car garage
Foundation	Slab

2nd Level

COVERED BALCONY
© Copyright by designer

DOWN

GUEST SUITE 3
13'-0"x14'-0"
COFFER CEIL.

W.I.C.

Main Living 91'-0"

Storage/Opt. Sitting 11⁸ x 16¹⁰
Master Bdrm. 17⁸ x 16¹⁰
M.Bath
Court Yard
Future Hot Tub
Bdrm.3 15⁶ x 11⁶
Pool
Living Area 19⁴ x 17⁸ 13' Ceiling
Computer Station
Bdrm.2 11¹⁰ x 15⁶
Patio
Brkfst. 14² x 13⁴
Kit. 12² x 13⁴
Dining 11⁸ x 15² 13' Ceiling
Foyer 7⁰ x 15² 13' Ceiling
Court Yard
Command Center
Lav.
Rec. Room 20² x 21⁴
Double Garage 23⁴ x 21⁴

© Copyright by designer

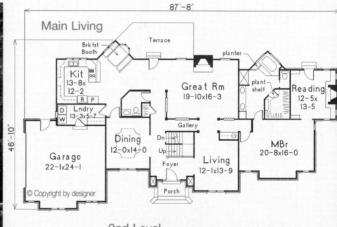

2nd Level
Future Finish 17⁶ x 11⁴
Future Finish 17⁶ x 13⁴
Full Bath

© Copyright by designer

Plan ID 71136 — Price Code: H

Total Living Area	3,190 sq.ft.
Main Living	3,190 sq.ft.
Bedrooms	3
Bathrooms	2.5
Dimensions	91'-0" x 83'-0"
Garage Type	Two-car garage
Foundation	Basement*, Crawlspace*, Slab

Main Living 87'-8"

Brkfst Booth
Terrace
planter
Kit 13-8x 12-2
Great Rm 19-10x16-3
plant shelf
Reading 12-5x 13-5
Lndry 13-3x5-7
Dining 12-0x14-0
Gallery
Garage 22-1x24-1
Living 12-1x13-9
MBr 20-8x16-0
Foyer
Porch

46'-10"

© Copyright by designer

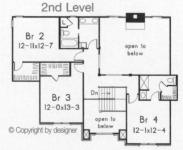

2nd Level
Br 2 12-11x12-7
open to below
Br 3 12-0x13-3
open to below
Br 4 12-1x12-4

© Copyright by designer

Plan ID 69001 — Price Code: H

Total Living Area	3,234 sq.ft.
Main Living	2,273 sq.ft.
2nd Level	961 sq.ft.
Bedrooms	4
Bathrooms	3.5
Dimensions	87'-8" x 46'-10"
Garage Type	Two-car garage
Foundation	Basement, Crawlspace, Slab

Plan ID **24803** Price Code: K

Total Living Area	3,047 sq.ft.
Basement	1,533 sq.ft.
Main Living	2,414 sq.ft.
Bedrooms	4
Bathrooms	2.5
Dimensions	82'-0" x 62'-0"
Garage Type	Three-car garage
Foundation	Basement

Basement

Br 2
13-6 x 11-10

Br 3
10-8 x 11-10

Family Rm
21-6 x 18-10

gas fireplace

Br 4
11-6 x 13-0

Lin

Storage
18-0 x 11-0

future wet bar

Storage
23-11 x 15-10

furn.

W/H

© Copyright by designer

Main Living

Brkfst
13-0 x 12-0

Deck

DN

Screened
Porch
12-8 x 13-8

Master Suite
15-0 x 16-0

built-ins

gas fireplace

Great Rm
21-8 x 19-0

Kit
11-0 x
25-0

decor clg.

cabinets

D

W

whirlpool

shelves

DN

railing

desk

pantry

Ldry

books

columns

Foyer

Dining Rm
14-0 x 11-0

Garage
33-8 x 21-8

© Copyright by designer

Study /
Guest
11-0 x 13-8

Plan ID 94169 Price Code: H

Total Living Area	3,042 sq.ft.
Main Living	2,186 sq.ft.
2nd Level	856 sq.ft.
Bedrooms	3
Bathrooms	2.5
Dimensions	73'-0" x 62'-0"
Garage Type	Three-car garage
Foundation	Basement

Plan ID 94179 Price Code: H

Total Living Area	3,079 sq.ft.
Main Living	2,211 sq.ft.
2nd Level	868 sq.ft.
Bedrooms	3
Bathrooms	2.5
Dimensions	71'-0" x 62'-0"
Garage Type	Three-car garage
Foundation	Basement

Plan ID	**94176**	Price Code: H

Total Living Area	3,090 sq. ft.
Main Living	2,320 sq. ft.
2nd Level	776 sq. ft.
Bedrooms	4
Bathrooms	2.5
Dimensions	91'-4" x 50'-10"
Garage Type	Three-car garage
Foundation	Basement

Breathtaking Details

Incredible details abound throughout this beautiful one-story design. Columns and ceiling details define the creatively configured dining area and parlor which flank the foyer. Further inside, the gourmet kitchen opens to a generously sized dinette and gathering room, perfect for entertaining. The secluded study provides a quiet setting for work or reflection. Spacious secondary bedrooms are separated from the luxurious master suite with roomy his and her walk-in closets, separate vanities, walk-in shower and beautiful oval tub positioned within an arched setting. Main living areas, as well as the master bedroom, access a comfortably shaded, covered lanai.

A beautifully detailed half-round wall on the front of the home conceals a hidden treasure – the elegantly appointed oval tub in the master bath. ▶

ORDER NOW 1-800-235-5700 or at **www.familyhomeplans.com**

The secluded master bedroom offers peaceful views onto to covered lanai. ◄

Plan ID **58901** Price Code: I

Total Living Area	3,316 sq.ft.
Main Living	3,316 sq.ft.
Bedrooms	3
Bathrooms	2.5
Dimensions	67'-6" x 110'-0"
Garage Type	Three car garage
Foundation	Slab

STUDY
13'-0"x11'-2"
COFFER CEIL.

COVERED LANAI

GATHERING ROOM
16'-0"x21'-0"

BDR 3
13'-0"x12'-0"

DINETTE
11'-0"x11'-0"

COVERED LANAI

Main Living

BDR 2
13'-0"x12'-0"

KITCHEN
16'-0"x16'-0"
COFFER CEIL.

PARLOR
16'-0"x17'-11"
COFFER CEIL.

MASTER SUITE
15'-0"x20'-0"
COFFER CEIL.

LAUN.

BUTLERS PANTRY

W.T.C.

DINING
15'-0"x15'-0"
COFFER CEIL.

FOYER

1 CAR GARAGE
12'-0"x20'-0"

ENTRY

W.T.C.

COFFER CEIL.

2 CAR GARAGE
21'-0"x24'-0"

© Copyright by designer

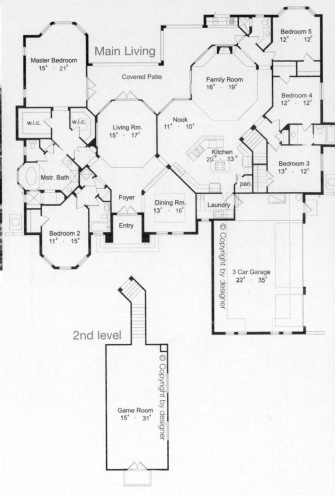

Main Living

Master Bedroom
15⁴ · 21²

Covered Patio

Bedroom 5
12⁰ · 12⁰

Family Room
16⁰ · 19²

Bedroom 4
12⁰ · 12⁰

w.i.c.   w.i.c.

Living Rm.
15⁰ · 17²

Nook
11⁰ · 10⁰

Kitchen
20¹⁰ · 13¹⁰

Bedroom 3
13⁴ · 12⁰

Mstr. Bath

pan.

Foyer

Dining Rm.
13⁰ · 16²

Laundry

Bedroom 2
11⁴ · 15⁰

Entry

3 Car Garage
22⁸ · 35⁰

2nd level

Game Room
15⁴ · 31⁴

© Copyright by designer

Plan ID 63021   Price Code: I

Total Living Area	3,434 sq.ft.
Main Living	3,434 sq.ft.
Bedrooms	5
Bathrooms	4
Dimensions	82'-4" x 83'-8"
Garage Type	Three-car garage
Foundation	Slab

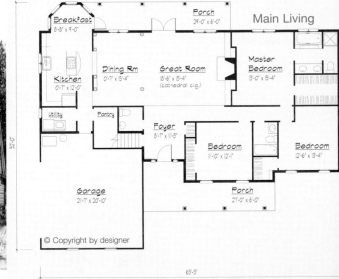

Main Living

Breakfast
8'-8" x 9'-0"

Porch
24'-0" x 6'-0"

Dining Rm
0'-7" x 15'-4"

Great Room
18'-6" x 15'-4"
(cathedral clg.)

Master Bedroom
18'-0" x 15'-4"

Kitchen
0'-7" x 12'-0"

Utility

Pantry

Foyer
8'-7" x 11'-3"

Bedroom
11'-0" x 12'-1"

Bedroom
12'-6" x 13'-4"

Garage
21'-7" x 20'-10"

Porch
27'-0" x 6'-0"

© Copyright by designer

2nd Level

line of 8' ceiling

Great Room
below

line of 8' ceiling

Bonus Rm.
21'-2" x 17'-0"

Bonus Rm.
22'-3" x 14'-4"

line of 8' ceiling

© Copyright by designer

Plan ID 41006   Price Code: H

Total Living Area	3,143 sq.ft.
Main Living	1,827 sq.ft.
2nd Level	1,316 sq.ft.
Bedrooms	3
Bathrooms	2.5
Dimensions	63'-6" x 52'-0"
Garage Type	Two-car garage
Foundation	Crawlspace

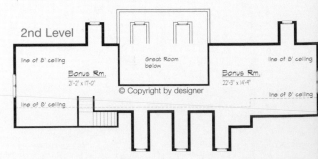

ORDER NOW 1-800-235-5700 or at www.familyhomeplans.com

Plan ID 94174   Price Code: K

Total Living Area	3,886 sq.ft.
Main Living	2,519 sq.ft.
2nd Level	1,367 sq.ft.
Bedrooms	3
Bathrooms	3.5
Dimensions	78'-8" x 60'-0"
Garage Type	Three-car garage
Foundation	Basement

Plan ID **64984** **Price Code: H**

Total Living Area	3,016 sq.ft.
Main Living	1,716 sq.ft.
2nd Level	1,300 sq.ft.
Bedrooms	6
Bathrooms	4.5
Dimensions	60'-0" x 47'-8"
Garage Type	Two-car garage
Foundation	Crawlspace

Main Living

10-8 X 11-8

12-8 X 15-0

11-8 X 15-0

16-4 X 12-0

16-0 X 15-8

© Copyright by designer

12-8 X 11-6

2-CAR GARAGE
22-4 X 20-4

47-8

60-0

2nd Level

11-8 X 10-0

12-8 X 15-8

© Copyright by designer

11-8 X 10-0

12-8 X 10-0

11-8 X 10-0

Basement

© Copyright by designer

11-1 x 13-8

14-1 x 15-8

STORAGE
19-11 x 15-1

21-10 x 13-10

Plan ID 64981 Price Code: J

Total Living Area	3,506 sq.ft.
Basement	1,247 sq.ft.
Main Living	1,604 sq.ft.
2nd Level	655 sq.ft.
Bedrooms	5
Bathrooms	3.5
Dimensions	59'-0" x 49'-8"
Garage Type	Two-car garage
Foundation	Finished basement with walkout

Main Living

© Copyright by designer

2-CAR GARAGE
20-0 x 25-8

14-4 x 13-10

49-8

13-8 x 17-10

21-8 x 13-10

19-11 x 15-4

59-0

2nd Level

© Copyright by designer

BONUS ROOM
10-10 x 25-8

10-10 x 13-0

13-0 x 10-0

Luxurious Entertaining

Few homes would be better suited for luxurious living and entertaining. An outside courtyard, adjacent to the entry, greets guests with a stunning first impression. Inside, the foyer centers on views through the formal parlor's bowed windows. Special ceiling details define the parlor's space, as well as that of the dining room. The gathering room and dinette offer expanded areas for friends and family to mingle. The master suite is certainly one to show visitors, with its corner fireplace, dual walk-in closets, his and her vanities and octagonal shower area. An upper-level guest suite beckons visitors to stay over. Outside, a columned portico separates two garages as a stylish setting for vehicles.

The covered lanai borders the entire rear of the home, creating a paradise for entertaining. ▲

The upper level guest suite, with private balcony, is one of the most captivating areas of the home. ▶

ORDER NOW 1-800-235-5700 or at www.familyhomeplans.com

The parlor's graceful array of bowed window offer unrestricted views to the outside. ◄

Angles and arches define the pampering master bedroom, with its breathtaking ceiling details. ▼

Plan ID	58907	Price Code: J
Total Living Area	3,680 sq.ft.	
Main Living	3,232 sq.ft.	
2nd Level	448 sq.ft.	
Bedrooms	3	
Bathrooms	3.5	
Dimensions	120'-0" x 103'-0"	
Garage Type	Three-car garage	
Foundation	Slab	

Main Living

2nd Level

IMPORTANT INFORMATION
to make your dream come true

Foundation Plan

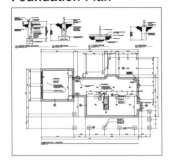

These plans will accurately show the dimensions of the footprint of your home, including load-bearing points and beam placement if applicable. The foundation style will vary from plan to plan. (Please note: There may be an additional charge for optional foundation plan. Please call for details.)

Detailed Floor Plans

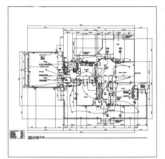

The floor plans of your home accurately depict the dimensions of the positioning of the walls, doors, windows, stairs, and permanent fixtures. They will show you the relationship and dimensions of rooms, closets, and traffic patterns. The schematic of the electrical layout may be included in the plan.

Roof Plan

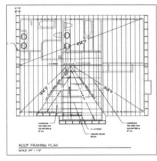

The information necessary to construct the roof will be included with your home plans. Some plans will reference roof trusses, while many others contain schematic framing plans. These framing plans will indicate the lumber sizes necessary for the rafters and ridgeboards based on the designated roof loads.

Typical Wall Section

This section will address insulation, roof components, and interior and exterior wall finishes. Your plans will be designed with either 2x4 or 2x6 exterior walls, but if you wish, most professional contractors can easily adapt the plans to the wall thickness you require.

Exterior Elevations

These fronts, rear, and side views of the home include information pertaining to the exterior finish materials, roof pitches, and exterior height dimensions.

Typical Cross Section

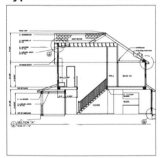

A cut-away cross section through the entire home shows your building contractor the exact correlation of construction components at all levels of the house. It will help to clarify the load bearing points from the roof all the way down to the basement. Available for most plans.

Stair Details

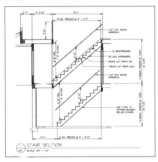

If the design you have chosen includes stairs, the plans will show the information that you need in order to build them-either through a stair cross section or on the floor plans.

Fireplace Details

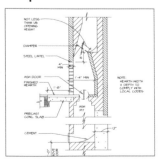

If the home you have chosen includes a fireplace, a fireplace detail will show typical methods of constructing the firebox, hearth, and flue chase for masonry units, or a wood frame chase for zero-clearance units. Available for most plans.

Cabinet Plans

These plans, or in some cases elevations, will detail the layout of the kitchen and bathroom cabinets at a larger scale.
Available for most plans.

Garlinghouse
Options & Extras

Reversed Plans can Make Your Dream Home Just Right

You could have exactly the home you want by flipping it end-for-end. Simply order your plans "reversed." We'll send you one full set of mirror-image plans (with the writing backwards) as a master guide for you and your builder. The remaining sets of your order will come as shown in this book so the dimensions and specifications are easily read on the job site. Most plans in our collection will come stamped "reversed" so there is no confusion. We can only send reversed plans with multiple-set orders. There is a $50 charge for this service. Some plans in our collection are available in "Right Reading Reverse." Right Reading Reverse plans will show your home in reverse. This easy-to-read format will save you valuable time and money. Please contact our Sales Department at 800-235-5700 to check for Right Reading Reverse availability. There is a $135 charge for this service.

Remember to Order Your Materials List

Available at a modest additional charge, the Materials List gives the quantity, dimensions, and specifications for the major materials needed to build your home. You will get faster, more accurate bids from your contractors and building suppliers and avoid paying for unused materials as well as waste. Materials Lists are available for all home plans except as otherwise indicated,but can only be ordered with a set of home plans. Due to differences in regional requirements and homeowner or builder preferences, electrical, plumbing and heating / air conditioning equipment specifications are not designed specifically for each plan.

What We Offer

Home Plan Blueprint Package

By purchasing a multiple-set package of blueprints or a Vellum from The Garlinghouse Company, you not only receive the physical blueprint documents necessary for construction, but you are also granted a license to build one (and only one) home. You can also make simple modifications, including minor non-structural changes and material substitutions, to our design as long as these changes are made directly on the blueprints purchased from The Garlinghouse Company and no additional copies are made.

Home Plan Vellums

By purchasing Vellums for one of our home plans, you receive the same construction drawings found in the blueprints, but printed on vellum paper. Vellums can be erased and are perfect for making design changes. They are also semi-transparent, making them easy to duplicate. But most importantly, the purchase of home plan Vellums comes with a broader license that allows you to make changes to the design (i.e., create a hand drawn or CAD derivative work), to make copies of the plan, and to build one home from the plan.

License to Build Additional Homes

With the purchase of a blueprint package or Vellums, you automatically receive a license to build one home and only one home. If you want to build more homes than you are licensed to build through your purchase of a plan, then additional licenses must be purchased at reasonable costs from The Garlinghouse Company. Inquire for more information.

Modifying
Your Design Easily

How to Modify Your Garlinghouse Home Plan

Simple modifications to your dream home, including minor non-structural changes and material substitutions, can be made by you and your builder with the consent of your local building official, by marking the changes directly on your blueprints. However, if you are considering making significant changes to your chosen design, we recommend that you use the services of the Garlinghouse staff. We will help take your ideas and turn them into a reality, just the way you want.

Here's our procedure:

Call 800-235-5700 and order your modification estimate. The fee for this estimate is $50. We will review your plan changes and provide you with an estimate to draft your specific modifications before you purchase the vellums. Please note: A vellum must be purchased to modify a home plan design. After you receive your estimate, if you decide to have Garlinghouse do the changes, the $50 estimate fee will be deducted from the cost of your modifications. If, however, you chose to use a different service, the $50 estimate fee is non-refundable. (Note: Personal checks cannot be accepted for the estimate.)

A 75% deposit is required before we begin making the actual modifications to your plans.

Ignoring Copyrights Laws Can Be A $100,000 Mistake

⊘ What You Can't Do
U.S. copyright laws allow for statutory penalties of up to $100,000 per incident for copyright infringement involving any of the copyrighted plans found in this publication. The law can be confusing. So, for your own protection, take the time to understand what you can and cannot do when it comes to home plans.

⊘ You Cannot Duplicate Home Plans
Purchasing a set of blueprints and making additional sets by reproducing the original is illegal. If you need more than one set of a particular home plan, you must purchase them.

⊘ You Cannot Copy Any Part of a Home Plan to Create Another
Creating your own plan by copying even part of a home design found in this publication without permission is called "creating a derivative work" and is illegal.

⊘ You Cannot Build a Home Without a License
You must have a specific permission or a license to build a home from a copyrighted design, even if the finished home has been changed from the original plan. It is illegal to build one of the homes found in this publication without a license.

Once the design changes have been completed to your vellum plan, a representative will call to inform you that your modified vellum plan is complete and will be shipped as soon as the final payment has been made. For additional information, call us at 800-235-5700. Please refer to the Modification Pricing Guide for estimated modification costs.

Reproducible Vellums for Local Modification Ease

If you decide not to use Garlinghouse for your modifications, we recommend that you follow our same procedure of purchasing vellums. You then have the option of using the services of the original designer of the plan, a local professional designer, or an architect to make the modifications.

With a vellum copy of our plans, a design professional can alter the drawings just the way you want, then you can print as many copies of the modified plans as you need to build your house. And, since you have already started with our complete detailed plans, the cost of those expensive professional services will be significantly less than starting from scratch.

MODIFICATION PRICING GUIDE

Prices for changes will vary depending on the number of modifications requested, the house size, quality of original plan, format provided and method of design used by the original designer. Typically, modifications cost around $1500, excluding the price of the (hand-drawn or computer generated) vellum.

Please contact us to get your $50 estimate at: 800-235-5700

Detail Plans

Information on Construction Techniques—NOT PLAN SPECIFIC

$19.95

per set (includes postage)
($47.95 for all three)

PLEASE NOTE: The detail plans are not specific to any one home plan and should be used only as a general reference guide.

Because local codes and requirements vary greatly, we recommend that you obtain drawings and bids from licensed contractors to do your mechanical plans. However, if you want to know more about techniques—and deal more confidently with subcontractors—we offer these remarkably useful detail sheets. These detail sheets will aid in your understanding of these technical subjects.

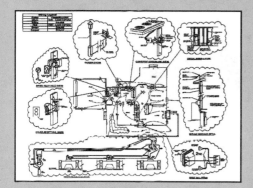

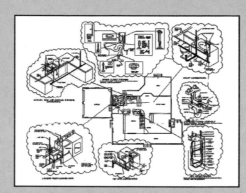

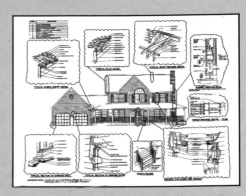

Residential Electrical Details

Eight sheets that cover all aspects of residential wiring, from simple switch wiring to service entrance connections. Details distribution panel layout with outlet and switch schematics, circuit breaker and wiring installation methods, and ground fault interrupter specifications. Conforms to requirements of National Electrical Code. Color coded with a glossary of terms.

Residential Plumbing Details

Eight sheets packed with information detailing pipe installation methods, fittings, and sized. Details plumbing hook-ups for toilets, sinks, washers, sump pumps, and septic system construction. Conforms to requirements of National Plumbing code. Color coded with a glossary of terms and quick index.

Residential Construction Details

Ten sheets that cover the essentials of stick-built residential home construction. Details foundation options—poured concrete basement, concrete block, or monolithic concrete slab. Shows all aspects of floor, wall and roof framing. Provides details for roof dormers, overhangs, chimneys and skylights. Conforms to requirements of Uniform Building code or BOCA code. Includes a quick index and a glossary of terms.

Your Blueprints Can Be Sealed by A Registered Architect

Many of our home plan construction drawings can be sealed by an architect that is registered in most states. Please call our Order Department for details. Although an architect's seal will not guarantee approval of your home plan blueprints, a seal is sometimes required by your state or local building department in order to get a building permit. Please talk to your local building officials, before you order your blueprints, to determine if a seal is needed in your area. You will need to provide the county and state of your building site when ordering an architect's seal on your blueprints, and please allow additional time to process your order (an additional five to fifteen working days, at least).

State Energy Certificates

A few states require that an energy certificate be prepared for your new home to their specifications before a building permit can be issued. Again, your local building official can tell you if one is required in your state. You will first need to fill out the energy certificate checklist available to you when your order is placed. This list contains questions about type of heating used, siding, windows, location of home, etc. This checklist provides all the information needed to prepare your state energy certificate. Please note: energy certificates are only available on orders for blueprints with an architect's seal.

Specifications & Contract Form

We send this form to you free of charge with your home plan order. The form is designed to be filled in by you or your contractor with the exact materials to use in the construction of your new home. Once signed by you and your contractor it will provide you with peace of mind throughout the construction process.

Questions?

Call our customer service department
1-800-235-5700.

Order Form

Price Level	1 Set	4 Sets	8 Sets	Vellums	CADD Files	Material List	Additional Sets
A	$ 485.00	$ 555.00	$ 595.00	$ 735.00	$ 1,235.00	$ 60.00	$ 50.00
B	$ 515.00	$ 585.00	$ 625.00	$ 765.00	$ 1,265.00	$ 60.00	$ 50.00
C	$ 545.00	$ 615.00	$ 655.00	$ 795.00	$ 1,295.00	$ 70.00	$ 50.00
D	$ 575.00	$ 645.00	$ 685.00	$ 825.00	$ 1,325.00	$ 70.00	$ 50.00
E	$ 605.00	$ 675.00	$ 715.00	$ 855.00	$ 1,355.00	$ 70.00	$ 50.00
F	$ 635.00	$ 705.00	$ 745.00	$ 885.00	$ 1,385.00	$ 70.00	$ 50.00
G	$ 665.00	$ 735.00	$ 775.00	$ 915.00	$ 1,415.00	$ 70.00	$ 50.00
H	$ 695.00	$ 765.00	$ 805.00	$ 945.00	$ 1,445.00	$ 80.00	$ 50.00
I	$ 725.00	$ 795.00	$ 835.00	$ 975.00	$ 1,475.00	$ 80.00	$ 50.00
J	$ 755.00	$ 825.00	$ 865.00	$ 1,005.00	$ 1,505.00	$ 80.00	$ 50.00
K	$ 785.00	$ 855.00	$ 895.00	$ 1,035.00	$ 1,535.00	$ 80.00	$ 50.00
L	$ 845.00	$ 915.00	$ 955.00	$ 1,095.00	$ 1,595.00	$ 90.00	$ 50.00

TO PLACE ORDERS
- To order your home plans
- Questions about a plan

To order your plan on-line
using our secure server, visit:
Visit www.familyhomeplans.com

1-800-235-5700

Order Code No. **H6BBB**

The Garlinghouse Company financially supports Homes
for Our Troops. Learn more at www.homesforourtroops.org

____ Set(s) of blueprints for plan # _____ $ _____

____ Vellum for plan # _____ $ _____

____ CADD files for plan # _____ $ _____

____ Foundation _____ $ _____

____ * Call for Pricing on alternate foundations _____ $ _____

____ Additional set(s) (Not available for 1 set-study set) $ _____

____ Mirror Image Reverse $ _____

____ Right Reading Reverse $ _____

____ Materials list for plan # _____ $ _____

Detail Plans (Not plan specific) @ $19.95 each - All 3 @ $ 47.95

❏ Construction ❏ Plumbing ❏ Electrical $ _____

Shipping $ _____

Subtotal $ _____

Sales Tax (VA and SC residents add 5%. Not required for other states.) $ _____

TOTAL AMOUNT ENCLOSED $ _____

Name: _____

Street: _____

City: _____

State: _____ Zip Code: _____

Daytime Phone: _____

Email Address: _____

Send your check, money order, or credit card information to:
(No C.O.D.'s Please) *Prices subject to change without notice.*

Please submit all UNITED STATES & OTHER NATIONS
orders to:
The Garlinghouse Company
Attn: Order Fulfillment Dept.
4125 Lafayette Center Drive, Suite 100
Chantilly, VA 20151
CALL: (800) 235-5700 FAX: (703) 222-9705

Please Submit all CANADIAN plan orders to:
The Garlinghouse Company
102 Ellis Street
Penticton, BC V2A 4L5
CALL: (800) 361-7526 FAX: (250) 493-7526

Credit Card Information
Charge To: ❏ Mastercard ❏ Visa ❏ American Express ❏ Discover

Card # | | | | | | | | | | | | | | | |

Signature _____ Exp. _____ / _____

Blueprint Order Information

Before ordering, please read all ordering information.

How Many Sets of Plans Will You Need?

The Standard 8-Set Construction Package

Our experience shows that you'll speed up every step of construction and avoid costly building errors by ordering enough sets to go around. Each tradesperson wants a set—the general contractor and all subcontractors: foundation, electrical, plumbing, heating/air conditioning, and framers. Don't forget your lending institution, building department, and, of course, a set for yourself.

* Recommended For Construction *

To Reorder, Call 800-235-5700

If you find after your initial purchase that you require additional sets of plans, a materials list, or other items, you may purchase them from us at special reorder prices (please call for pricing details) provided that you reorder within six months of your original order date. There is a $28 reorder processing fee that is charged on all reorders. For more information on reordering plans, please contact our Sales Department.

An Important Note About Building Code Requirements

All plans are drawn to conform to one or more of the industry's major national building standards. However, due to the variety of local building regulations, your plan may need to be modified to comply with local requirements—snow loads, energy loads, seismic zones, etc. Do check them fully and consult your local building officials. A few states require that all building plans used be drawn by an architect registered in that state. While having your plans reviewed and stamped by such an architect may be prudent, laws requiring non-conforming plans like ours to be completely redrawn forces you to unnecessarily pay very large fees. If your state has such a law, we strongly recommend you contact your state representative to protest. The rendering, floor plans, and technical information contained within this publication are not guaranteed to be totally accurate. Consequently, no information from this publication should be used either as a guide to constructing a home or for estimating the cost of building a home. Complete blueprints must be purchased for such purposes.

Customer Service/Exchanges Call 800-895-3715

If for some reason you have a question about your existing order, please call 800-895-3715. Your plans are custom printed especially for you once you place your order. For that reason we cannot accept any returns. If for some reason you find that the plan you have purchased from us does not meet your needs, then you may exchange that plan for any other plan in our collection. We allow you 60 days from your original invoice date to make an exchange. At the time of the exchange, you will be charged a processing fee of 30% of the total amount of your original order, plus the difference in price between the plans (if applicable), plus the cost to ship the new plans to you. Call our Customer Service Department for more information. Please Note: Reproducible Vellums can only be exchanged if they are unopened.

Important Shipping Information

Please refer to the shipping charts on the order form for service availability for your specific plan number. Our delivery service must have a street address or Rural Route Box number—never a post office box. (PLEASE NOTE. Supplying a P.O. Box number will only will delay the shipping of your order.) Use a work address if no one is home during the day. Orders being shipped to APO or FPO must go via First Class Mail. Please include the proper postage. For our International Customers, only Certified bank checks and money orders are accepted and must be payable in U.S. currency. For speed, we ship international orders Air Parcel Post. Please refer to the chart for the correct shipping cost,

Important Canadian Shipping Information

To our friends in Canada, we have a plan design affiliate in Penticton, BC. This relationship will help you avoid the delays and charges associated with shipments from the United States. Moreover, our affiliate is familiar with the building requirements in your community and country. We prefer payments in U.S. currency. Please call our Canadian office at toll free 1-800-361-7526 for current Canadian prices.

Design, Build & Decorate Your New Home on Your Table

Plan Index

PLAN #	SQ.FT.	PRICE CODE	PAGE #	PLAN #	SQ.FT.	PRICE CODE	PAGE #	PLAN #	SQ.FT.	PRICE CODE	PAGE #
64983	1168	A	12	62086	1597	B	85	64977	1779	C	136
58311	1193	A	19	41022	1604	B	94	96808	1784	C	99
65003	1295	A	12	41021	1604	B	97	58903	1789	C	113
97334	1295	A	16	94522	1606	B	74	69017	1791	C	61
92431	1296	A	20	94682	1609	B	76	77045	1791	C	108
68096	1311	A	22	97760	1611	B	89	99680	1793	C	81
58310	1312	A	18	94683	1618	B	75	67042	1795	C	65
97731	1315	A	24	24701	1625	B	48	59012	1799	C	117
92372	1334	A	27	65246	1625	B	134	59017	1802	C	119
97332	1340	A	17	24717	1642	B	43	93293	1803	C	129
92458	1343	A	26	93171	1642	B	54	77049	1815	C	111
24402	1346	A	14	79005	1643	B	104	64986	1816	C	137
79002	1360	A	20	99175	1649	B	54	24651	1821	C	38
94688	1363	A	22	82011	1654	B	82	79012	1821	C	107
99639	1366	A	24	59009	1654	B	118	65380	1832	C	139
82003	1379	A	28	65635	1655	B	58	40021	1833	C	124
99673	1380	A	25	24725	1661	B	48	64978	1838	C	136
77015	1418	A	21	69515	1679	B	77	97777	1861	C	88
92459	1420	A	26	40005	1680	B	120	73005	1867	C	52
77017	1434	A	23	64988	1680	B	135	68170	1867	C	72
20164	1456	A	14	20075	1682	B	32	93107	1868	C	57
97137	1461	A	15	65677	1682	B	59	63114	1868	C	92
93165	1472	A	16	99187	1683	B	52	98956	1869	C	130
94154	1477	A	23	68525	1688	B	68	71032	1869	C	130
65001	1480	A	10 & 11	79007	1688	B	105	71033	1870	C	132
64985	1484	A	13	40010	1688	B	123	65624	1891	C	58
62143	1485	A	28	68432	1694	B	68	69503	1892	C	78
61033	1485	A	29	41003	1694	B	95	77058	1896	C	109
58301	1495	A	18	41000	1694	B	96	24743	1900	C	35
94517	1500	A	74	96824	1698	B	102	67046	1905	C	64
59050	1500	A	116	24250	1700	B	33	10785	1907	C	49
40027	1501	B	120	59065	1700	B	118	94157	1912	C	125
59052	1502	B	116	65616	1704	B	60	94153	1916	C	125
92442	1507	B	112	69016	1708	B	62	77063	1919	C	110
92649	1508	B	88	71067	1715	B	128	82051	1921	C	84
71022	1532	B	126 & 127	77031	1720	B	108	40004	1927	C	121
24721	1539	B	39	69014	1721	B	63	99683	1945	C	80
68149	1539	B	73	40030	1730	B	122	58309	1948	C	115
93161	1540	B	56	20100	1737	B	37	65012	1953	C	138
71023	1553	B	132	24249	1741	B	44 & 45	96811	1954	C	98
24738	1554	B	30 & 31	82050	1746	B	83	65556	1955	C	134
34603	1560	B	46	79235	1747	B	104	92461	1963	C	87
34602	1560	B	47	34376	1748	B	34	67036	1974	C	66
58306	1560	B	114	41008	1749	B	94	41013	1974	C	96
20220	1568	B	36	97757	1755	C	86	97405	1984	C	69
79233	1573	B	106	63095	1758	C	93	92446	1992	C	90
99641	1579	B	79	62177	1760	C	82	92421	1992	C	91
97178	1591	B	55	93133	1763	C	53	20230	1995	C	50 & 51
67044	1593	B	67	71028	1765	C	133	40014	1997	C	122
24242	1595	B	42	96525	1771	C	103	59070	2000	C	192

| The Best Baby Boomer Home Plans — ORDER NOW 1-800-235-5700 or at www.familyhomeplans.com

PLAN #	SQ.FT.	PRICE CODE	PAGE #	PLAN #	SQ.FT.	PRICE CODE	PAGE #	PLAN #	SQ.FT.	PRICE CODE	PAGE #
77135	2000	C	197	44054	2261	E	155	44063	2688	F	252
65626	2002	D	152	65143	2265	E	209	69011	2723	F	232
92697	2017	D	184	41012	2276	E	195	20407	2753	G	214
69510	2018	D	176 & 177	69512	2282	E	178	71004	2753	G	219
62317	2022	C	186	77087	2297	E	198	20233	2768	G	216
59026	2024	D	193	96865	2302	E	179	44067	2788	G	226
67027	2028	D	164	71042	2322	E	188	94177	2792	G	248
69019	2029	D	172	96833	2327	E	180	58904	2793	G	254
67028	2036	D	166	65678	2328	E	156	96825	2795	G	239
65125	2037	D	211	50023	2332	E	185	94175	2797	G	249
63050	2041	D	204	77095	2333	E	199	58900	2797	G	254
24736	2044	D	142	92428	2340	E	190	65126	2802	G	247
40013	2046	D	169	67043	2350	E	164	69005	2806	G	230
79156	2069	D	202	63005	2363	E	205	69007	2828	G	234
92463	2071	D	188	20368	2372	E	144 & 145	44039	2843	G	227
79000	2079	D	202	65633	2393	E	158	94163	2843	G	251
65686	2085	D	157	94611	2406	E	159	64987	2849	G	255
40019	2085	D	173	62136	2413	E	186	24702	2859	G	217
96529	2089	D	181	94173	2421	E	206	69520	2874	G	212 & 213
63364	2089	D	204	77103	2440	E	196	69000	2874	G	235
41010	2099	D	194	50012	2449	E	182	63181	2887	G	253
41009	2105	D	194	24959	2464	E	147	94644	2898	G	222
44045	2109	D	153	24703	2465	E	143	94994	2957	G	233
24557	2110	D	150	40007	2465	E	172	41002	2977	G	244
65368	2111	D	208	44061	2471	E	154	64980	2992	G	246
40018	2122	D	171	94670	2471	E	162 & 163	64984	3016	H	276
64979	2122	D	210	62045	2476	E	187	94169	3042	H	270
67045	2126	D	167	24252	2478	E	148 & 149	94179	3079	H	270
63365	2140	D	203	44066	2478	E	152	94176	3096	H	271
77080	2143	D	200	50049	2506	F	241	20105	3131	H	258
68148	2144	D	174	79243	2507	F	245	41006	3143	H	274
64982	2146	D	210	20173	2511	F	214	94622	3149	H	264
92631	2157	D	182	97486	2517	F	228	71136	3190	H	268
44069	2159	D	156	41001	2525	F	244	94666	3194	H	264
44037	2164	D	154	65673	2542	F	224	69001	3234	H	268
24952	2179	D	140 & 141	62195	2553	F	218	58901	3316	I	272 & 273
92443	2184	D	189	96827	2571	F	236	24613	3323	I	259
67002	2185	D	166	24989	2592	F	231	58906	3341	I	266 & 267
40020	2197	D	170	69003	2597	F	232	65613	3372	I	265
97710	2198	D	183	96839	2599	F	237	63021	3434	I	274
59073	2200	D	192	59079	2601	F	240	64981	3506	J	277
67038	2204	D	165	44042	2613	F	226	58907	3680	J	278 & 279
65426	2204	D	207	24953	2614	F	215	94174	3886	K	275
92643	2209	D	184	71119	2614	F	242 & 243	44068	3887	K	263
94673	2232	D	168	99473	2639	F	229	24803	3947	K	269
20193	2250	D	146	96823	2645	F	238	24802	4064	L	256 & 257
59092	2250	D	201	94178	2652	F	248	44051	4212	L	262
59074	2251	E	193	63011	2660	F	252	20166	4403	L	260 & 261
68162	2252	E	175	94663	2665	F	223				
20234	2257	E	151	97946	2688	F	225				